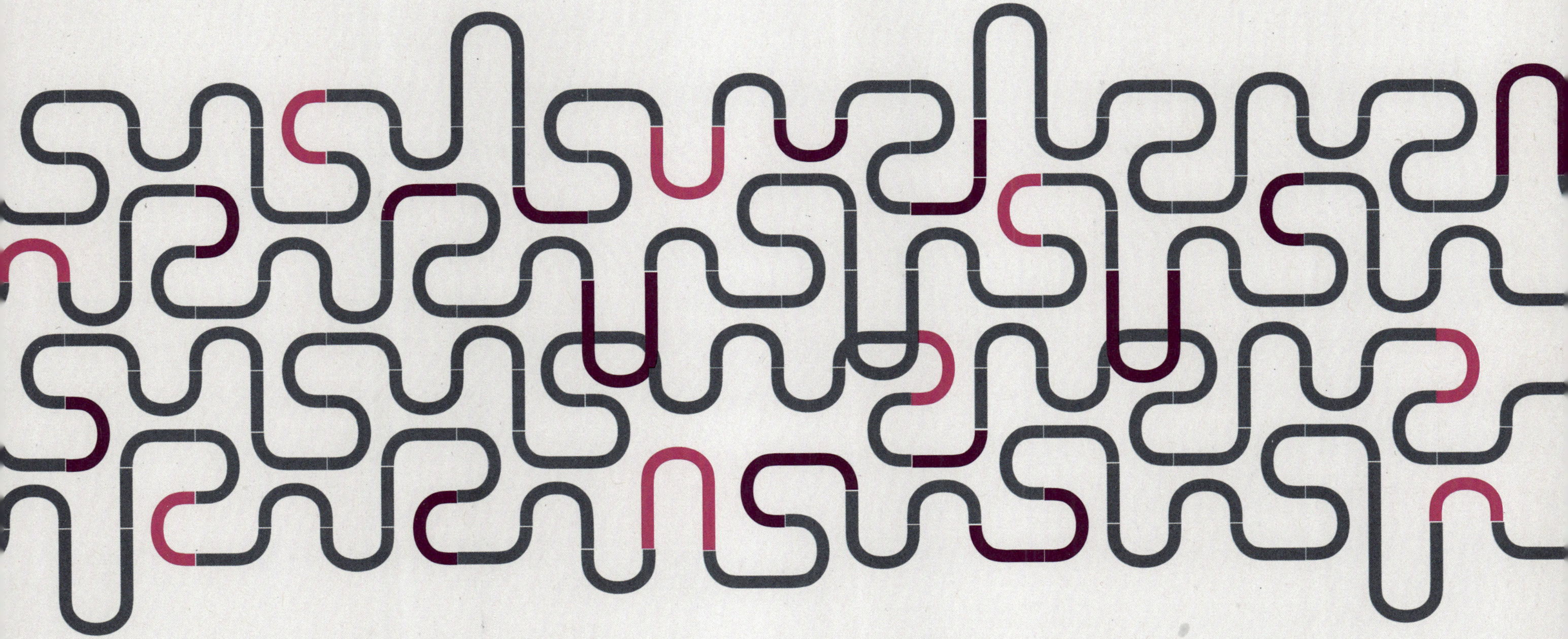

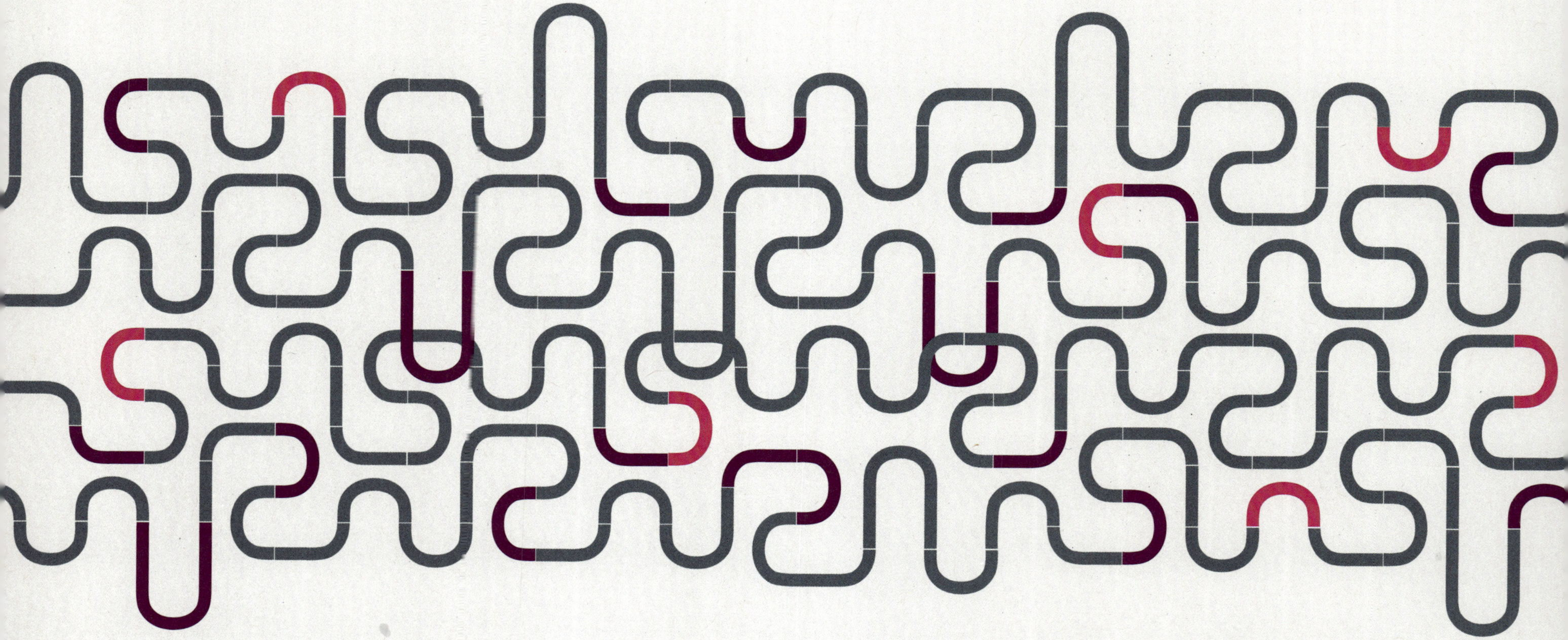

COSMOPOLITAN ROUTES

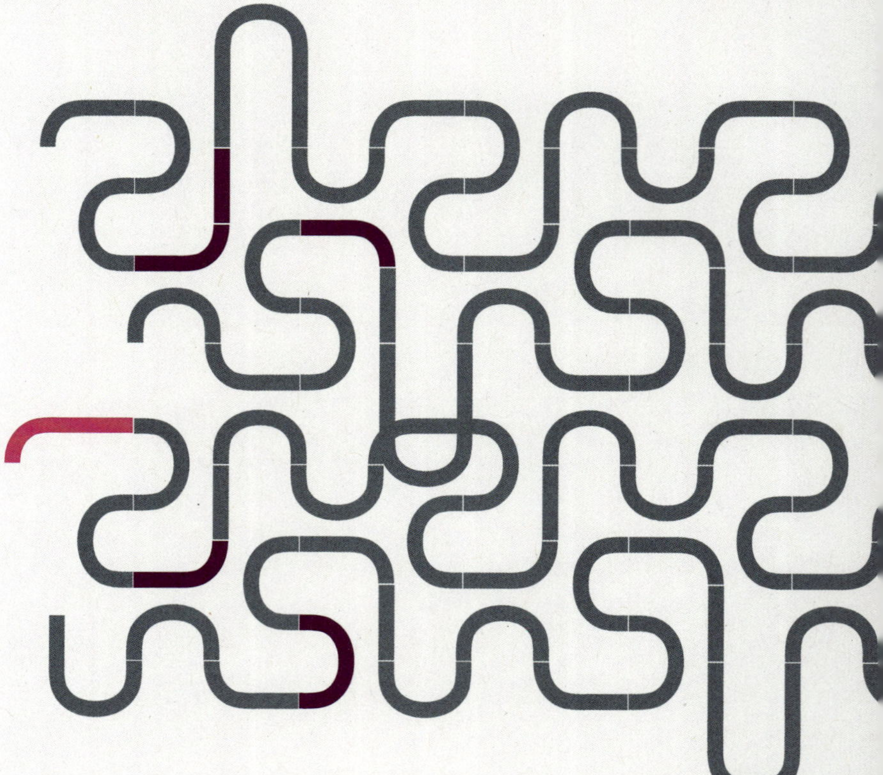

COSMOPOLITAN ROUTES
HOUSTON COLLECTS LATIN AMERICAN ART

GILBERT VICARIO
WITH CONTRIBUTIONS BY MARI CARMEN RAMÍREZ
AND ELIZABETH CEREJIDO

THE MUSEUM OF FINE ARTS, HOUSTON DISTRIBUTED BY YALE UNIVERSITY PRESS, NEW HAVEN AND LONDON

This book was published to accompany the exhibition of the same title that was presented at the Museum of Fine Arts, Houston, from October 24, 2010, through February 6, 2011. The book also commemorates the tenth anniversary of the founding of the Latin American Art Department and the International Center for the Arts of the Americas at the Museum of Fine Arts, Houston.

Generous funding for *Cosmopolitan Routes: Houston Collects Latin American Art* was provided by

Continental Airlines

Additional funding was provided by Mr. and Mrs. Louis K. Adler; Puffer-Sweiven/Emerson Process Management; Leslie and Brad Bucher; Macy's; and Mr. Samuel F. Gorman.

Produced by the International Center for the Arts of the Americas (ICAA) and the Publications Department of the Museum of Fine Arts, Houston

Distributed by Yale University Press, New Haven and London
www.yalebooks.com/art

Library of Congress Cataloging-in-Publication Data

Vicario, Gilbert.
Cosmopolitan routes : Houston collects Latin American art / by Gilbert Vicario ; with essays by Mari Carmen Ramírez and Elizabeth Cerejido.
p. cm.
Includes index.
ISBN 978-0-300-16933-5 (hardcover)
1. Art, Latin American–20th century–Exhibitions. 2. Art, Latin American–21st century–Exhibitions. 3. Art–Collectors and collecting–Texas–Houston–Exhibitions. I. Ramírez, Mari Carmen, 1955– II. Cerejido, Elizabeth. III. Title. IV. Title: Houston collects Latin American art.
N6502.5.V53 2011
709.8'0747641411–dc22
2010041978

THIS BOOK IS DEDICATED TO
THE LATIN MAECENAS

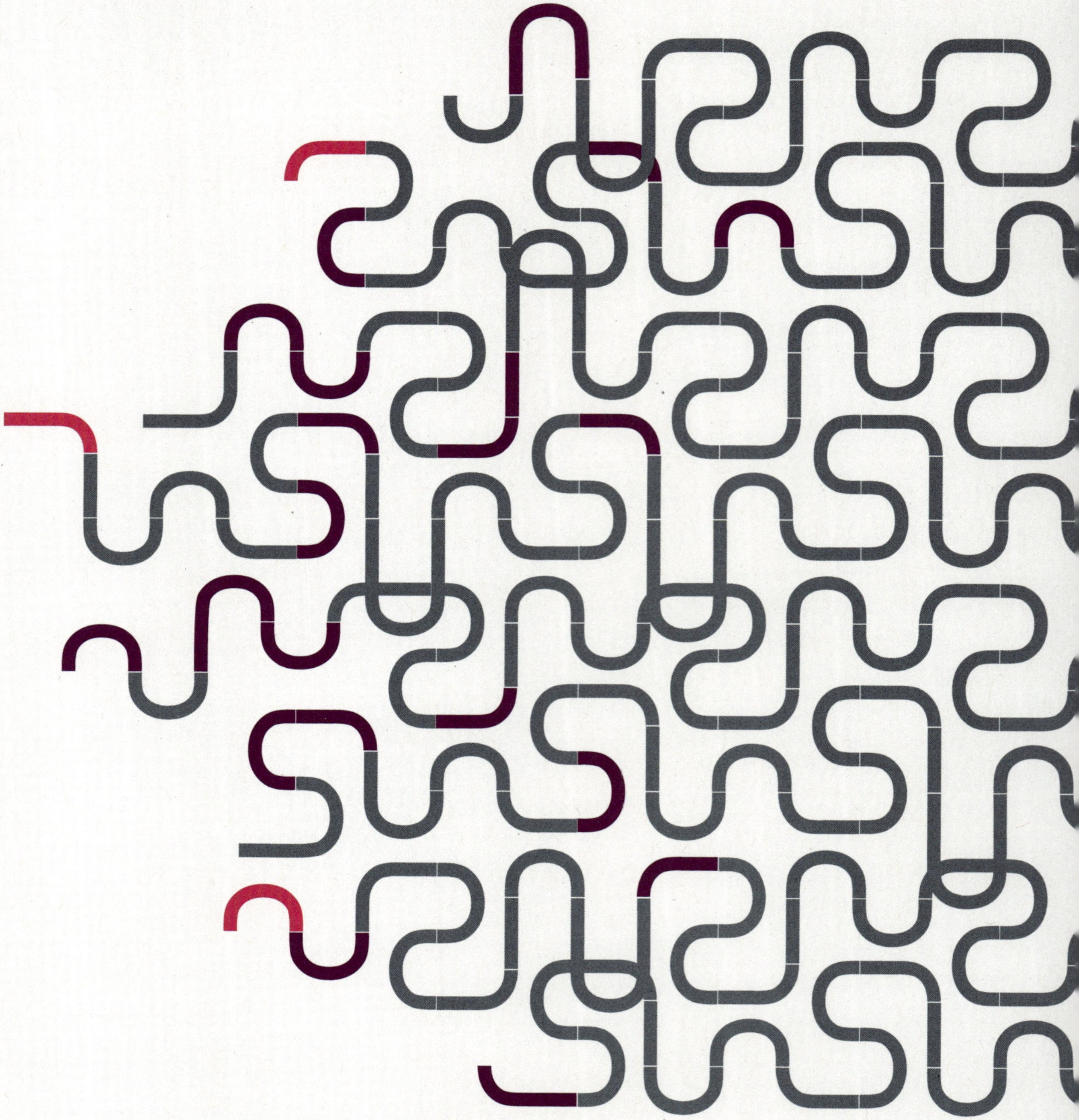

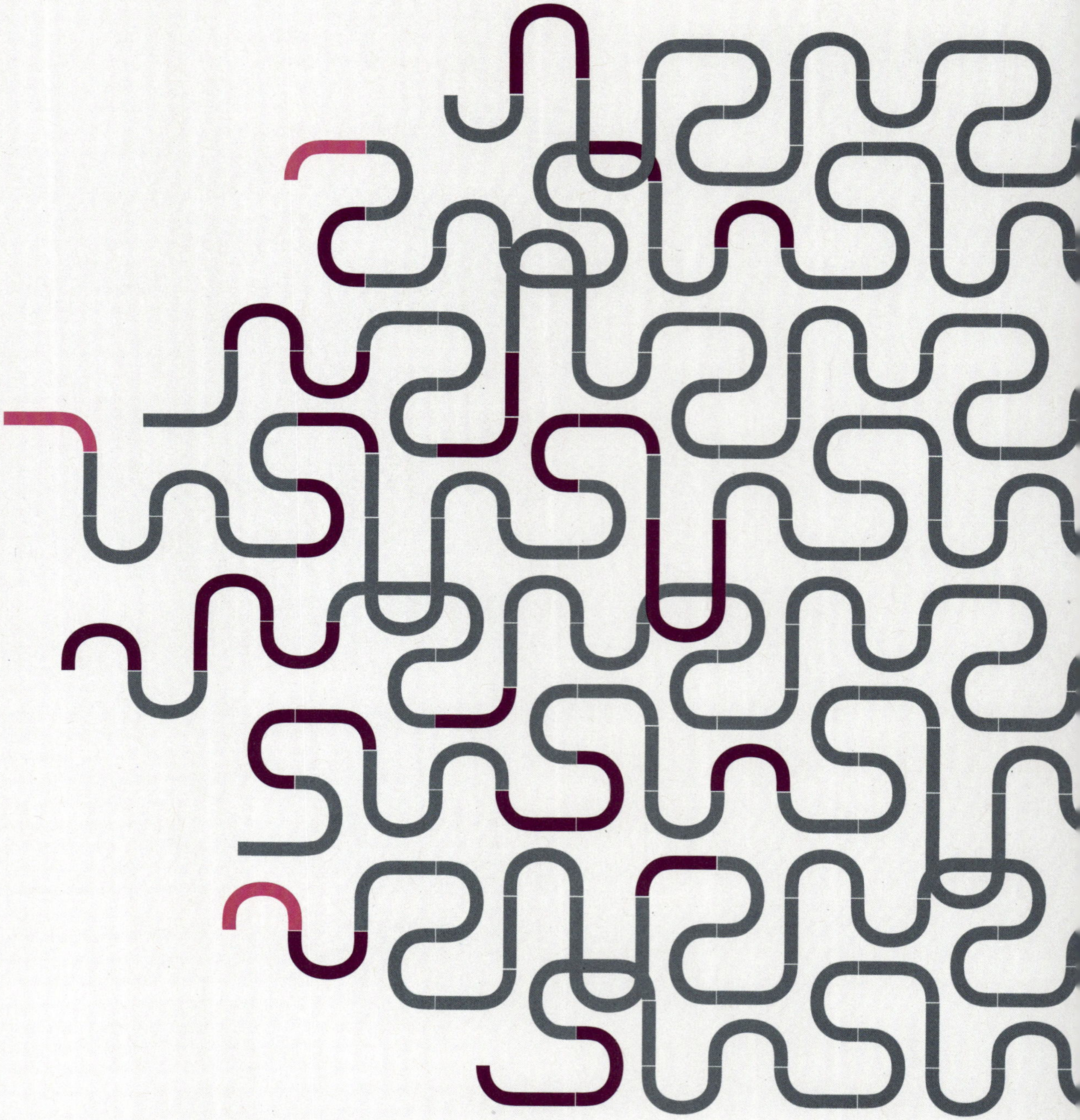

LATIN AMERICAN ART SUBCOMMITTEE THE MUSEUM OF FINE ARTS, HOUSTON

CHAIRMAN
Mr. Richard W. Wortham III

Ms. Sofia Adrogué
Dr. Bernardino Arocha**
Mr. José Luis Barragán**
Mr. Luis Benshimol**
Ms. Tanya Brillembourg
Mr. Brad Bucher
Dr. Luis T. Campos
Mr. Carlos Cruz**
Mrs. Roy H. Cullen**
Mr. Germán Curá**
Mrs. Araceli Diederichs**
Ms. Susan Dunwoody**
The Honorable Sylvia R. Garcia
Mr. Alfred C. Glassell III
Mr. Samuel F. Gorman
Mr. Eduardo Grüneisen**
Mr. Tomás Gunz**
Ms. Celina Hellmund**
Mr. William C. Helms
Mr. George B. Kelly**
Mr. Adolpho Leirner
Mrs. Meredith J. Long
Mrs. Sara S. Morgan
Mr. John C. Moriniere**
Mr. Ernesto Poma**
Mrs. Charles W. Tate

**Committee Consultant

FOUNDERS OF THE LATIN AMERICAN ART COLLECTION AND THE INTERNATIONAL CENTER FOR THE ARTS OF THE AMERICAS AT THE MUSEUM OF FINE ARTS, HOUSTON

PLATINUM FOUNDERS
AT&T Inc.
Cruz-Diez Foundation
The Bruce T. Halle Family Foundation
Caroline Wiess Law Foundation
The Wortham Foundation, Inc./
Mr. and Mrs. R. W. Wortham III

GOLD FOUNDERS
Fundación Gego
Petrobras America, Inc.

SILVER FOUNDERS
Leslie and Brad Bucher
Dr. Luis and Cecilia Campos
The J. Paul Getty Trust

BRONZE FOUNDERS
Celina Hellmund
Bernard Chappard
Mary and Roy Cullen
Fulbright & Jaworski L.L.P.
Linnet F. Deily
Ada Atuña de Matto
Cecilia de Torres
The Ford Foundation
Alfred C. Glassell III
Eduardo Carlos Grüneisen and Maria Eugenia Salimei de Grüneisen
Olive McCollum Jenney
The Henry Luce Foundation
The Latin Maecenas
Frank Ribelin
The Rockefeller Foundation
Andy Warhol Foundation

SUSTAINING FOUNDERS
Sofia Adrogué and Sten L. Gustafson
Antonio Asis
Jean and Benbow Bullock
Ms. Patricia Phelps de Cisneros
Fundación Pan Klub-Xul Solar, Ciudad Buenos Aires
The Favrot Fund
Samuel F. Gorman
Linda and George Kelly
Karol Kreymer and Dr. Robert J. Card
Anne and Jack Moriniere
Cecilia and Ernesto Poma
Kristi and John Schiller
Sotheby's
Judy and Charles Tate
Juan Carlos Uriarte

FOUNDERS
Mary and Bernardino Arocha
Patricia and José Luis Barragán
Frances and Donald E. Baxter, M.D.
Mr. Luis Benshimol
Suzette and Darrell Betts
Jean-Marie and Araceli Diederichs
Susan and Mac Dunwoody
Claudia Alemán Gallegos
Ms. Cecily E. Horton
Lee and Joe Jamail
Adolpho Leirner
Mr. and Mrs. Paul S. Madan
Daniel Joseph Martinez
Oscar Muñoz
Dr. Michele Sartori
María Inés Sicardi, Allison and David Ayers, and Carlos Bacino
Carolina and Sergio Weitzman
Gabriel Werthein

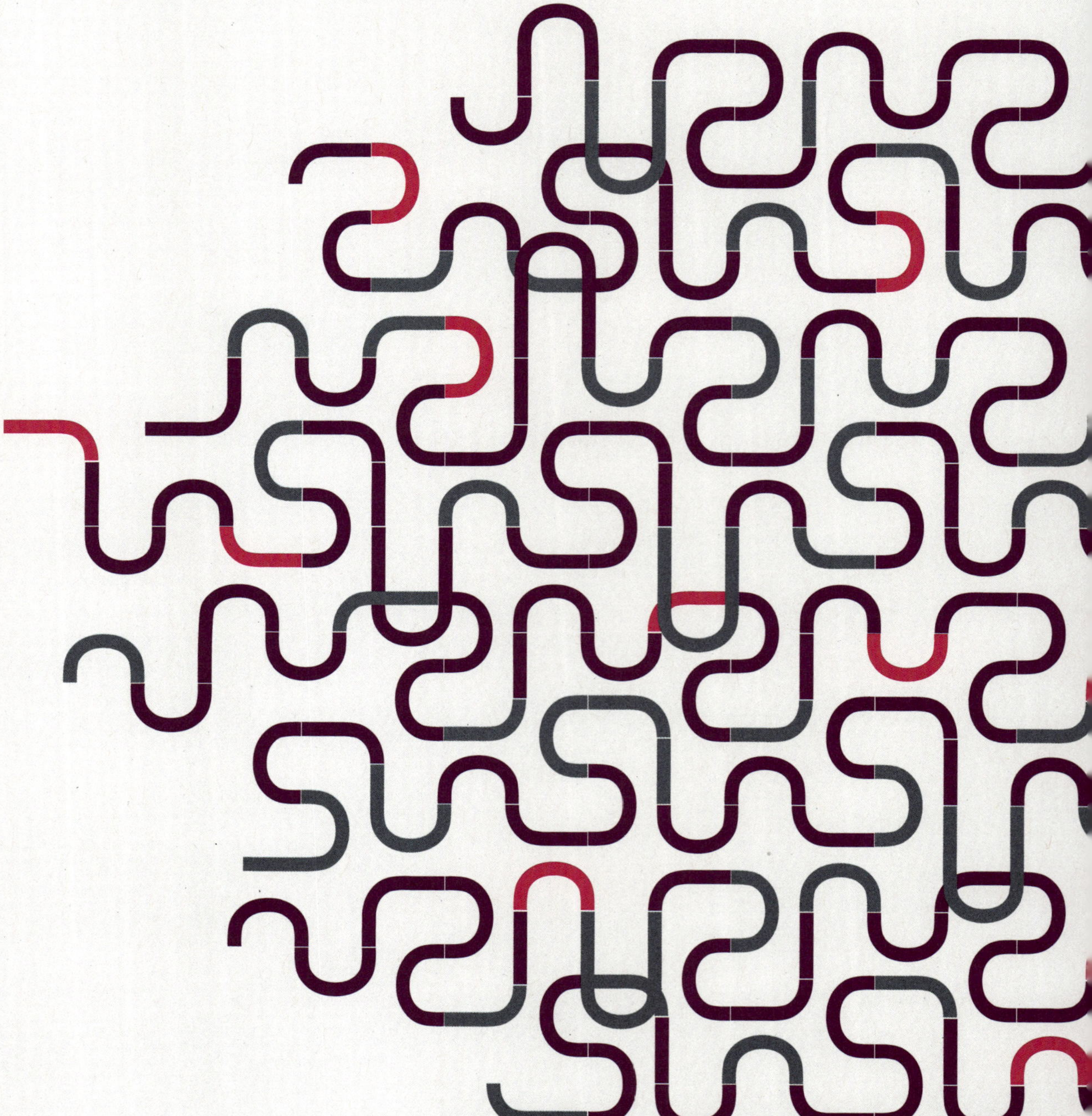

The Museum of Fine Arts, Houston, is committed to collecting, exhibiting, preserving, conserving, and interpreting modern and contemporary art of Latin America and Latino art. During the past nine years, the MFAH trustees have established a department of Latin American art, endowed a curatorship, and built an important research program in the International Center for the Arts of the Americas. The permanent collection has grown at an astounding rate, and private collectors have often led the way with their own individual passions and points of view.

Cosmopolitan Routes is an exhibition conceived as a celebration of collectors and their visions. From Houston to Chicago, Miami, New York, Scottsdale (Arizona), Carmel (California), and other cities, U.S. collectors have united with their neighbors in Mexico, Argentina, Venezuela, Brazil, Chile, and Peru to lend masterworks for this exhibition. In addition, important European collectors, especially those from Spain, have enriched the presentation.

FOREWORD PETER C. MARZIO, DIRECTOR

The exhibition also anticipates the tenth anniversary of the Latin American Art Department and the ICAA, as well as the Latin Maecenas, one of the MFAH's key fund-raising and support organizations. The Latin Maecenas has been the primary patron group that has made the ICAA and the Latin American Art Department possible in the first place.

The professional staff that made this exhibition possible includes guest curator Gilbert Vicario, curator, Des Moines Art Center; Elizabeth Cerejido, assistant curator, Latin American art; Magdalena Grüneisen and Mariana Hartenthal, curatorial interns; Diane Lovejoy, publications director; John Obsta, registrar; Marty Stein, photographic and imaging services manager; and Thomas R. DuBrock and Will Michels, photographers. My thanks go to all of them and to Mari Carmen Ramírez, the Wortham Curator of Latin American Art and director, International Center for the Arts of the Americas, who oversaw the project from its inception. The Board of Trustees joins me in thanking the collectors who willingly shared their artworks with the museum to make this exhibition possible.

Finally, the museum received generous funding from Continental Airlines. Additional support was provided by Mr. and Mrs. Louis K. Adler, Puffer-Sweiven/Emerson Process Management, Leslie and Brad Bucher, Macy's, and Mr. Samuel F. Gorman.

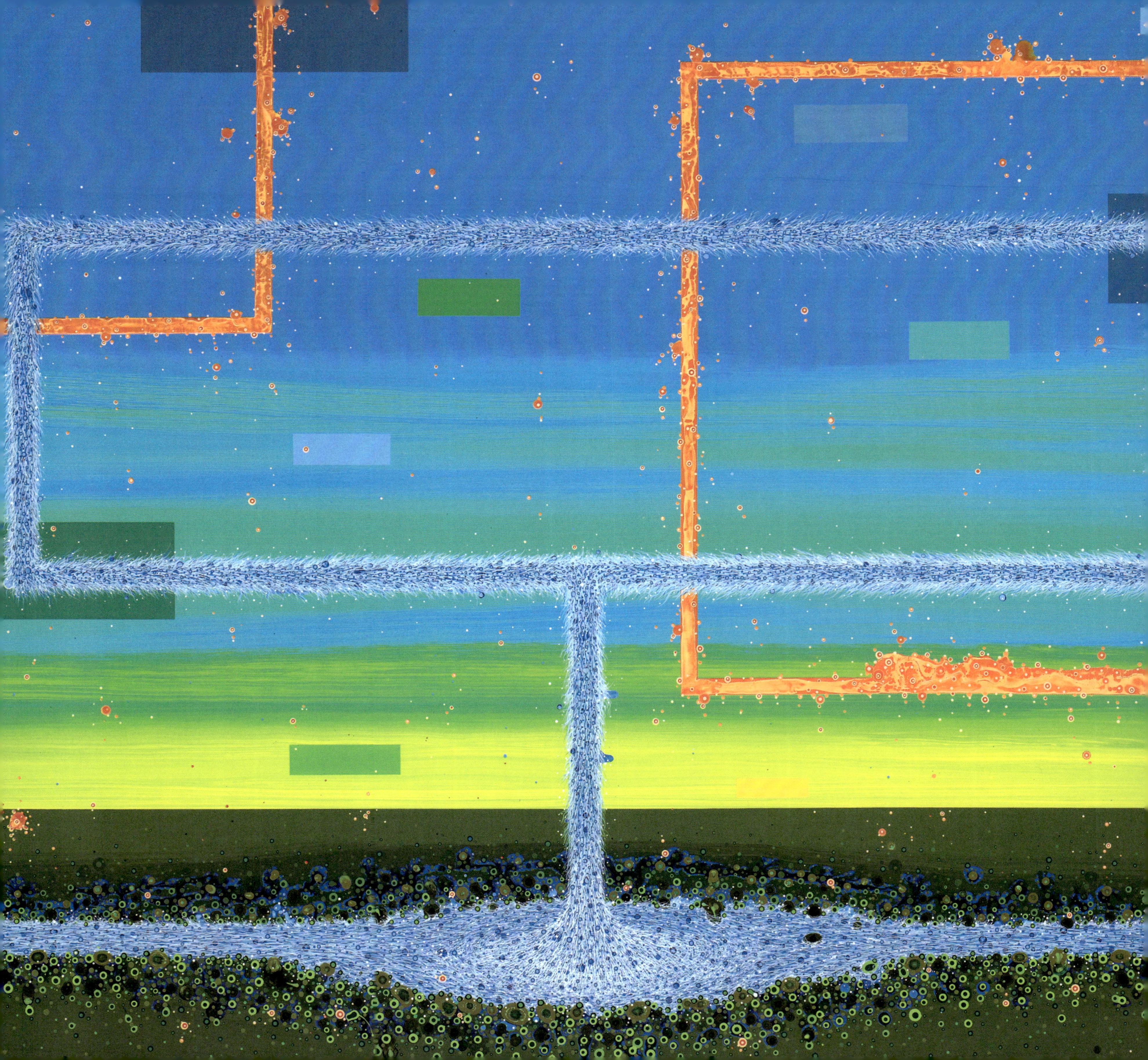

In October 2001, a large group of curators, artists, art historians, collectors, and art-world professionals descended on Houston to take part in the two-day international symposium *Collecting Latin American Art for the 21st Century.* Organized only a few months after the establishment of the Latin American Art Department and the International Center for the Arts of the Americas (ICAA) at the Museum of Fine Arts, Houston, the symposium was the first event organized by both entities with the aim of assisting the museum in charting its course in the deeply heterogeneous fields of Latin American and Latino art. Such an initiative sought to take advantage of the momentum generated by the boom in Latin American art that accompanied the arrival of the new millennium in the United States and abroad. In both formal presentations and informal discussions, presenters and audience members debated the role that a major museum like the MFAH could play in significantly stimulating the growth and development of what was then an emergent field of knowledge and collecting.[1] Among the key questions raised at the

LATIN AMERICAN ART IN HOUSTON
TEN YEARS LATER MARI CARMEN RAMÍREZ

time were: How does an institution or an individual begin to build a collection of the art of such a complex region? What are the challenges involved in these efforts? How could a museum promote sound collecting in this area among members of its constituent audiences? How could the MFAH take advantage of Houston's strategic geographic position and surge in Latino demographics in order to assume a leadership position in the field? At stake was the increasingly visible profile of Latin American art collectors in the global art circuits and the influential role they were being called to play in the fluid arena of contemporary art. With very few collectors of Latin American art in Houston at that time, could our city play such a prominent role, and succeed?

As it turned out, the most optimistic predictions leveled at the time fell short in light of the extraordinary accomplishments of the last decade. Indeed, so much has happened in Houston with regard to Latin American art since the inaugural ICAA symposium that I suspect many of these questions have either been answered or have become irrelevant. As thoroughly illustrated by the present exhibition – *Cosmopolitan Routes: Houston Collects Latin American Art*, guest-curated by Gilbert Vicario – one of the most significant outcomes of the launching of the Latin American

Marcelo Pombo, Argentinean, born 1959
Atardecer junto al arroyo [Sunset by the Stream], (detail), 2001
(See plate 82)

program was the consolidation of an enthusiastic, forward-looking community of Latin American art collectors. In response to the collectors' profound support, the MFAH formally established an organization, the Latin Maecenas. This community of collectors is not limited to Houston but – by way of vividly exemplifying the fluidity of today's global artistic circuits – extends as far south as São Paulo, Santiago, and Buenos Aires. It is precisely the multifarious mix of collectors from North and South America that lends the particular zest and spark to the group's profile and activities. Above all, this is an independent-minded group of individuals brought together first, by their passion for knowledge, and, second, by their evolving interests and strong ties – family, business, or professional – to Latin American art and culture.

Indeed, the selection of works in this exhibition reflects the inquisitiveness and vitality spurring these individuals' efforts to develop and mature as collectors. Because of their focus on the production of a complex region that for decades had been reduced to the biased construct of "the fantastic," it is no surprise that the Latin Maecenas' collecting activities go beyond prevailing stereotypes. In addition to the Latin American sui generis versions of Cubism, Constructivism, and Surrealism, the fifty-eight artists from fourteen countries in *Cosmopolitan Routes* stand for movements as diverse as the River Plate School of the South, Argentinean Neo-Figuration, Brazilian Neo-Concretismo, Venezuelan Cinetismo, and U.S. Latino art, as well as the plural, media-transgressive manifestations of contemporary art. Yet if anything characterizes the ensemble of artists and works on display, it is the lack of inhibition with regard to canonical standards of either taste or artistic fashion. By and large, there is a fresh quality to these collectors' choice of artists that takes them away from the predictable staples of the mainstream art world, placing them instead in unpredictable and more-or-less unexplored and venturesome territory. From this point of view, the works and movements that the title of the exhibition underscores reveal new routes and connections well beyond academic or trendy art-world coordinates.

Despite the challenges involved, the growth of this collecting community has not happened in a void. On the contrary, it has been supported from the beginning by an ambitious, long-term institutional vision that aims to position Houston as a cultural destination – housing radical innovators and experimental contributors – on the map of world art. Indeed, under the visionary, twenty-eight-year leadership of Director Peter C. Marzio, the MFAH has not only grown to become one of the leading encyclopedic museums in the United States. It has also evolved from an institution anchored in the beauty and glory of the art of past civilizations to become an "ecumenical" museum, solidly grounded in the global dynamics of our present times. That is, a museum where the plural, multicultural communities that make up the city and the region – North American, European, Latin American, Asian, African, African-American, Hindu, Islamic – are incorporated, not just as revenue-contributing audiences but as *active and equal co-participants* or *shareholders* of the museum's malleable identity. Such an inclusive paradigm – perhaps the only viable one for encyclopedic museums seeking to reinvent themselves in the twenty-first century –

implies a leadership position based on the principles of gregariousness and cultural dialogue. In such an all-embracing, nonhierarchical museum, Latin American art has found a resonant, synergistic context in which to unfold its meanings. At the same time, this paradigm has provided the fertilizing agent for dynamic communities of collectors like the Latin Maecenas to flourish. Where previously invisible, Houston collectors have emerged as critical partners in the museum's effort to represent and promote the rich legacy of world art represented by its constituent communities.

Such a set of achievements, in turn, speaks volumes about the MFAH's commitment to the field of modern and contemporary Latin American art, automatically answering many of the questions posed in the 2001 symposium. Furthermore, it must be duly stressed that, in the case of this rapidly emergent field, the so-called ecumenical model is complemented by the museum's four-pronged initiative comprising the following key areas: collection-building, exhibitions, research, and education. Armed with a strategic plan – and supported by a growing community of trustees and patrons exemplified by the Latin Maecenas – the MFAH set out to aggressively build an exemplary collection of twentieth- and twenty-first century Latin American art that today comprises more than four hundred works, including the prestigious Adolpho Leirner Collection of Brazilian Constructive Art. The museum has also established innovative, long-term partnerships with the Gego Foundation, the Cruz-Diez Foundation, and the Capriles Brillembourg Collection of Latin American Art. These multifaceted partnerships involve collection-sharing, exhibitions, research, publications, and conservation efforts, as well as the creation of a special fund for acquisitions in under-represented areas such as Central American and Caribbean art. Since the inception of the Latin American program, the Latin American Art Department has organized a number of research-based exhibitions aimed at introducing under-recognized values to the U.S. art scene.[2] And, through its research arm – the ICAA – it not only has published fourteen books and catalogues but also has organized the monumental initiative *Documents of Twentieth-Century Latin American and Latino Art: A Digital Archive and Publications Project*. The latter brings together a network of close to one hundred researchers located in ten Latin American and U.S. cities who for the last six years have been recovering, scanning, cataloguing, and uploading primary documents to an Internet-based website, where they will be available free of charge to users worldwide. The main objectives of this program are to make accessible the intellectual production of twentieth-century Latin American and Latino creators while simultaneously establishing the bases for a comparative history of Latin American and Latino art.

Under such parameters, *Cosmopolitan Routes: Houston Collects Latin American Art* is not only a concrete testimony of the undeniable inroads that both the museum and the city have made in this area over the last decade. It also exemplifies the impact these Houston-based initiatives have had in the field at-large during this brief period of time. This fact becomes clear when we consider that, ten years ago, the key factor missing from the international map of Latin American art was official legitimization and stable institutional support of the kind that could only be provided by major art museums. Everything else – abundant artistic production, active markets, specialized auctions, impassioned collectors, and exhibition circuits – was duly in place. In this context, the MFAH was, indeed, the first museum in its class to grasp the potential long-term transformative boost of such a move in a hegemonic country like the United States. That is, a country that not only houses the primary market for this art but is also home to the largest ascendant minority population of Latin descent in the world. Until then, no other major museum here or abroad had programmatically invested in an artistic and research venture of this scope in a sustained way. Hence, insofar as it stimulated other key institutions to enter the game, the outcome of that decision – we now know – had deep repercussions outside of Houston. Together with a host of other factors, the participation of the MFAH and others on the playing field of Latin American art contributed to turn a previously marginalized field into a highly competitive arena for the exchange of both private and institutional symbolic capital. Believe it or not, as can be attested by the enhanced presence of Latin American artists in global exhibition circuits and institutional collections, the result is the long-awaited consolidation of Latin American art as a global exhibition and collecting phenomenon.

This type of success, however, generally brings to light the limitations and contradictions of the developments at hand. Not surprisingly, in addition to a steep rise in prices and sales – not a bad development if decades of outright neglect are to be considered – the last ten years have also seen the increased "mainstreaming" of this art as more institutions and collectors seek access to its first-rate (yet still under-recognized) artists. More importantly, globalization has transformed Latin American art from a marginal investment into a strategic economic resource. That is, thanks to the activities of both private and institutional collectors, this art has become a favorite commodity in international markets. While there is no doubt that all this frantic back-and-forth is extremely positive for a growing field seeking long-term validation, it also brings with it potential pitfalls. The "mainstreaming" of Latin American art, for example, has sought to take away the specificity of its multifarious manifestations by reducing them to yet other instances of de-territorialized, "global" art. As collectors from across the globe vie for the historic "reserves" of this art, local museums in Latin American countries – unable to compete with such powerful agents – are left without works to fill their own institutional collections. And, as the markets demand more and more art from major players like Mexico, Brazil, Argentina, and Venezuela, the production of West Coast, Caribbean, Central American, and even U.S. Latino artists still awaits due recognition and validation.

Considering such a shifting – even volatile – context leads me to raise the following question: What will the next ten years bring for Latin American art? Although it is impossible to answer this question, it is important to keep in mind that, at least in Houston, what ten years ago seemed unreachable or exaggerated, today – thanks to the concerted efforts of the Museum of Fine Arts, Houston, and the community of collectors and supporters it has stimulated – has taken the concrete shape of a work-in-progress. From this perspective, I will argue, however, that the future of this field in the United States and elsewhere lies in the ability of institutions to ground this art in initiatives that combine ambitious collecting and exhibition efforts with solid research about the art, the artists who produced it, and the context – both local and international – that nurtured it. In this regard, only museums that have actively partnered with their communities and are attuned to the needs of the art and artists represented in their collection can both preserve the artistic production and make it relevant for generations of visitors. In this regard, the MFAH paradigm, insofar as it brings together a dynamic community of collectors with a powerhouse museum committed to collection-building, research, and education in the context of an inclusive, "ecumenical" vision of world art, has the possibility to once more re-draw the map of Latin American and Latino art for decades to come.

Finally, it would be naïve to think that the impact of the developments in the field of Latin American and Latino art of the last decade are restricted to the limited scope of the art world. The collaborative experience of the last ten years – undertaken through exhibitions, publications, and debates, as well as deep questioning – has led me to the conviction that what is at stake in such undertakings is not so much the long-term value or legitimization of Latin American art. To the extent that they have the potential to give a visible face to ascendant countries and communities, the repercussions of this project extend way beyond Houston. *Cosmopolitan Routes* is thus only a first encouraging step in this process.

Houston, October 2010

NOTES

1 See Mari Carmen Ramírez and Teresa Papanikolas, eds., *Collecting Latin American Art for the Twenty-First Century* (Houston: International Center for the Arts of the Americas, 2002).

2 Among the numerous significant exhibitions are *Inverted Utopias: Avant-Garde Art in Latin America* (2004); *Gego, Between Transparency and the Invisible* (2005); *Hélio Oiticica: The Body of Color* (2006); *Constructing a Poetic Universe: The Diane and Bruce Halle Collection of Latin American Art* (2007); *Building on a Construct: The Adolpho Leirner Collection of Brazilian Constructive Art at the Museum of Fine Arts, Houston* (2009).

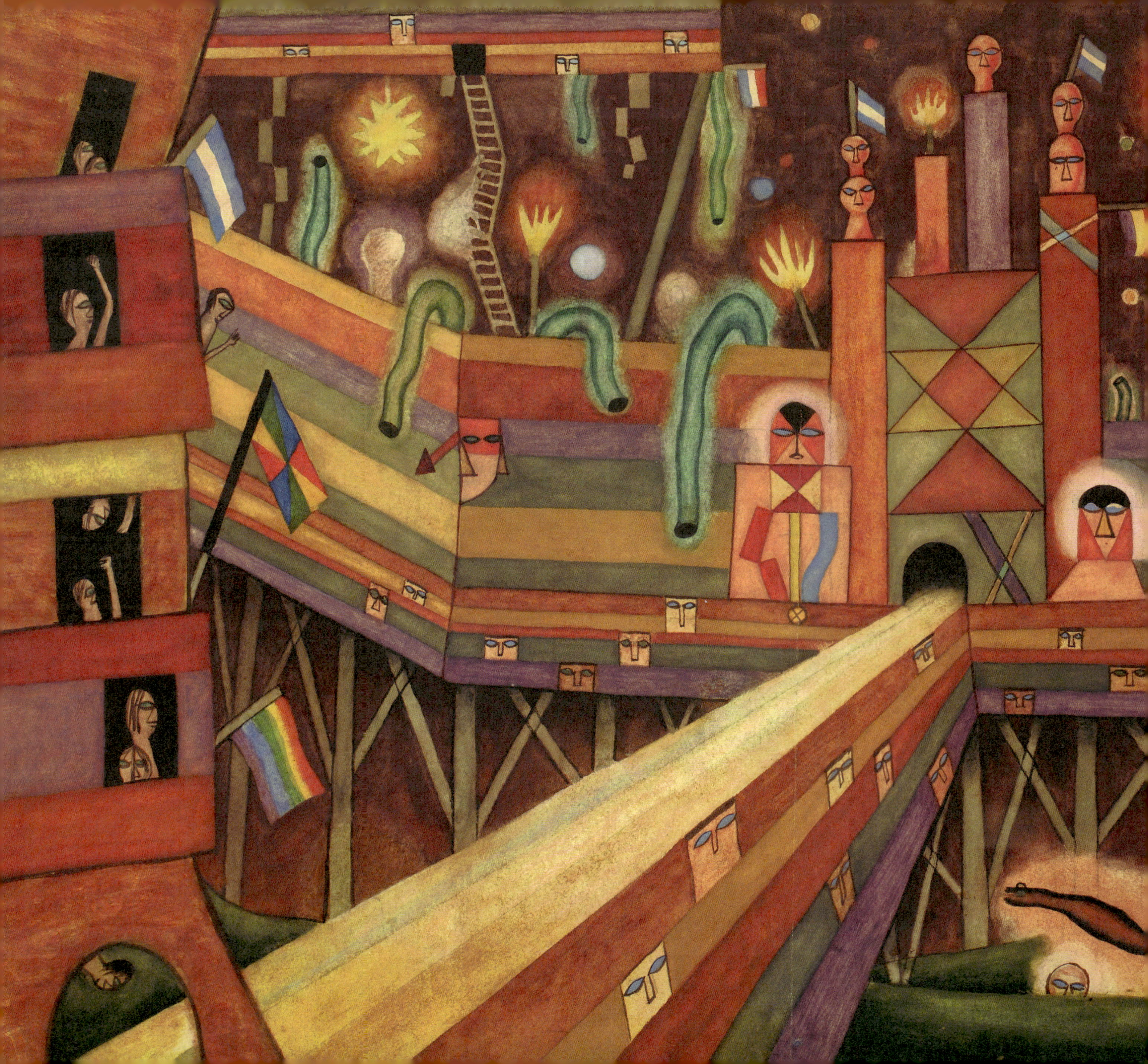

Cosmopolitan Routes: Houston Collects Latin American Art is an exhibition and publication project that highlights private holdings of Latin American art in the community at large and offers insights into the relationship between the art museum and the art collector. The diverse cultural makeup of the individuals themselves is reflected in their holdings of art. Certain collections gravitate toward one particular country, while in other cases a particular movement or style has informed the collectors' interests. The exhibition is organized into operative categories that take these idiosyncrasies into account while grouping together artists commonly found among many of the collectors and introducing new and lesser-known artists into the fold.

The exhibition frames the correspondences between the work produced in Latin America in the twentieth century and the larger artistic movements that have come to define modern and contemporary art on a global level. The works by Latin American and Latino artists are part of

COSMOPOLITAN ROUTES HOUSTON COLLECTS LATIN AMERICAN ART GILBERT VICARIO

a complex dialogue that mixes political, social, and cultural issues across geographic and national boundaries. Mexico, for example, has always held a special place in the intellectual imagination of European artists and writers and has served as a refuge for expatriates who have contributed to the artistic legacy. While in South America, many artists successfully combined their appreciation of European avant-garde movements with local sources to create a uniquely Latin American Modernist vision.

Cosmopolitan Routes situates Latin American art not as a monolithic school, but rather as a continually evolving discourse that occurs among individual impulses, universal themes, and shared ideas, all across vast networks of knowledge. The artists and works span about one hundred years, and, therefore, not every aspect of Latin American art is covered in the scope of this exhibition. Instead, the curatorial parameters have been defined by two guiding principles: that Latin American artists have always operated within sophisticated, global circuits, and that these artists have embarked on singular artistic trajectories. Sometimes these paths converge, or they move in opposite directions, or they run on parallel tracks. *Cosmopolitan Routes* also acknowledges that collectors

Xul Solar, Argentinean, 1887-1963
El túnel [The Tunnel] (detail), 1923
(See plate 20)

follow their own paths in choosing works that resonate personally and engage them in art collecting; this participatory act, in turn, reinforces the critical role played by the individual in the construction of culture through this practice. In keeping with this theme, it is significant to note that although the majority of the museum's patrons of Latin American art reside in Houston, an important constituent lives at least part-time in other places around the world. The Houston community extends to Carmel, Chicago, Miami, New York, and Scottsdale; and to our neighbors in the Southern Hemisphere: Monterrey, Mexico; Buenos Aires, Argentina; Caracas, Venezuela; São Paulo, Brazil; Santiago, Chile; and Madrid, Spain.

Cosmopolitan Routes is loosely organized around nine intersections. "Pioneers of Modernism" lays the groundwork and presents artists whose works are steeped in the artistic milieu of Europe in the early decades of the twentieth century, and who spent their formative years in Paris. "Automatism" explores André Breton's influence in Latin America and the symbiotic relationship between his sympathizers and Surrealist-inclined European artists living and working in Mexico after World War I. "The Inverted Map" acknowledges the influential role that Joaquín Torres-García played in South America upon his return to Montevideo in 1934 after spending more than forty years in Europe; this intersection also examines the numerous directions taken by some of his best students. "Constructed Identities" features work from Argentina, Uruguay, and Brazil that articulates the multiple ways in which abstraction and Concrete art exemplify their relationship to place. "Conceptual Realism" outlines covert strategies employed by South American artists to comment on political and social injustices, using both Post-Abstract Expressionist and figurative styles. "Unstable Visions" highlights the work of Kinetic artists who were primarily from Venezuela and Argentina, but who moved to Paris to join a larger international movement centered on optic or retinal concerns. "Discursive Play" initiates a conversation that addresses how contemporary artists sometimes quote from or readdress the contributions of an earlier generation of artists as a means of inscribing historical context into their own practice. "Connecting the Dots" focuses on how contemporary Latin American artists have used photography, video, and other digital reproductive technologies to produce work. "Borders Crossed" juxtaposes work by artists of Latin American descent with that of artists who simply use Latin America as their subject, providing curatorial commentary on the ever-expanding definition of what it means to be Latin American.

PIONEERS OF MODERNISM

Although work by the early pioneers of Latin American art is increasingly difficult to acquire, many Houston collectors have continued to search for and to embrace examples by artists such as Diego Rivera, Emilio Pettoruti, and Xul Solar as a way of deepening and expanding the reach of Modernism. Rivera, who spent nearly fourteen years in Europe, beginning in 1907, was initially informed by Spanish Modernism, yet he went on to explore Cubist tendencies that were starting to take shape in nearby Paris. Rivera's *Still Life with Lemons* (1916; plate 1), for example, with its bright palette and collapsed

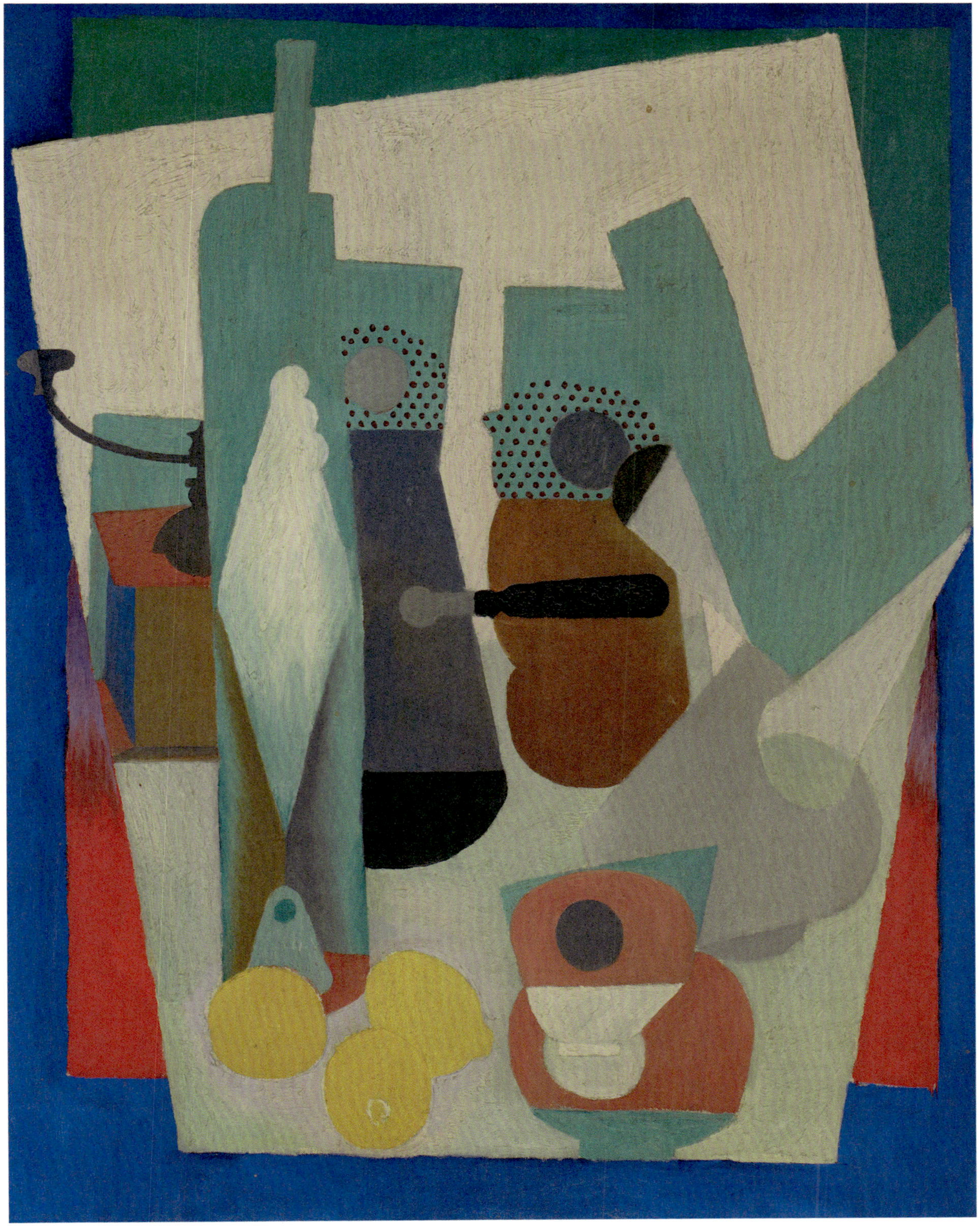

Plate 1
Diego Rivera, Mexican, 1886–1957
Still Life with Lemons, 1916
Oil on canvas
41 1/2 x 35 3/4 x 2 in. (105.4 x 90.8 x 5.1 cm)
The Brillembourg Capriles Collection
of Latin American Art at the Museum of
Fine Arts, Houston

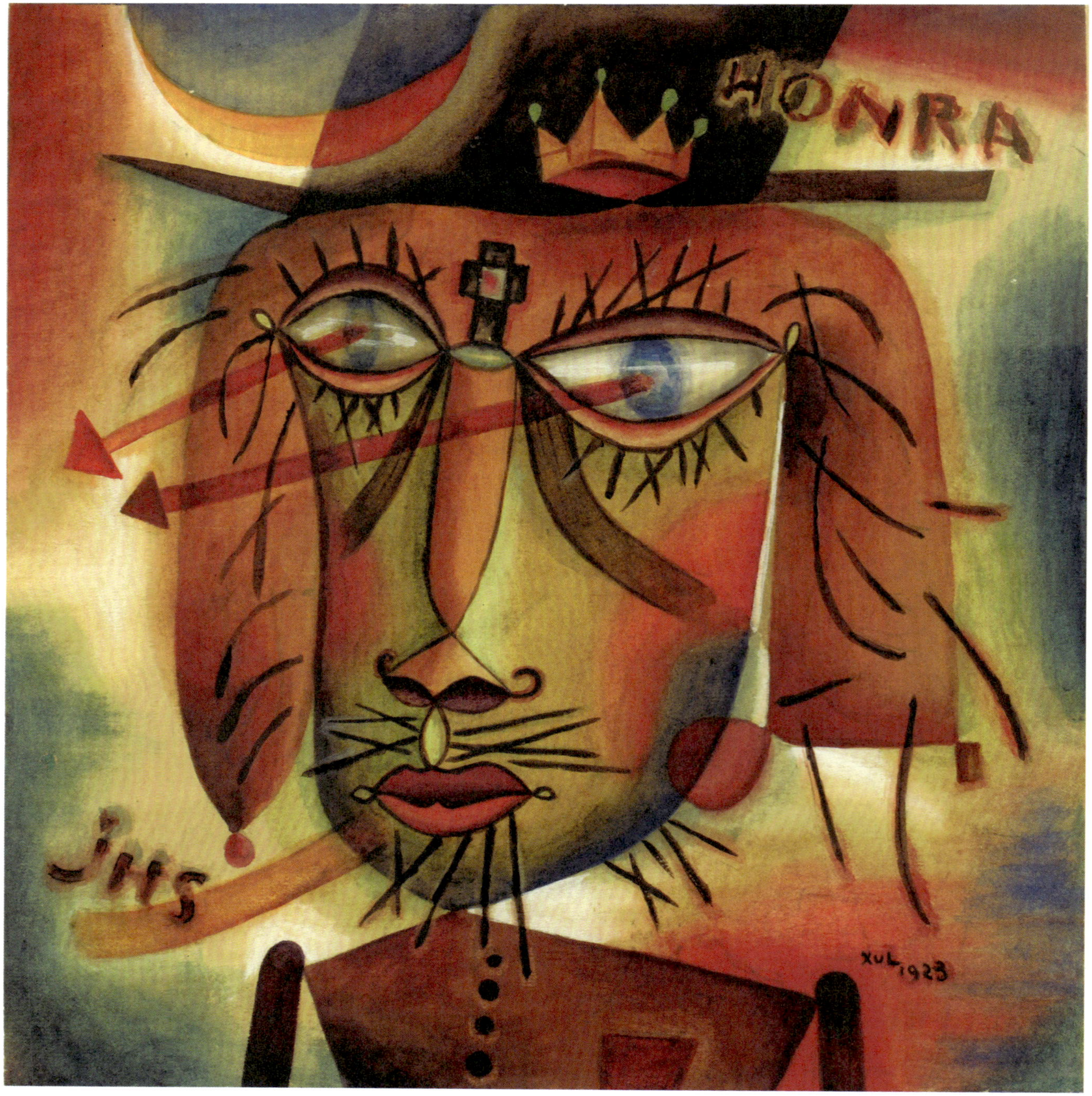

Plate 2
Xul Solar, Argentinean, 1887-1963
Jefa honra [Patroness Honor], 1923
Watercolor on paper
11 x 10 1/4 in. (28 x 26 cm)
Private collection

perspective, demonstrates how the artist began experimenting with the Synthetic Cubism more closely associated with the Spanish-born artist Juan Gris. In Rivera's composition, traditional still-life components are reduced to two-dimensional forms that emphasize their placement against shifting planes; these defy both gravity and depth. Toward the center of the composition, Rivera added Pointillist dots, which mirror Pablo Picasso's and Georges Braque's style at the time. Similarly, the Argentinean painter Emilio Pettoruti's work was deeply influenced by Gris's Synthetic Cubism. *La Voce* (1916; see plate 13) demonstrates how Pettoruti adapted Gris's collage technique, thereby continuing the exploration of two- and three-dimensional space on the surface of the canvas. Unlike Pettoruti with his European influences, Xul Solar leaned toward the visual poetry of Vassily Kandinsky and the playfulness of Paul Klee, although there were far more profound undercurrents at work. Xul Solar's vision is epitomized in *Jefa honra* (1923; plate 2), which features an animal figure with cosmological references, a crown, and the word "Honra" spelled out across the top of the composition. Imagined architecture was a leitmotif in his career. *El túnel [The Tunnel]* (1923; see plate 18), with its vibrant color palette of mauves and ochres, celebrates his cosmopolitan vision, expressed in the numerous and different imaginary flags that jut out from the eccentrically shaped structures. The stilts supporting the buildings refer to the many summer homes built on the flood-prone banks of the Tigre River outside of Buenos Aires. Although his works are sometimes mistaken for Surrealist art, Xul Solar's oeuvre was far removed from the Bretonian activities that emerged from World War I.

AUTOMATISM

From the 1920s on, the Surrealist movement spread across the globe, eventually impacting the visual arts, literature, film, and music of many countries and languages, as well as political thought and practice, philosophy, and social theory. As the poet and Surrealist theorist André Breton asserted, Surrealism was a form of revolution and was deeply connected to his own experiences of working in a neurological hospital treating soldiers suffering from shell shock. Breton was trained in medicine and psychiatry and applied Sigmund Freud's psychoanalytic principles to the battlefield. Back in Paris, Breton started the literary journal *Littérature* with Louis Aragon and Philippe Soupalt. In 1938, Breton accepted an invitation to a conference on Surrealism held at the National Autonomous University of Mexico (UNAM). There, Breton, after getting lost in Mexico City, famously stated, "I don't know why I came here. Mexico is the most surrealist country in the world." Diego Rivera and Frida Kahlo were among the small community of intellectuals and artists that entertained the French poet while in Mexico, whose itinerary included an important visit with the exiled Russian revolutionary Leon Trotsky. Breton and Rivera cowrote a manifesto, "*Pour un art révolutionaire indépendent*," which called for the freedom of art during an increasingly difficult time in the world.

From this point on, Mexico, and specifically Mexico City, became strongly associated with the Surrealist movement. Many artists from Europe were attracted to the artistic milieu found there, in part by the international attention focused on Rivera and Kahlo. In 1939, Kahlo began to receive critical attention for her own work and was given an exhibition in Paris at the Reno & Cole Gallery. *Moses* (1945) is one of Kahlo's most important contributions to Surrealism. An essay by Freud that established a link between ancient Egyptian beliefs, Moses, and the origins of monotheistic religion inspired the painting that depicts the infant Moses with a third eye of wisdom, a device Kahlo sometimes used in her portraits of Rivera. Another artist who integrated into the Mexican art scene at that time was Leonora Carrington, who had arrived in Mexico in 1942 after an emotional breakdown triggered by her separation from Max Ernst at the outbreak of World War II. Like Remedios Varo, the Spanish-born painter who had moved to Mexico a year earlier, Carrington had a passionate interest in the occult; many allusions to agnostic doctrines appear in her work, as do references to techniques of divination and to ancient Celtic mythology. Carrington's *The Journey of Prester John* (1953; see plate 27), which makes these connections, is a double-sided painting coauthored by the British poet Edward James, who was the visionary architect of Las Pozas, near Tampico, Mexico, and one of Carrington's greatest supporters. The art critic Salomon Grimberg writes that *Casting the Runes* (1951; see plate 28) is Carrington's visual adaptation of a fictional ghost tale written by Montague Rhodes James, provost of Eton College, involving alchemy, revenge, and a spell cast on the Academy using the runes (secrets) of the god Odin's magic alphabet. At the lower right of the composition are red-hooded priests responsible for conducting initiation rites; the central composition is dominated by a golden animal said to represent the moon.[1]

THE INVERTED MAP

While Surrealism continued to flourish in Mexico during the 1940s, the Constructive Universalist movement, centered on Joaquín Torres-García's influential teachings, asserted itself as a progressive melding of European abstraction and Pre-Columbian and indigenous art forms. Torres-García made significant inroads into European intellectual circles that were advancing the aesthetic values of Constructive and abstract-geometric art. Back in Paris in 1926–32, he met and interacted with important artists such as Theo van Doesburg, Jean Hélion, Georges Vantongerloo, and Piet Mondrian. Torres-García's contribution to this discourse included the order and logic found in rules of composition, such as the golden ration, and he included in his works symbolic figures that represent man, knowledge, science, and the city. *Composition symetrique #525 en rouge* (1932; plate 3), for example, illustrates his approach to the vertical-horizontal grid by incorporating a unique vocabulary of pictographic symbols that harmoniously balance intellectual, emotional, and earthly elements. By 1934, Torres-García had returned to his native country, where he began applying progressive artistic theories at the Uruguay Society of Arts, and also began teaching and exhibiting his work at the Escuela Taller de Artes Plásticas. In 1943, he founded the Taller Torres-García for young artists, an arts-and-crafts workshop that operated until the early 1960s. Torres-García died in 1949, leaving an indelible legacy that forever changed the aesthetic

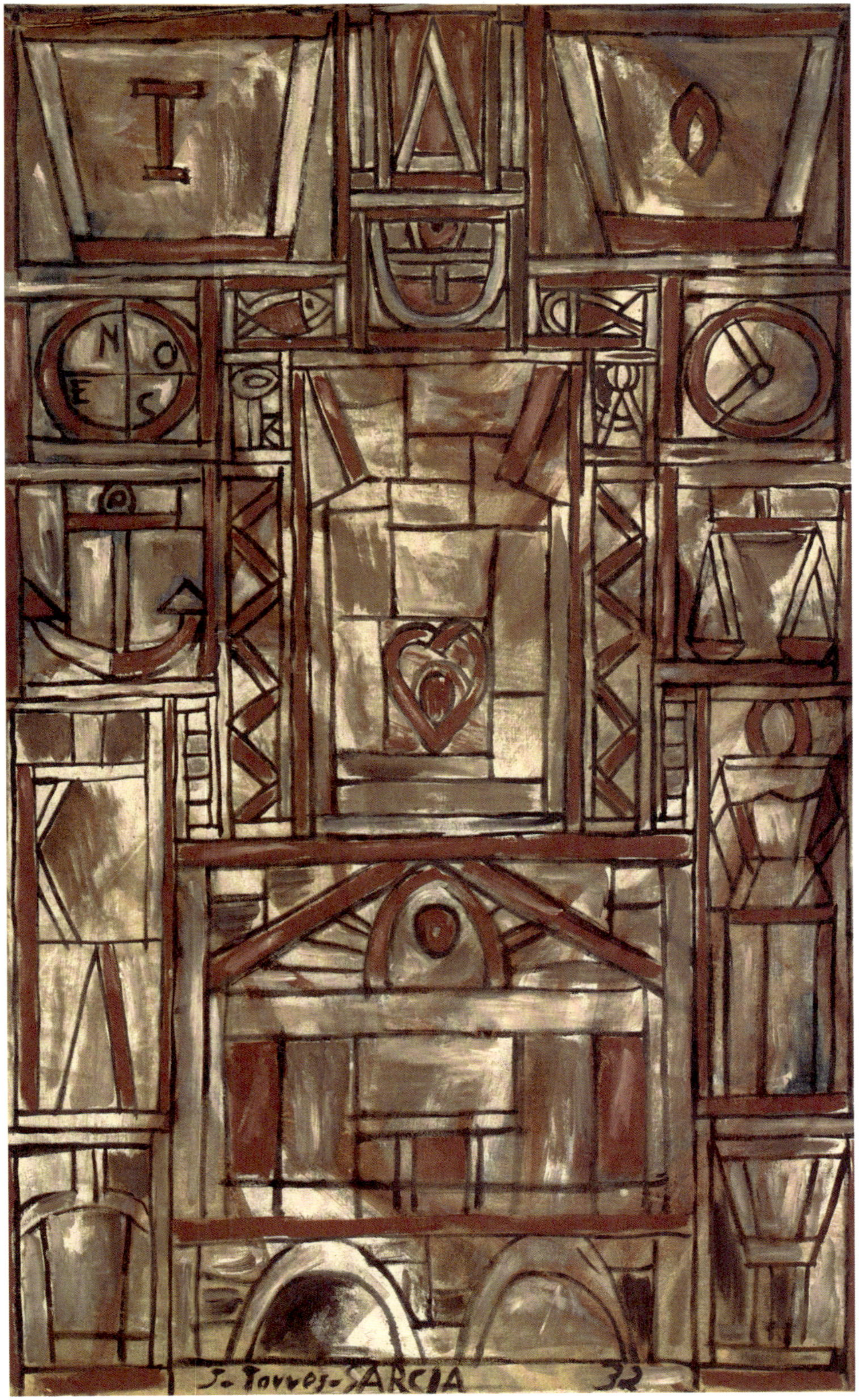

Plate 3
Joaquín Torres-García, Uruguayan, 1874-1949
Composition symetrique #525 en rouge
[Composición simétrica # 525 en rojo]
[Symmetric Composition #525 in Red], 1932
Oil on canvas
50 1/2 x 31 1/4 in. (128.3 x 79.4 cm)
Collection of Mr. and Mrs. Meredith J. Long

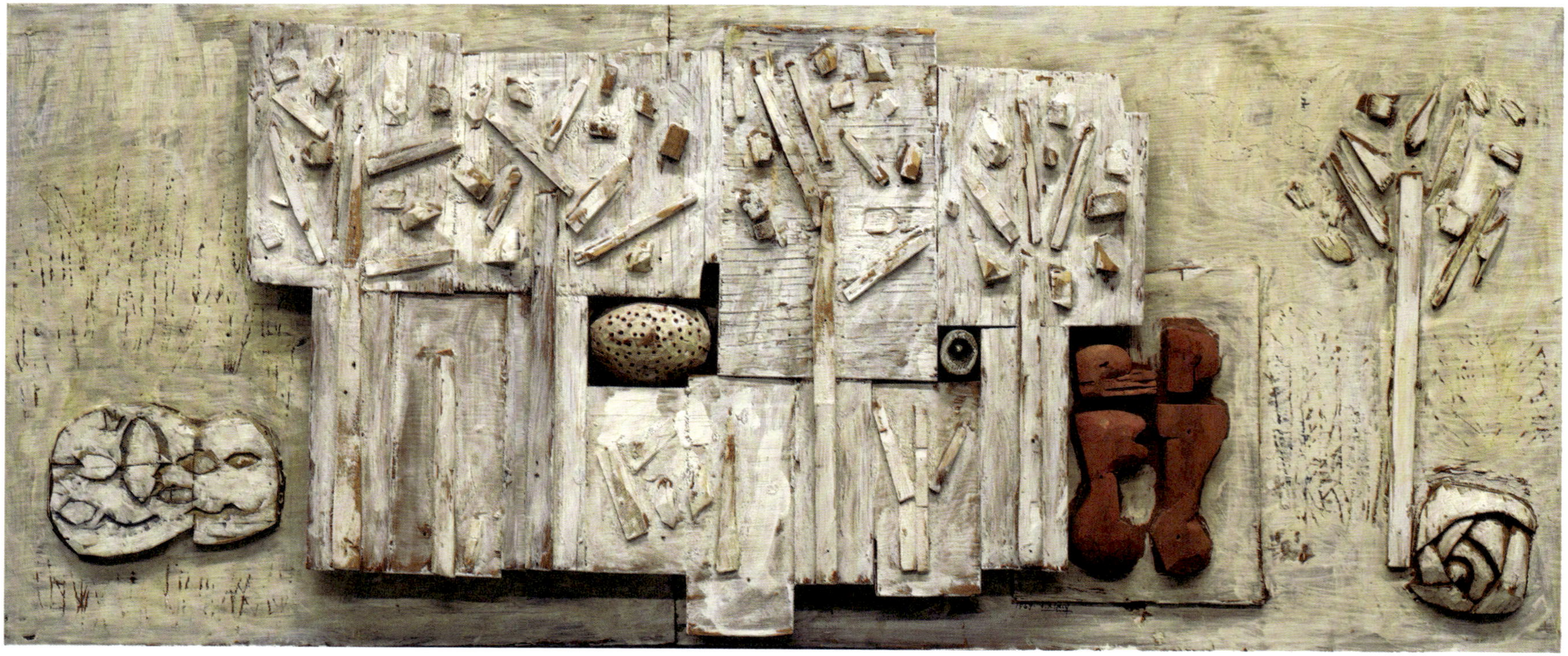

Plate 4
Julio Alpuy, Uruguayan, 1919-2009
Sin título (Bosque con pareja) [Untitled (Forest with Couple)], 1969
Oil on carved and incised wood
22 x 57 1/2 in. (56 x 146.5 cm)
Collection of Celina Hellmund

language of modern South America. His most dedicated students went on to develop their own independent styles, charting new territories by incorporating elements that enabled their work to emerge collectively as singular identities, distinct from work of the Constructive Universalist program. Julio Alpuy, for example, who was first a student and then a teacher at the Taller, expanded his vocabulary by immersing himself in travels that led him through Latin America, Europe, the Middle East, and eventually to New York, where he settled in 1961. Alpuy believed that these travels helped him to establish a universal language that ultimately refined his view of the figure, landscape, and spirituality. Works such as *Sín titulo (Bosque con pareja)* [Untitled (Forest with Couple)] (1969; plate 4) demonstrate a radical departure from the Constructive grid to a more earthly composition, typified by his use of rough-hewn incisions into solid wood supports, primitive carvings, pockmarks, and organic depictions of primeval and cosmological landscapes. On the other hand, Gonzalo Fonseca's body of work is more purely sculptural in form than Alpuy's. Favoring wood, stone, and marble, Fonseca looked toward architecture and the ancient ruins of Bolivia and Peru for inspiration, fueled, in part, by a desire to collapse ancient and modern times through the construction of imagined microcosms. *Dos cabezas* [Two Heads] (1968; plate 5), considered to be an unusual piece for Fonseca, is made of found wood elements that he collected on the streets of New York. Nestled within the two boxlike niches are two busts; one contains a carved head choked by a ball stuffed in its mouth, and the other makes a playful reference to sex. This piece may be Fonseca's response to the compartmentalization that Jasper Johns frequently employed in works such as *Target with Four Faces* (1955), or perhaps it is simply an adaptation of Fonseca's architectonic structures to the sophisticated artistic milieu of New York City.

CONSTRUCTED IDENTITIES

By the mid-1940s, the legacy of Constructive and geometric art extended well beyond the borders of Uruguay to include important regional manifestations in Argentina and Brazil. The Madí movement began about 1946 in Argentina and included Carmelo Arden Quin, Gyula Kosice, Ennio Iommi, Diyi Laañ, and Martín Blaszko. The movement emphasized nonfigurative expressions that articulated geometry and color within nontraditional forms. The Madí artist Antonio Llorens made a significant impact at the São Paulo Biennale in 1958 when his painting *Geométrico con cuadrado* (1952; see plate 40) was exhibited. The work consists of a flat plane juxtaposing orthogonal squares with sinuous lines and forms. In Brazil, the Constructive and Concrete art movements manifested in both the Grupo Frente (1954–56) in Rio de Janeiro and the Grupo ruptura (1952) in São Paulo. Hélio Oiticica, who at age seventeen qualified as the youngest member of Grupo Frente, developed a unique oeuvre that shifted the notion of color into conceptual and interactive territories, forever changing the relationship of color to figure and ground. The Metaesquemas series consists of more than 350 gouache-on-board studies of color and geometry; its title combines the Portuguese words "meta" (beyond vision) and "esquema" (structure). Oiticica reduced his vocabulary to an arrangement of positive and negative spaces. He produced interplays between shapes and backgrounds by using a "mirror effect" that repeats on a grid, creating a strict visual logic out of seeming chaos and irregularity (plates 6–7). Lygia Clark, who with Oiticica, Lygia Pape, and Ferreira Gullar founded the Neo-Concrete movement, in 1957, produced stark, two-dimensional works that create three-dimensionality out of flat planes of line and surface. As was the case with Oiticica, in the Superficies Moduladas series of 1956–58, Clark initiated what became an evolutionary process of breaking down the relationship between the traditional work of art and the spectator by beginning to separate illusion from reality.

CONCEPTUAL REALISM

The influential artist Antonio Berni used the representational power of the human figure to express through caricature the character of the Argentinean people. He devoted a substantial body of work to two stock characters he invented: Juanito Laguna, a poor boy from the slums of Buenos Aires, and Ramona Montiel, a woman who in trying to make a living, eventually becomes a prostitute (see plate 64). Berni's work is marked by great technical innovation, and his skill at creating assemblages of recycled materials is without equal in Latin America. His innovative printing technique, called "xilocollage relief," creates a thick textured surface with impressions made of recycled objects. In works such as *Ley marcial* [Martial Law], the grotesque figure of a general is rendered as a combination of painted surface and assemblage. Only plastic eyes and wiry facial hair counterbalance his face, a bizarre combination of teal and purple colors, while metal shoe taps adorn his uniform. Jorge de la Vega, Luis Felipe Noé, and Leon Ferrari in Argentina, and José Balmes in Chile picked up on the rebellious and chaotic potential of figuration and gestural painting as a means of expressing political uncertainty. Noé's *Alias el chancho*, 1962, is a grizzly depiction of a pig devouring its prey while a group of individuals appears emotionless in the background. At the bottom of the painting, the words *viva la patria* (long live the nation) are scrawled in red paint, clearly articulating its political message. De la Vega similarly produced large-scale canvases, filled with jarring images of ferocious-looking creatures that exemplified a collective fear of chaos and distrust at the hands of an unstable and violent government. Ferrrari's untitled drawings from 1962 predate the Carta a un general (Letter to a General) (1963) series that were made in response to the military dictatorship. The earlier drawings, while not directly related to his covert admonition of the ruling government, exemplify how the incomprehensibility of his cursive drawings can deeply convey contemporary social angst through a psycho-linguistic framework.

UNSTABLE VISIONS

Running parallel to the Expressionist tendencies of the aforementioned artists was the transcontinental movement of optical and Kinetic art. The Argentines Julio Le Parc, Horacio García Rossi, Martha Boto, Luis Tomasello, and Gregorio Vardanega practiced or continue to practice in Paris, while the Venezuelans Jesús Rafael Soto and

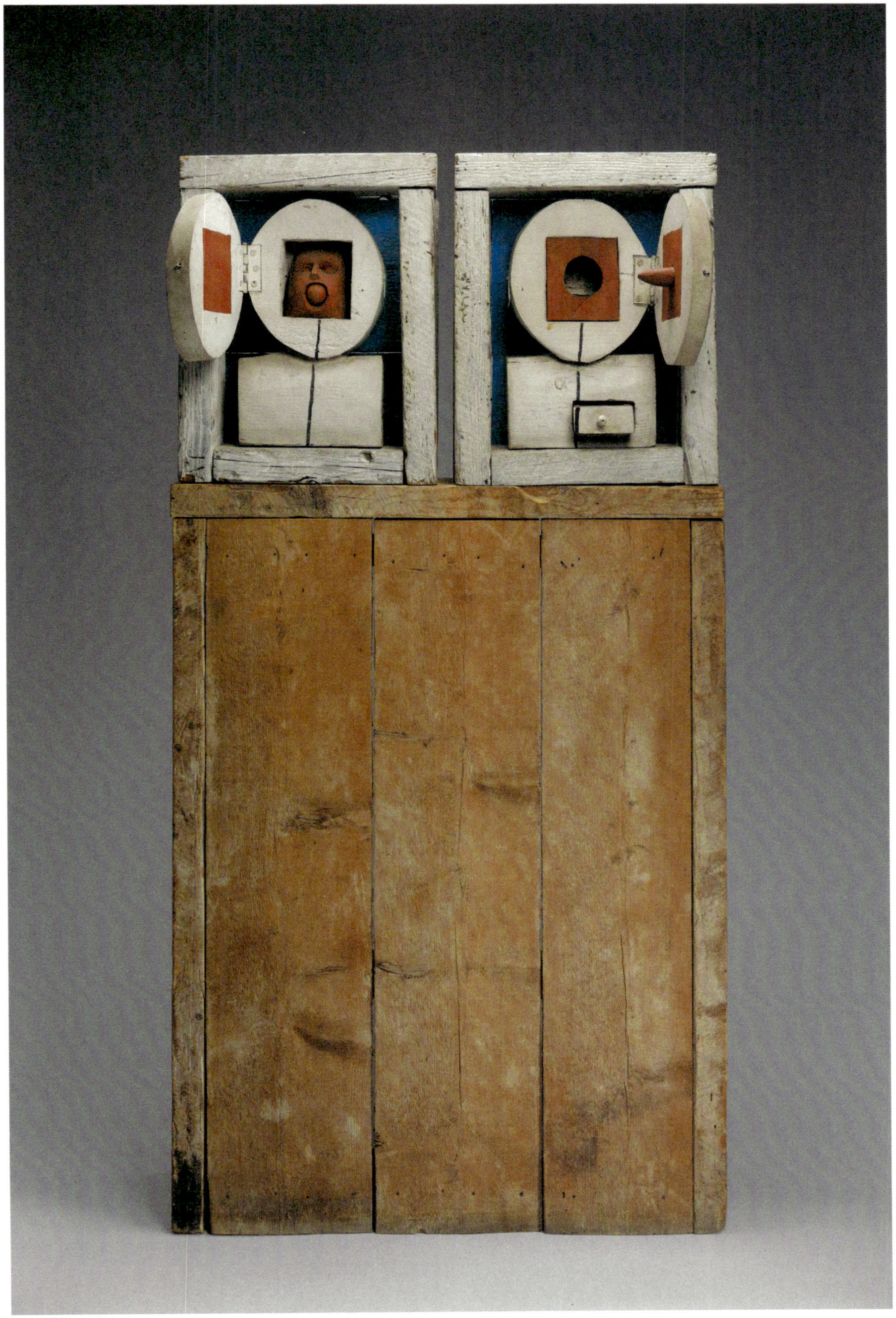

Plate 5
Gonzalo Fonseca, Uruguayan, 1922-1997
Dos cabezas [Two Heads], 1968
Wood, paint and metal hinges
57 5/8 x 30 x 9 in. (146.3 x 76.2 x 22.9 cm)
Estate of Frank Ribelin Collection,
courtesy of McClain Gallery

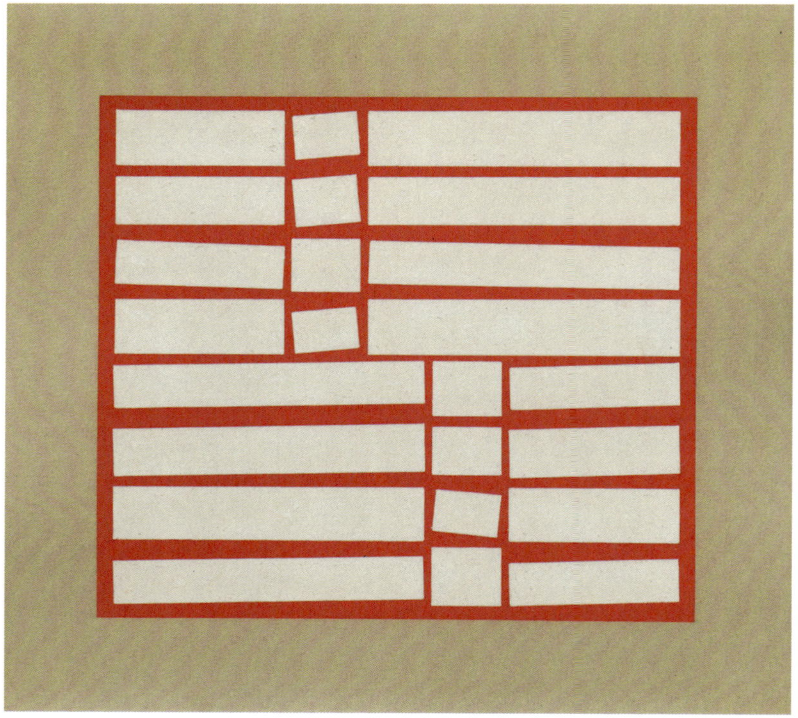

Plate 6
Hélio Oiticica, Brazilian, 1937-1980
Metaesquema #428, c. 1956-57
Gouache on cardboard
17 x 14 in. (43.2 x 35.6 cm)
Collection of Luis and Cecilia Campos

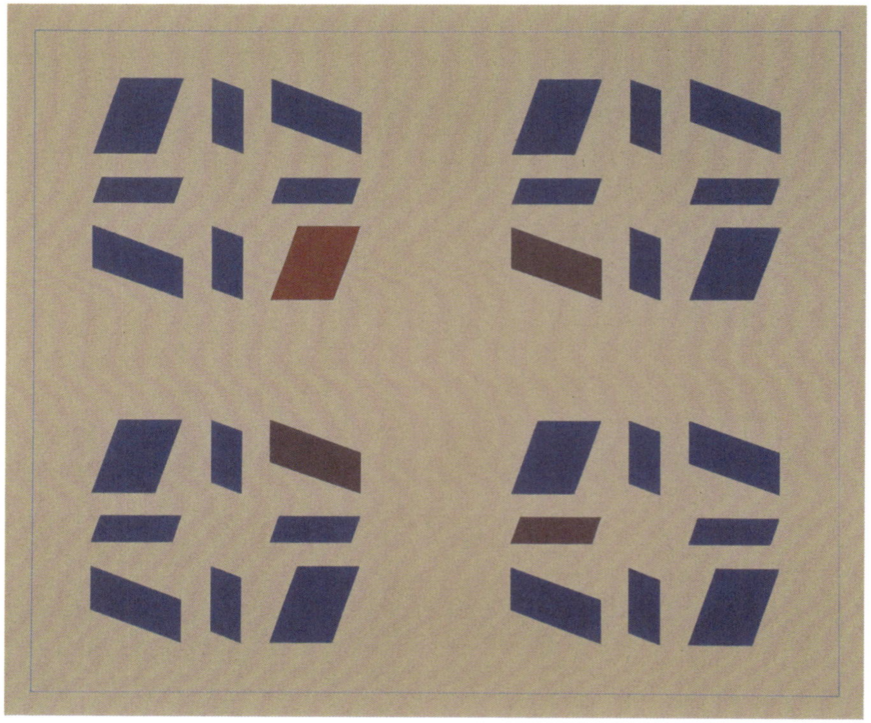

Plate 7
Hélio Oiticica, Brazilian, 1937-1980
Metaesquema, 1957
Gouache on cardboard
19 1/4 x 16 1/2 in. (48.9 x 41.9 cm)
Private collection

Carlos Cruz-Diez worked more independently in Paris. Gego (Gertrud Goldschmidt), who emigrated from Germany, developed her work in Venezuela and the United States. Although similarities can be found among all of these artists' Kinetic works, Jesús Rafael Soto's contribution to optically charged art was radically different from that of many of his contemporaries because his work never depended on a mechanical apparatus. Soto's process relied on the vibrational movement created by the spectator's retinal and physical interaction with the work. *Sphere de Bale* (1977; plate 50) is a sculptural maquette made of thin metal rods used to create volume and movement. This piece relates to Soto's larger vibrational environments, called Penetrables, which require a participatory engagement that begins with the viewer entering the work of art. Ricardo Pau-Llosa writes:

> In Soto's work, movement is always linked to presence, in most instances to the body itself. When shifts in point of view create optical illusions in Soto's works, these illusions are a natural effect of the pursuit of a higher goal. This primary goal consists of forging an ambiguous sense of aesthetic space. On the one hand, there is the space defined "within" the work; on the other, the space defined by the viewer's position vis-à-vis the work. Soto's appropriation of this second manifestation of aesthetic space predates, by at least a decade, Conceptual artists' view of the context which gallery and museums provide as an inextricable element of the act of apprehending works of art.[2]

The idea of eliciting vibrational quality from static objects was an early preoccupation in the work of Gego. *Una de cinco variantes* (1967; plate 52) demonstrates her early approach to this problem. Like Soto, Gego employed the use of thin lines constructed of wire to achieve volume and form but at the same time to dissolve it. The question of how to balance positive and negative space became an obsessive inquiry that led her to push beyond the notion of a self-contained sculpture by isolating the single line. This radical approach ultimately propelled her to pursue a conceptual direction that would forever link the work with the transparent space it occupied. Her Dibujos sin papel [Drawings without Paper] series (1985; see plate 53) furthered this philosophical position by insisting that the shadows cast by these sculptures on the walls complete the relational dialogue between line, space, and volume.

DISCURSIVE PLAY

Contemporary artists continue to elaborate on many of the artistic traditions set in motion by their predecessors, such as Magdalena Fernández, Elías Crespín, and Gabriel de la Mora. Although Fernández produces work related to the optic and Kinetic art traditions of her native Venezuela, the Brazilian Hélio Oiticica is the subject of her video installation titled *2pmHOoo8N (Homenaje a Helio Oiticica)* (2008), in which the artist conceptually appropriates Oiticica's Metaesquemas to create a continuously shifting environment of light, color, and movement. By animating the geometric components of the Oitician grid, Fernández engages in a discursive, trans-generational dialogue that incorporates the spectator's physical and psychological relationship in the work. In essence, she is taking the fundamental principles of the Metaesquemas and pushing them toward a perceptual conclusion. Like her contemporary Alexander Apostol, Fernández examines the utopian aspirations of modern Latin American aesthetics in order to make sense of the sociopolitical realities of the present day. Elías Crespín, who is also from Venezuela, but lives and works in Caracas and Paris, continues the tradition of his fellow Kinetic artists who worked in both cities. Although his early work bears a slight resemblance to that of Gego's *Reticuláreas*, Crespín's work delves deeper into mathematical concerns. In a scientific sense, his electro-kinetic sculptures are based on Cartesian geometric principles comprising shifting points, lines, surfaces, and volumes. *Tetra Circular Azul* [Tetra Circular Blue] (2009; plate 8) moves Crespín in to a recent preoccupation with light and color by creating a constantly changing kinetic dance of square Plexiglas cutouts. Carefully choreographed to cycle through subtly shifting configurations, Crespín's sculptures become philosophic meditations on time and space. The Mexican Gabriel de la Mora, known for precisely rendered illustrations using single strands of hair instead of pens or pencils, as seen in *E.P.R.B.A.X.L.J.* (2007; see plate 77), has recently produced more abstract work. Looking like one of Buckminster Fuller's geodesic domes or Gego's Reticuláreas, Mora's *M.E.A.I* (2008; see plate 77) embraces both references with conviction. The delicately knotted strands, however, create a surprisingly sturdy yet ephemeral structure that ironically offers a feminine response to Gego's seemingly masculine steel-and-iron armatures.

CONNECTING THE DOTS

For the purposes of this exhibition, examining every Latin American work in Houston's private collections was not viable or even pertinent to the

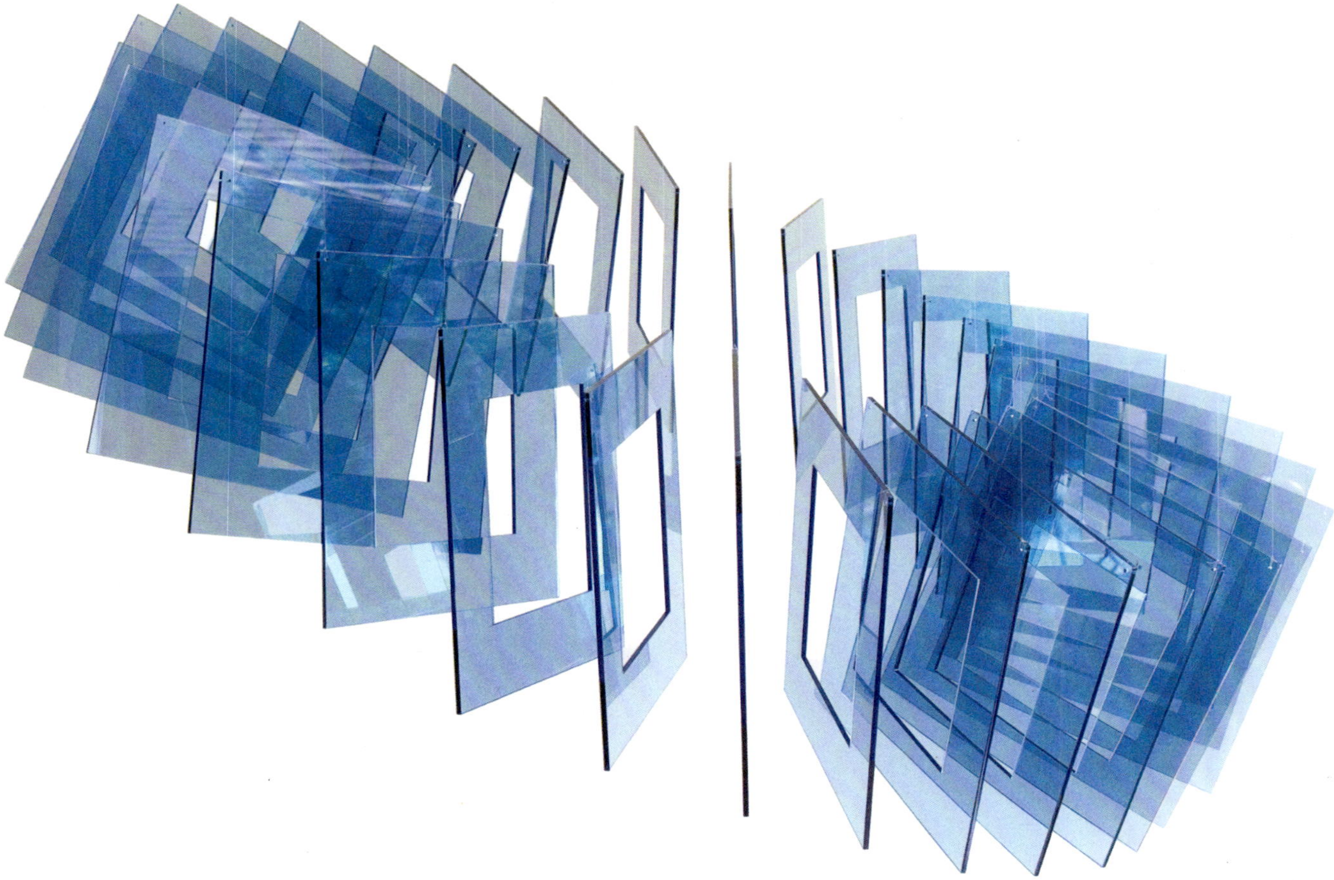

Plate 8
Elías Crespín, Venezuelan, born 1965
Tetra Circular Azul [Tetra Circular Blue], 2009
Acrylic, wood, computer
10 x 5 x 5 in. (25.4 x 12.7 x 12.7 cm)
Collection of Leslie and Brad Bucher

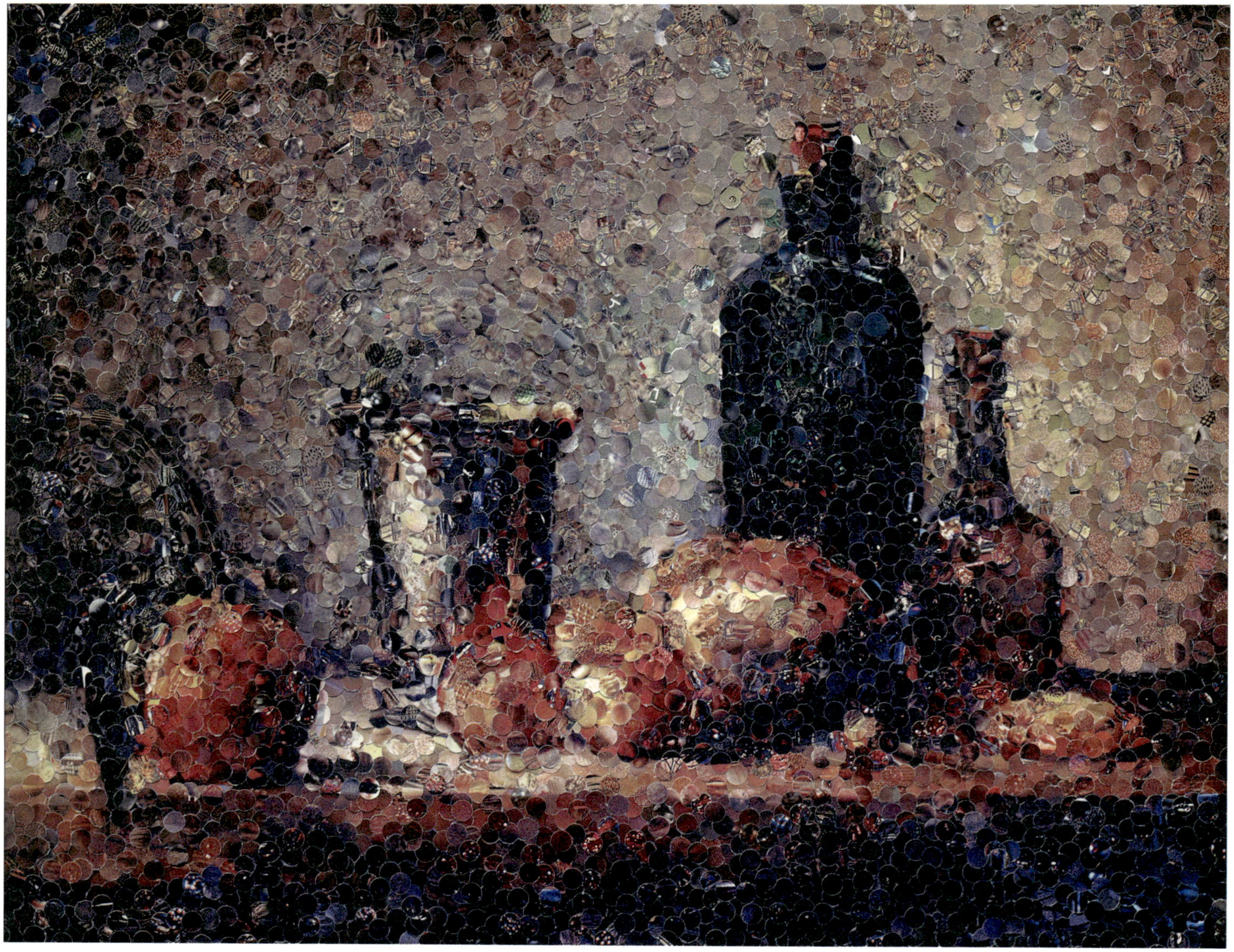

Plate 9
Vik Muniz, Brazilian, born 1961
Still Life after Chardin (Pictures of Magazine, Still Life), 2004
Chromogenic print
46 x 50 in. (116.8 x 127 cm)
Collection of Barbara and Michael Gamson

project's objectives. Yet it is still important to acknowledge the strong impulse to collect contemporary art among Houston collectors at-large. For many individuals, acquiring historical works is of little interest because of both economic limitations and the difficulty in finding appropriate works. The possibility of building a cogent body of work exists with contemporary and emerging artists and truly enables collectors to share in an international dialogue as it unfolds in real time. Much of the work of contemporary Latin American artists is informed by conceptual vocabularies that have circulated around the world in the last thirty years. These vocabularies reflect the humanistic impulse of artists who aspire to create dialogues that reach beyond geographic and cultural borders. Information has flowed more readily in the last few decades than it did in the early modern period, and the advent of the Internet has enabled artists to embark on virtual routes that, in turn, have transformed what were previously local artistic tendencies. Ideas centered on the urban landscape, everyday life, and conceptual photographic strategies allow artists to participate in larger, global dialogues while examining how they relate back to local vernacular, cultural specificities, and political and social dynamics. Many of the contemporary artists represented in *Cosmopolitan Routes* do double duty, first by representing the multivalent artistic and intellectual rigor of contemporary art production, and second by enabling a discursive relationship to develop across trans-generational lines.

In this context, one of the most innovative artists to emerge from Latin America is Vik Muniz, who creates photographic portraits and landscapes out of unusual materials, including chocolate syrup, caviar, diamonds, junk, earth, and pigment. These materials are shaped and accumulated to form images of everything – from celebrities and artistic icons to canonical works of art. Muniz's *Still Life after Chardin (Pictures of Magazine, Still Life)* (2004; see plate 9), constructed out of small disks of magazine paper, is an appropriation of a painting by the French eighteenth-century still-life master Jean-Baptiste-Siméon Chardin. Muniz's interest in appropriation led him recently to complete his Verso series of trompe l'oeil sculptures. A radical departure from his photographic portraits, the Verso series consists of nine famous works of art whose versos, or backs, are faithfully re-created, down to every stretcher bar, bare canvas, hanging hardware, and institutional labels bearing the exhibition histories of each work of art. *Verso (Woman with Parrot)* (2008) is a copy of the back of Pierre-Auguste Renoir's *Woman with Parrot* (1871) in the collection of the Solomon R. Guggenheim Museum in New York. In Muniz's work, the painting rests on pads and leans against the wall, as if waiting to be hung in the gallery. The Colombian artist Miguel Angel Rojas creates both photographic images and works inspired by mechanical reproductive technologies. He often uses coca leaves cut into confetti-like disks to build words and images that refer to controversial issues, or specifically to drug-trafficking related to the politics of his country. *Nowadays* (2005; see plate 66) is constructed of coca leaves that spell out the title of the famous Richard Hamilton collage that is considered to be the first work of Pop Art, *Just what is it that makes today's homes so different, so appealing?* The accompanying collage, *Bratatata*, uses punched dollar bills to illustrate the Roy Lichtenstein painting *As I Opened Fire* (1964).

Together, the Rojas works featured in this exhibition create dense layers of meaning that ricochet between the pervasiveness of violence in Colombian society and the impact of Pop Art on artists of his generation. In *David 8* (2005; plate 10), Rojas creates a life-size black-and-white portrait of a government soldier who stepped on a land mine. Posed in *contrapposto* like Michelangelo's *David* (1504), with the full weight of the figure resting on the right leg while the left arm taps the left shoulder, Roja's subject is somehow dignified through a surreal irony that bespeaks his lamentable fate as a land-mine victim.

BORDERS CROSSED

As *Cosmopolitan Routes* seeks to elucidate networks and points of convergence that link artistic movements and styles operating between multiple centers, both in Europe and Latin America, how do American artists of Latin American descent fit within this new framework? Although Carlos Almaraz was born in Mexico, he lived and worked primarily in Los Angeles, producing vivid, Expressionistic landscapes that were inspired by the color palettes of Claude Monet and Henri Matisse. The urban landscapes of Los Angeles and Southern California provided the basis for many compositions that center on Echo Park, an oasis within the city that offered Almaraz an ever-changing panorama of atmosphere and light, which was a sharp yet poetic departure from his activist murals of the early 1970s (see plate 88). Although it is difficult to categorize the work of Martín Ramírez, a self-taught artist diagnosed as a catatonic schizophrenic, he produced an astonishing group of drawings within the confines of DeWitt State Hospital in northern California, where he resided for the last fifteen years of his life. His work was first discovered by Tarmo Pasto, a visiting professor of psychology and art who noted that Ramirez's complex drawings were executed on brown paper bags, scraps of examination-table paper, and book pages glued together with a paste made of potatoes and human saliva. Ramírez's work is populated with images of Madonnas, horseback riders, and trains entering and exiting stations, and imbued with decorative patterns and undulating fields of concentric lines. Luis Jiménez, born in El Paso, Texas, is known for his large polychrome fiberglass sculptures, usually incorporating southwestern and Latino themes, including *vaqueros* (cowboys), folk dancers, and Native Americans. *Cruzando el Rio Bravo* [Crossing the River Bravo] (1989; plate 11) commemorates the hundreds of thousands of individuals who have crossed the border illegally to gain access to better employment and education. *The End of the Trail (with Electric Sunset)* (1971; see plate 89) is a spectacular rendition of an archetypal sunset scene within the genre of American cowboy art.

The work of Dario Robleto defies easy categorization. By choosing to identify less with the specifics of his cultural heritage and more with larger themes related to history and popular culture, Robleto has created an idiosyncratic practice rooted in his childhood observations of the honky-tonk bar where his mother worked and later in his observations of a hospice where he witnessed the frailty of human life. The artist is known for using rare and archaic materials, including vinyl records, dinosaur fossils, impact glass formed by meteorites, human tears and

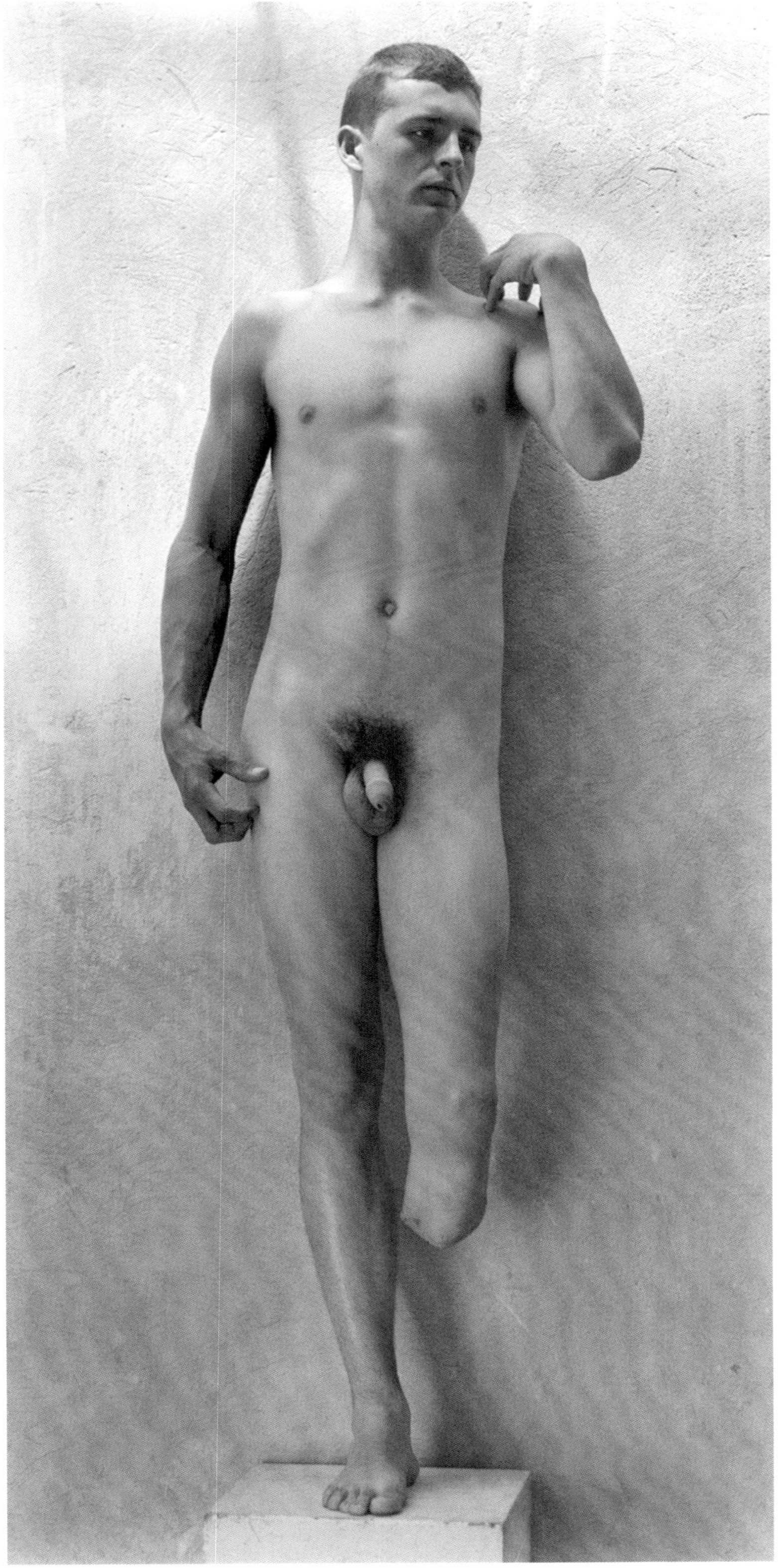

Plate 10
Miguel Ángel Rojas, Colombian, born 1946
David 8, 2005
Digital print
79 1/2 x 39 1/2 in. (201.9 x 100.3 cm)
Collection of Carlos Bacino

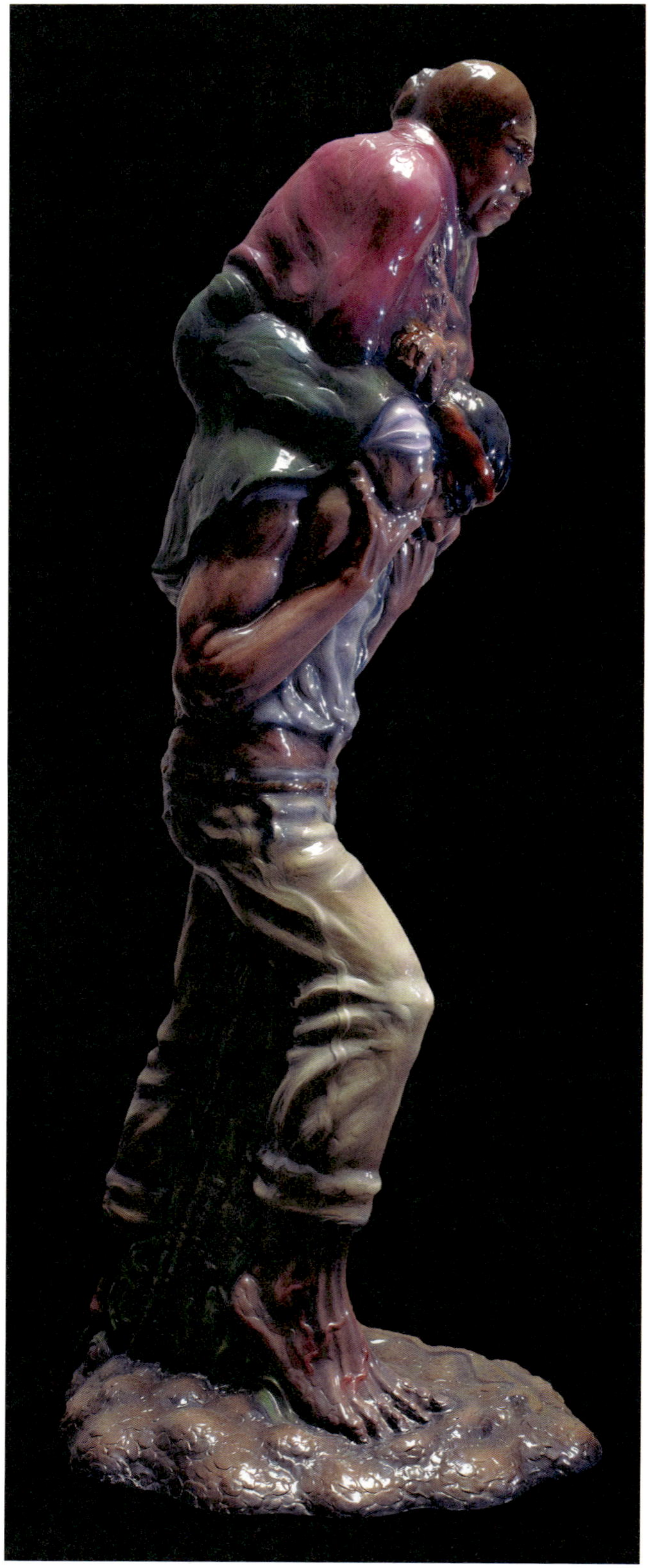

Plate 11
Luis Jiménez, American, 1940-2006
Cruzando el Rio Bravo [Crossing the Rio Bravo], 1989
Fiberglass with urethane finish
127 x 34 x 54 in. (322.6 x 86.4 x 137.2 cm)
The Museum of Fine Arts, Houston,
museum purchase with funds provided by
the Caroline Wiess Law Accessions Endowment Fund

heartbeats to create poetic narratives that challenge our faith in the everyday objects that shape our lives. The records that played in the jukebox at the bar inspired a body of work that uses both the syntax of music and the actual vinyl disk to create sculpture. *A Rosary for Rhythm* (2007), which consists of melted and carved vinyl records of Jerry Lee Lewis's and Little Richard's "Whole Lotta Shakin' Goin' On," ground hip bone dust, cast pewter, and metal chain, conflates the early criticism of rock music as the work of the devil with a rosary intended to counteract its sins. *Shaker Apothecary* (2007; plate 94) is a Shaker chest containing twenty-eight drawers in which hand-ground vinyl dance-craze records are paired with various medicinal herbs. By teaming "The Hustle" with devil's claw root, "Do the Hand Jive" with the Rose of Jericho, and "Peppermint Twist" with dandelion root, Robleto makes the correlation between the curative properties of music and those of botanical science.

Although Robleto's apothecary cabinet suggests the celebrated eighteenth-century Enlightenment practice of museum collections and the scientific process of archiving and cataloging objects, there are inherent shortcomings of a curatorial project such as *Cosmopolitan Routes*. Nonetheless, these shortcomings are revealing. The fact that not every Latin American artist, artistic style, or movement can be covered in the scope of this essay or in the exhibition speaks strongly to the heterogeneity and vastness of the field. The artworks selected for *Cosmopolitan Routes*, therefore, do not intend to provide a fixed view of Latin American art; instead, the goal is to suggest the salient characteristics of Latin American art and to offer clues to their evolution. More importantly, especially when seen together, the artworks offer new possibilities of interpretation, free from geopolitical barriers and with the potential for a shared construction of meaning. This framework is not a wholesale rejection of the encyclopedic one that has traditionally governed the museum and its collections, but rather an opportunity for exploring an expanded and perhaps utopian system of classification. The participation of the collector is critical to this equation and highlights his or her commitment to building knowledge through community. During the last decade, the Latin Maecenas of the Museum of Fine Arts, Houston, embarked on a path of discovery that is just unfolding. Their limitless quest for discovery is motivated both by the imagination of the artist and by their open willingness to build a legacy that will inspire generations to come.

NOTES

1 Salomon Grimberg, Lot 213, The Latin American Sale, Christie's, New York, June 1–2, 2000.

2 Ricardo Pau-Llosa, "Jesús Soto: Feeling the Infinite," in *Sculpture* 16, no. 6 (July/August 1997).

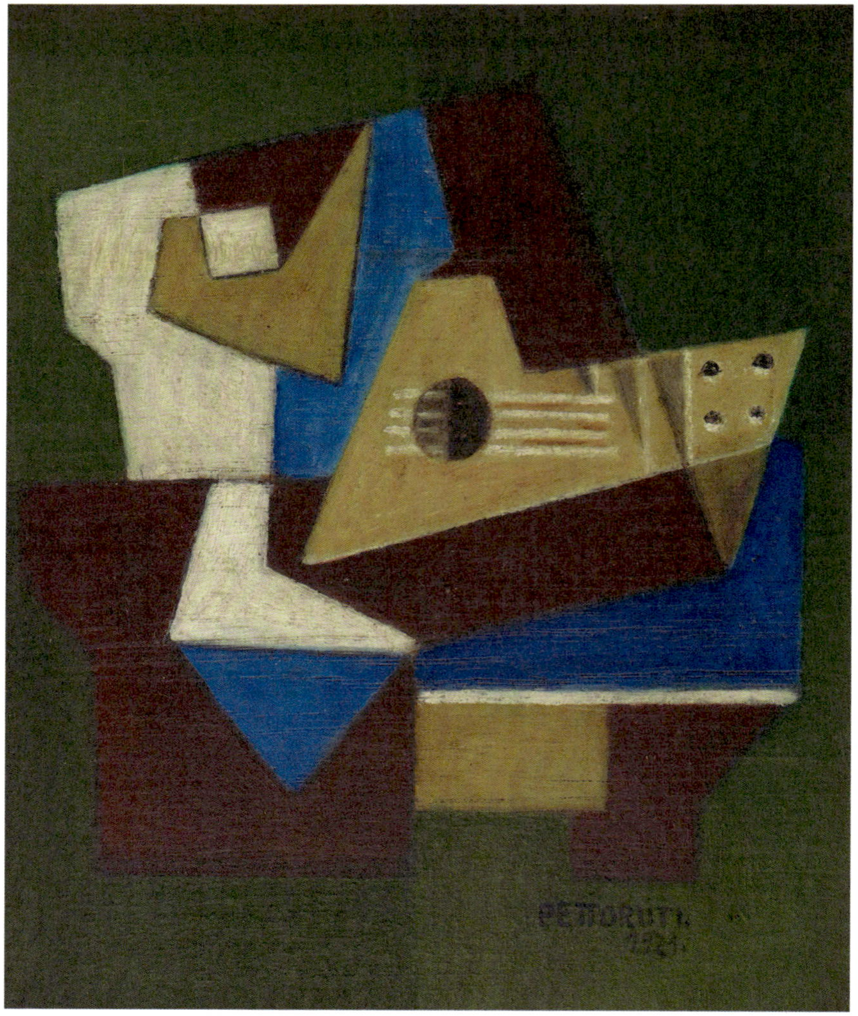

Plate 12
Emilio Pettoruti, Argentinean, 1892–1971
Composición (sin título)
[Composition (Untitled)], 1921
Oil on board
7 1/8 x 5 7/8 in. (18.2 x 15 cm)
Private collection

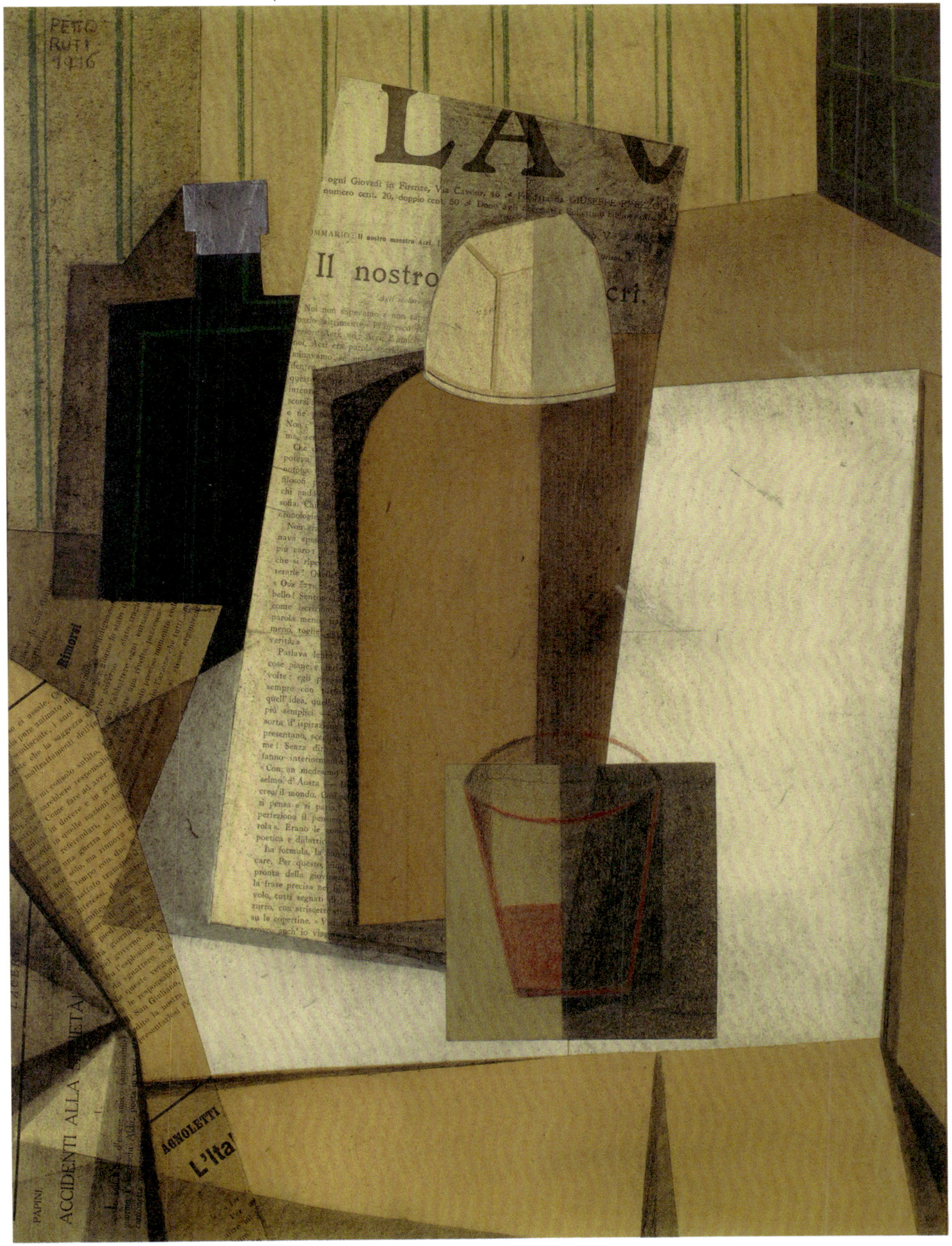

Plate 13
Emilio Pettoruti, Argentinean, 1892–1971
La Voce [The Voice], 1916
Collage
38 x 30 1/2 x 2 1/2 in. (96.5 x 77.5 x 6.4 cm)
The Brillembourg Capriles Collection
of Latin American Art at the
Museum of Fine Arts, Houston

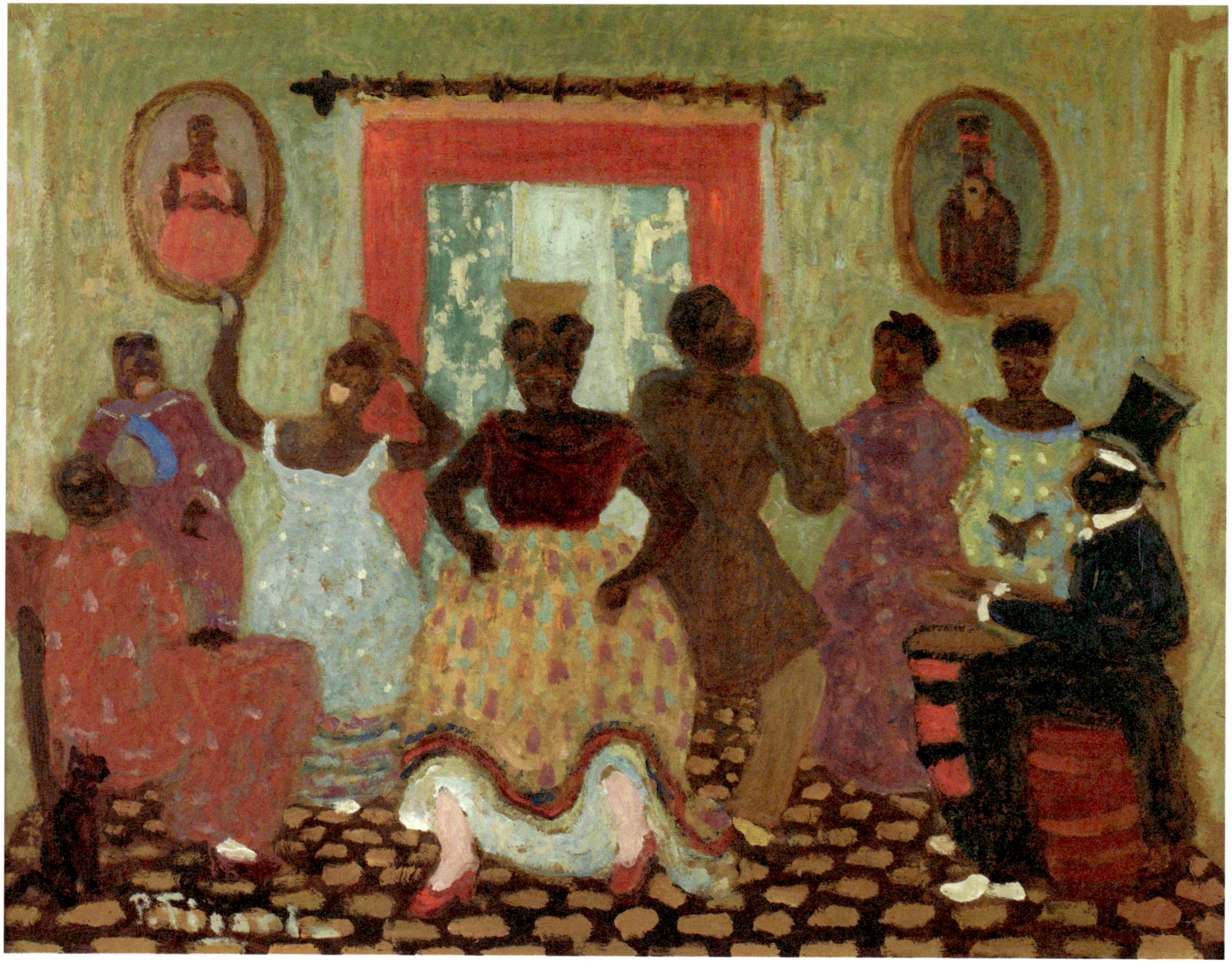

Plate 14
Pedro Figari, Uruguayan, 1861-1938
Candombe, 1921
Oil on cardboard
23 5/8 x 31 1/2 in. (60 x 80 cm)
Private collection

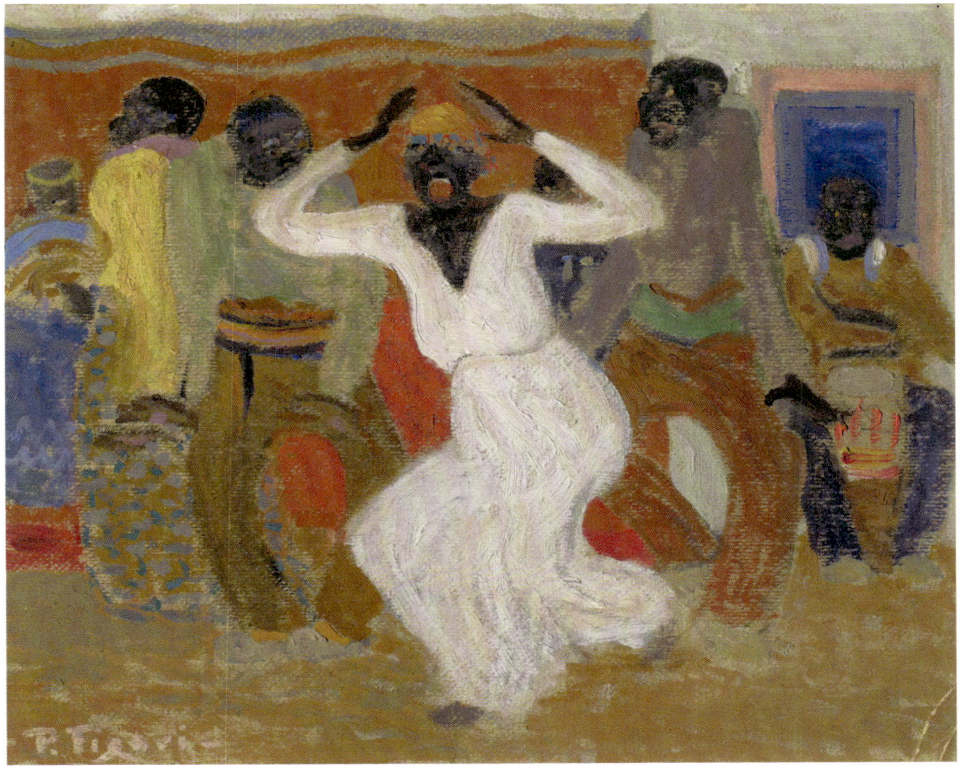

Plate 15
Pedro Figari, Uruguayan, 1861-1938
El último Candombe [The Last Candombe], 1921-25
Oil on cardboard
18 7/8 x 24 7/16 in. (48 x 62 cm)
Private collection

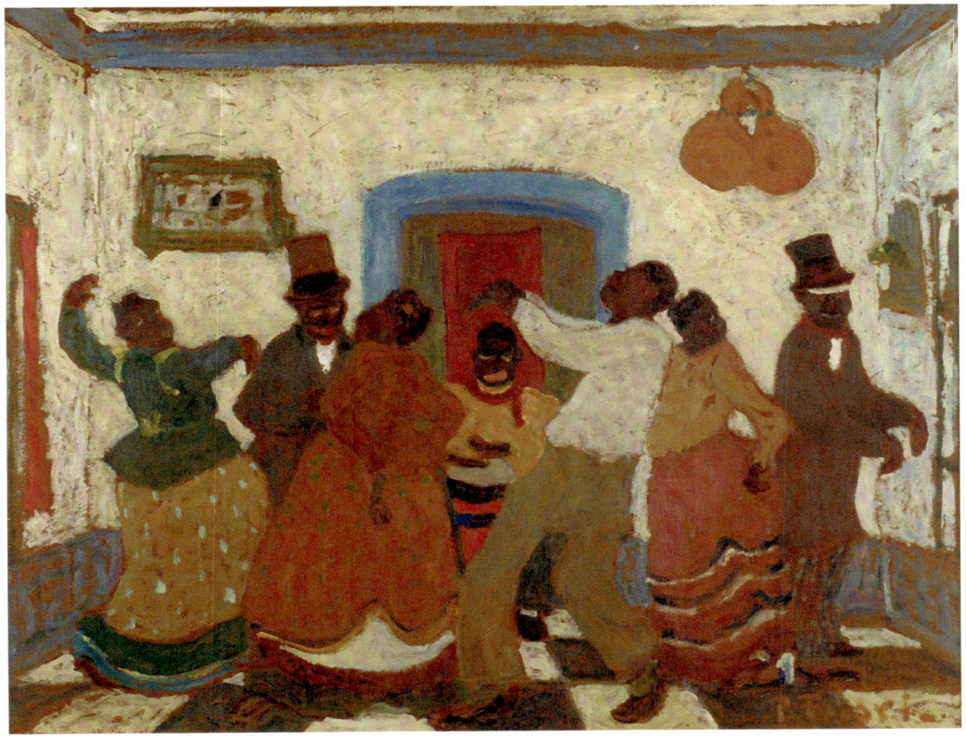

Plate 16
Pedro Figari, Uruguayan, 1861-1938
Candombe, c. 1930
Oil on board
22 x 26 in. (55.9 x 68 cm)
Private collection

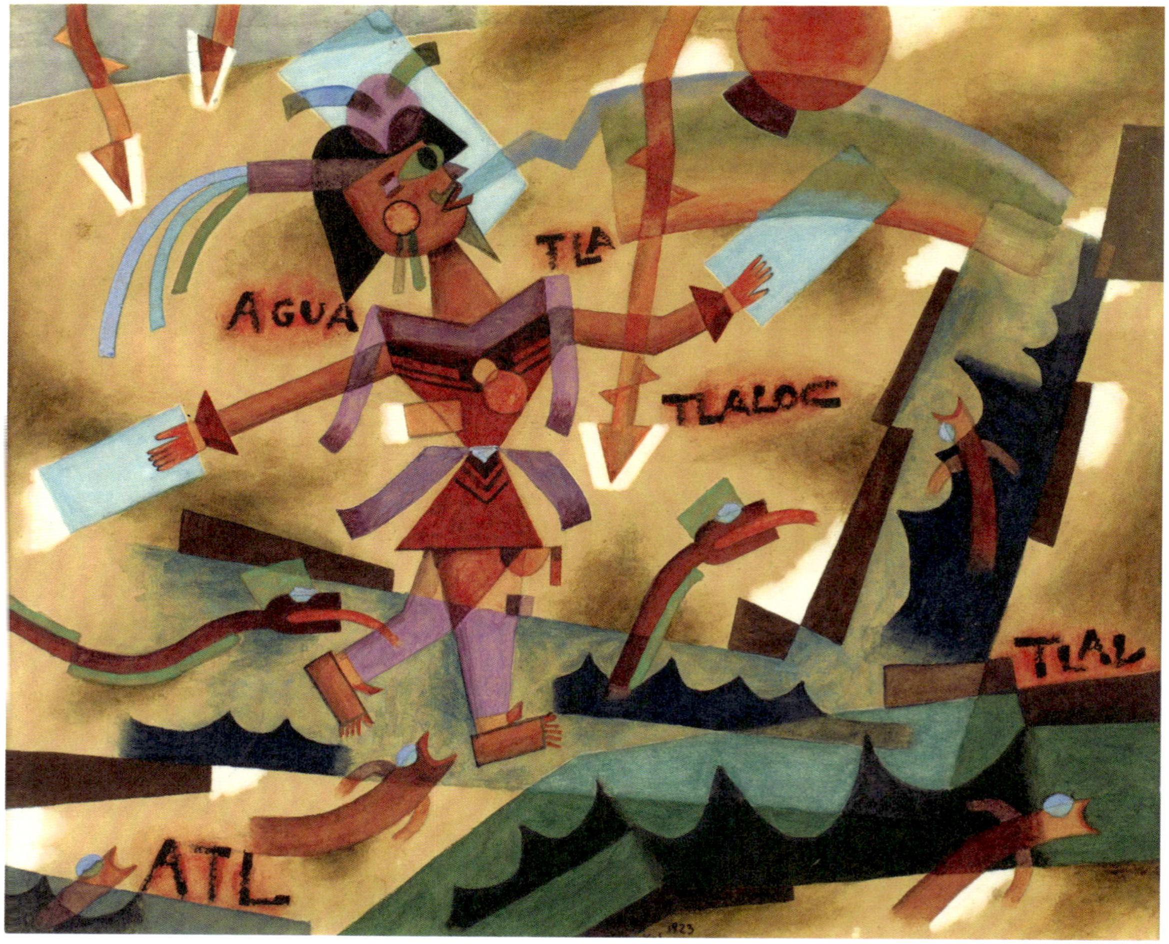

Plate 17
Xul Solar, Argentinean, 1887-1963
Tlaloc, 1923
Watercolor on paper
10 1/4 x 12 5/8 in. (26 x 32 cm)
Private collection

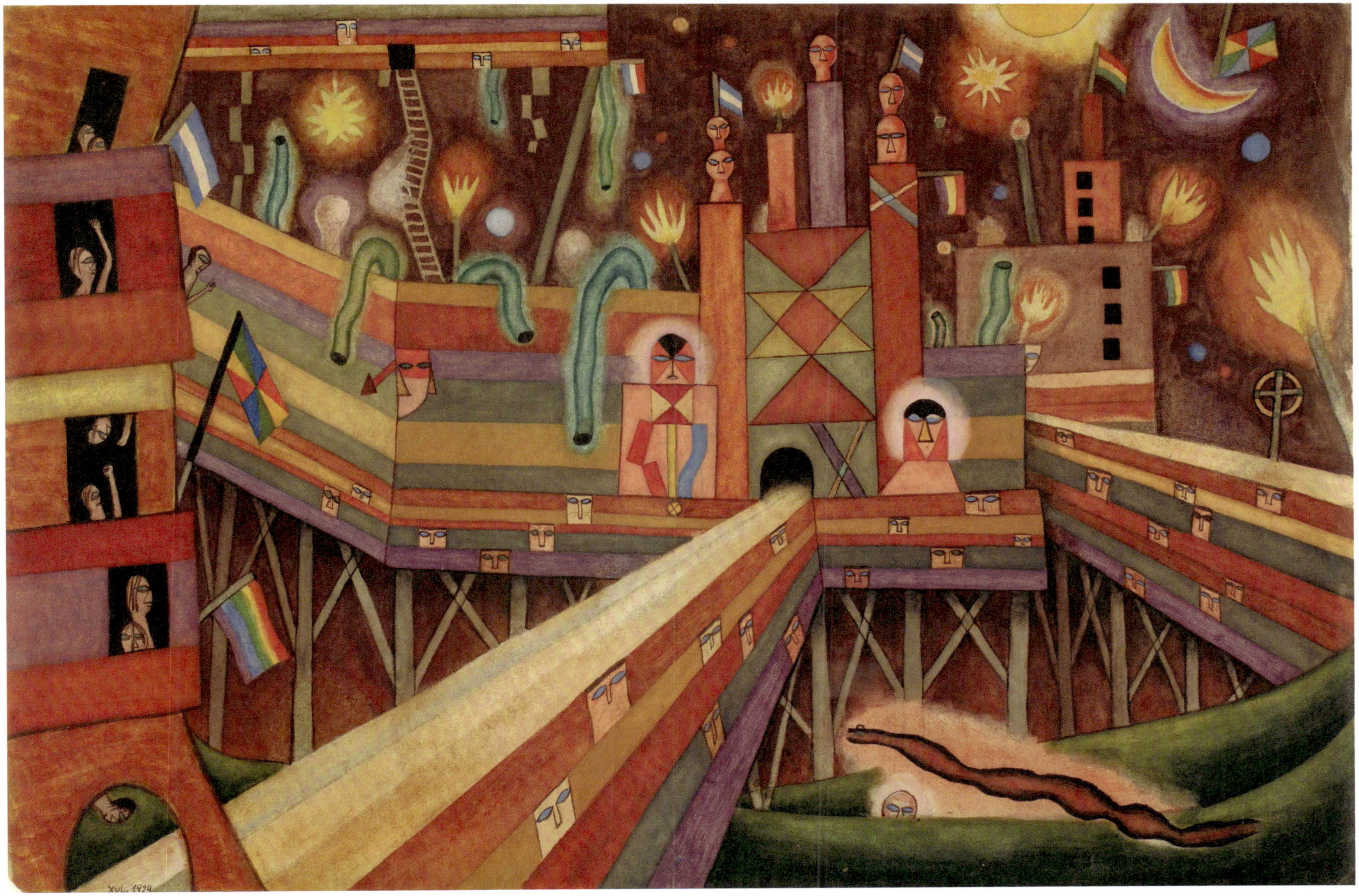

Plate 18
Xul Solar, Argentinean, 1887-1963
El túnel [The Tunnel], 1923
Watercolor on paper
18 7/8 x 24 7/16 in. (48 x 62 cm)
Private collection

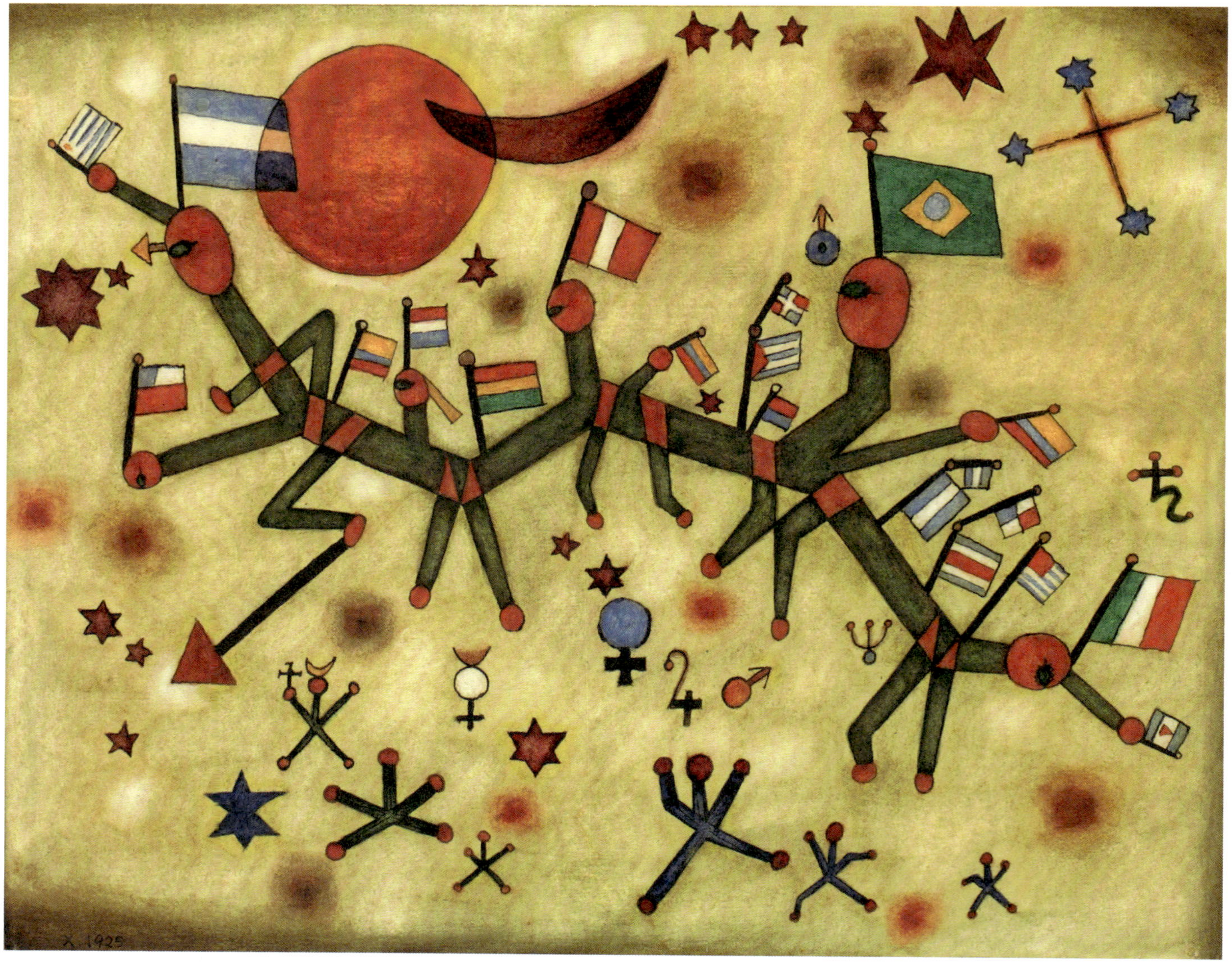

Plate 19
Xul Solar, Argentinean, 1887-1963
País [Country], 1925
Watercolor on paper
9 15/16 x 12 7/8 in. (25.2 x 32.7 cm)
Private collection

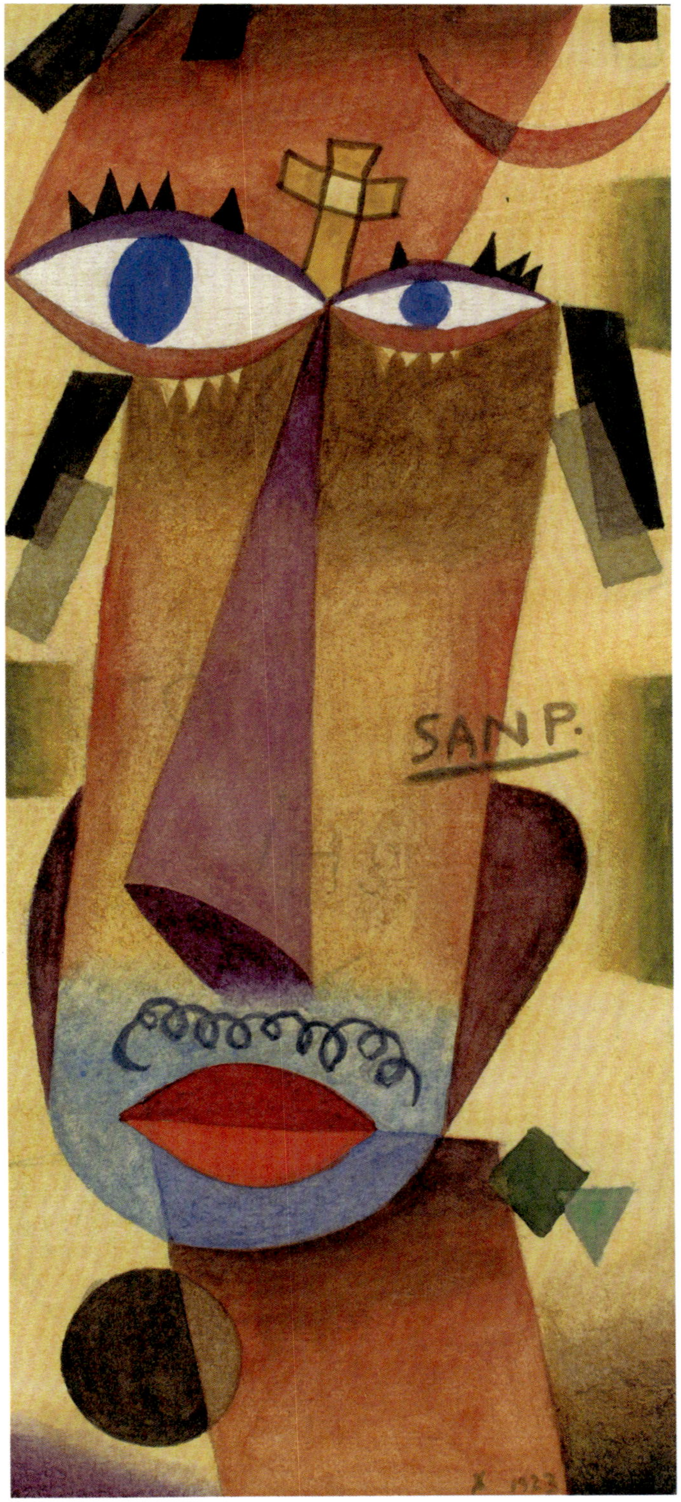

Plate 20
Xul Solar, Argentinean, 1887-1963
San P, 1923
Gouache on paper
11 13/16 x 7 7/8 in. (30 x 20 cm)
Collection of Mary and Roy Cullen

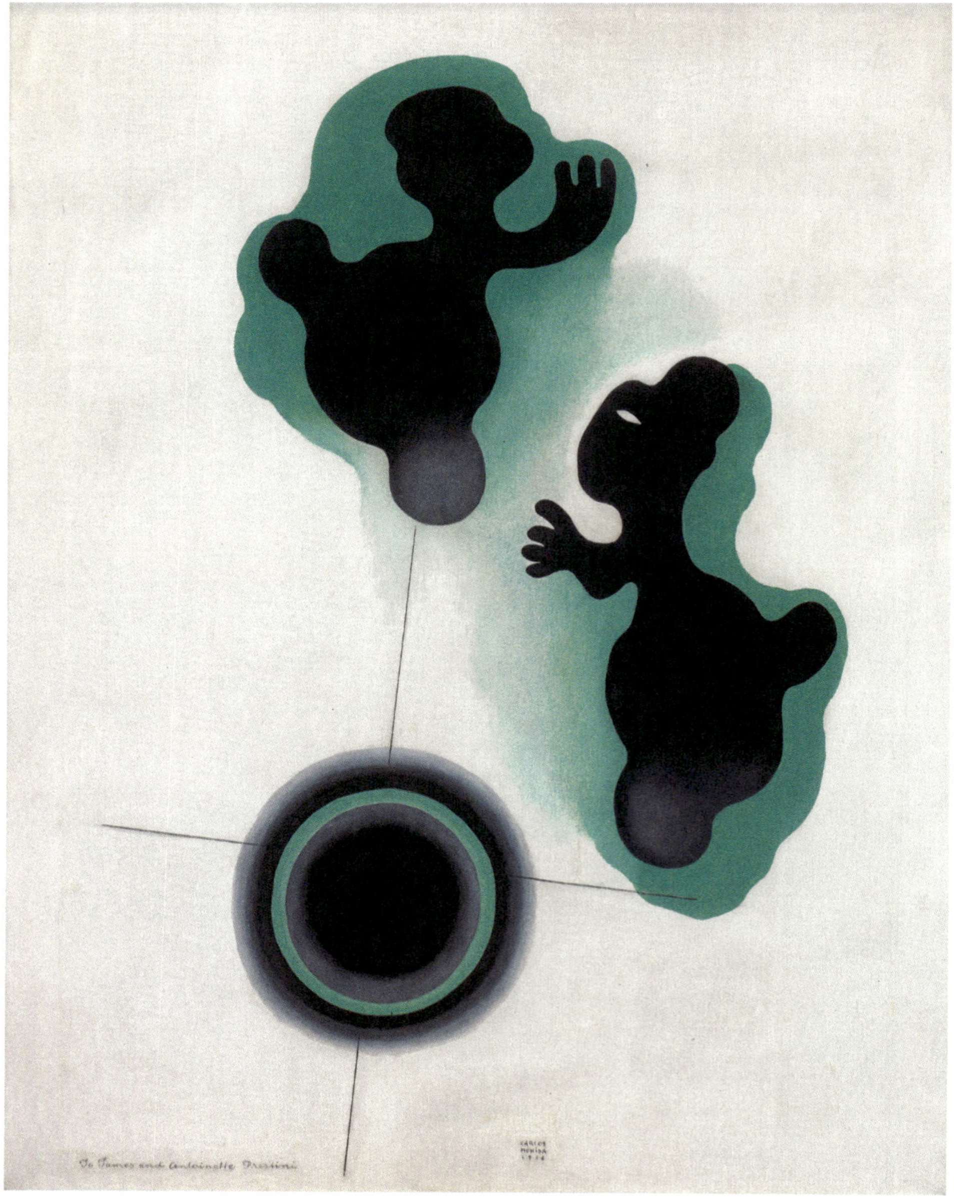

Plate 21
Carlos Mérida, Guatemalan,
active in Mexico, 1891-1984
Untitled (Floating Forms), 1936
Oil on canvas
25 x 19 1/2 in. (63.5 x 49.5 cm)
Collection of Mary and Roy Cullen

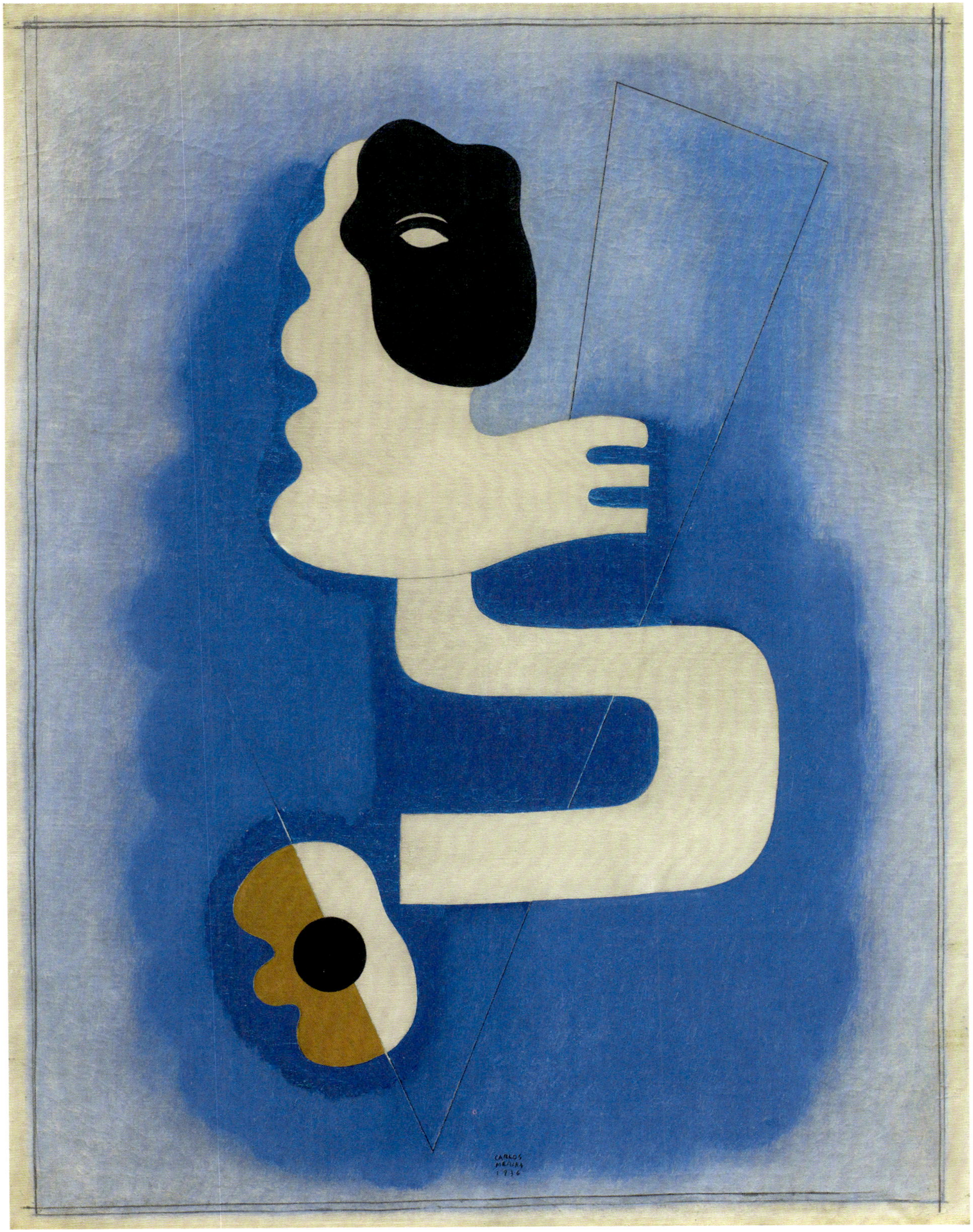

Plate 22
Carlos Mérida, Guatemalan, active in Mexico, 1891-1984
Canción de cuna [Lullaby], 1936
Oil on canvas
31 x 25 in. (78.7 x 63.5 cm)
Private collection

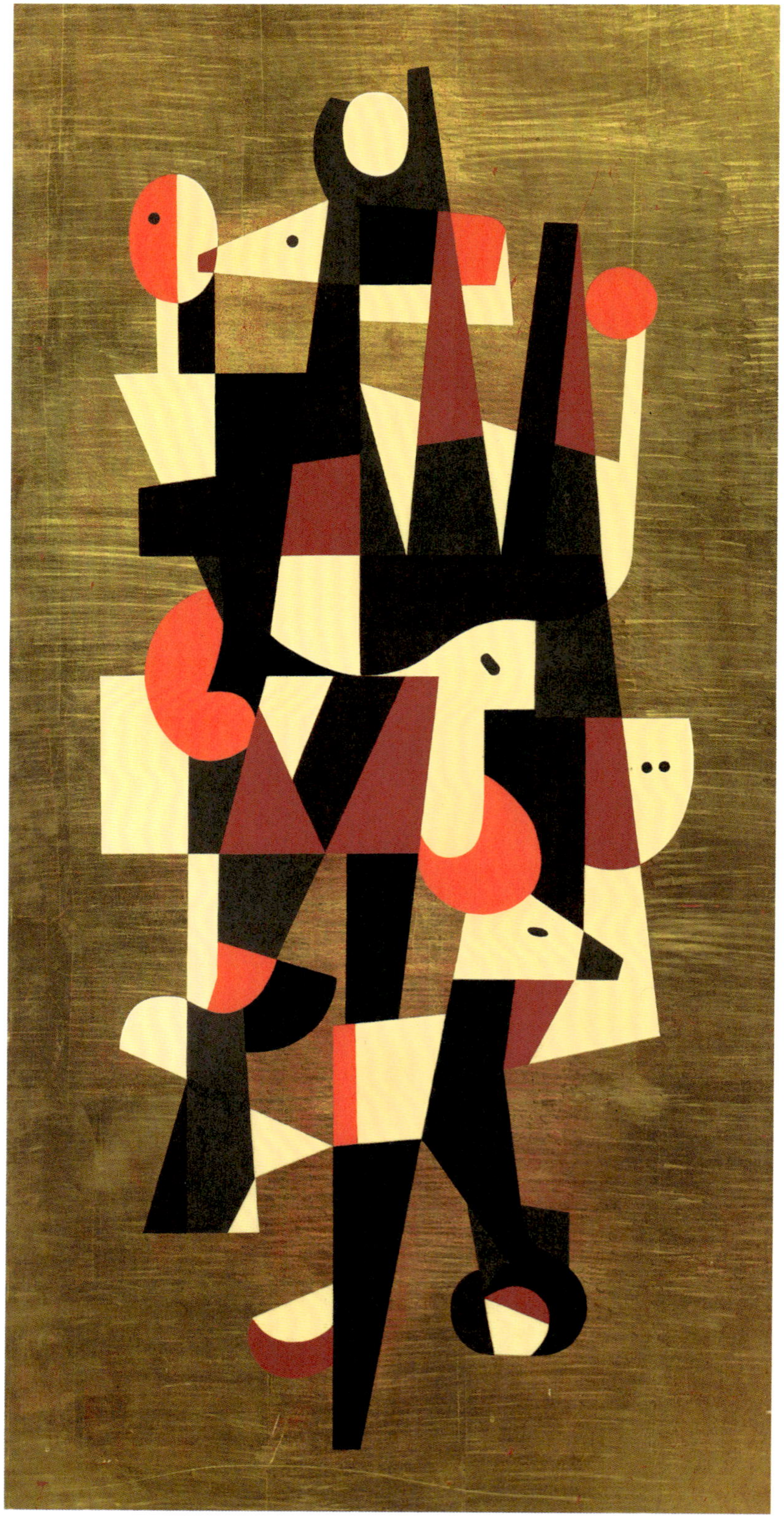

Plate 22
Carlos Mérida, Guatemalan,
active in Mexico, 1891-1984
Untitled, 1936
Petro plastic and gold leaf on wood
46 7/8 x 24 1/2 in. (119.1 x 62.2 cm)
Collection of Charles and Judy Tate

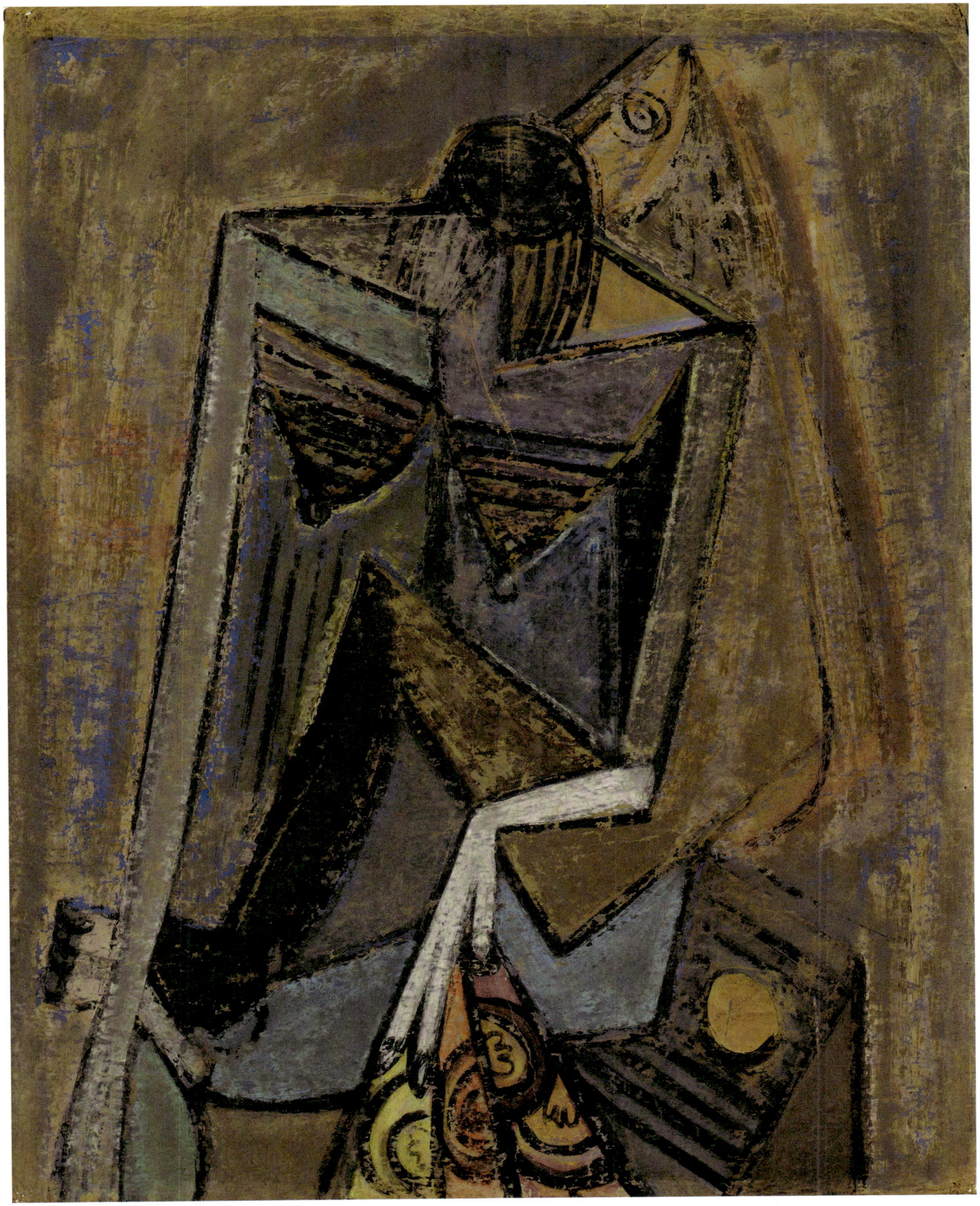

Plate 24
Wifredo Lam, Cuban, 1902–1982
Mujer con abanico [Woman with Fan], 1942
Gouache on paper
41 1/2 x 34 1/2 in. (105.4 x 87.6 cm)
The Brillembourg Capriles Collection
of Latin American Art at
the Museum of Fine Arts, Houston

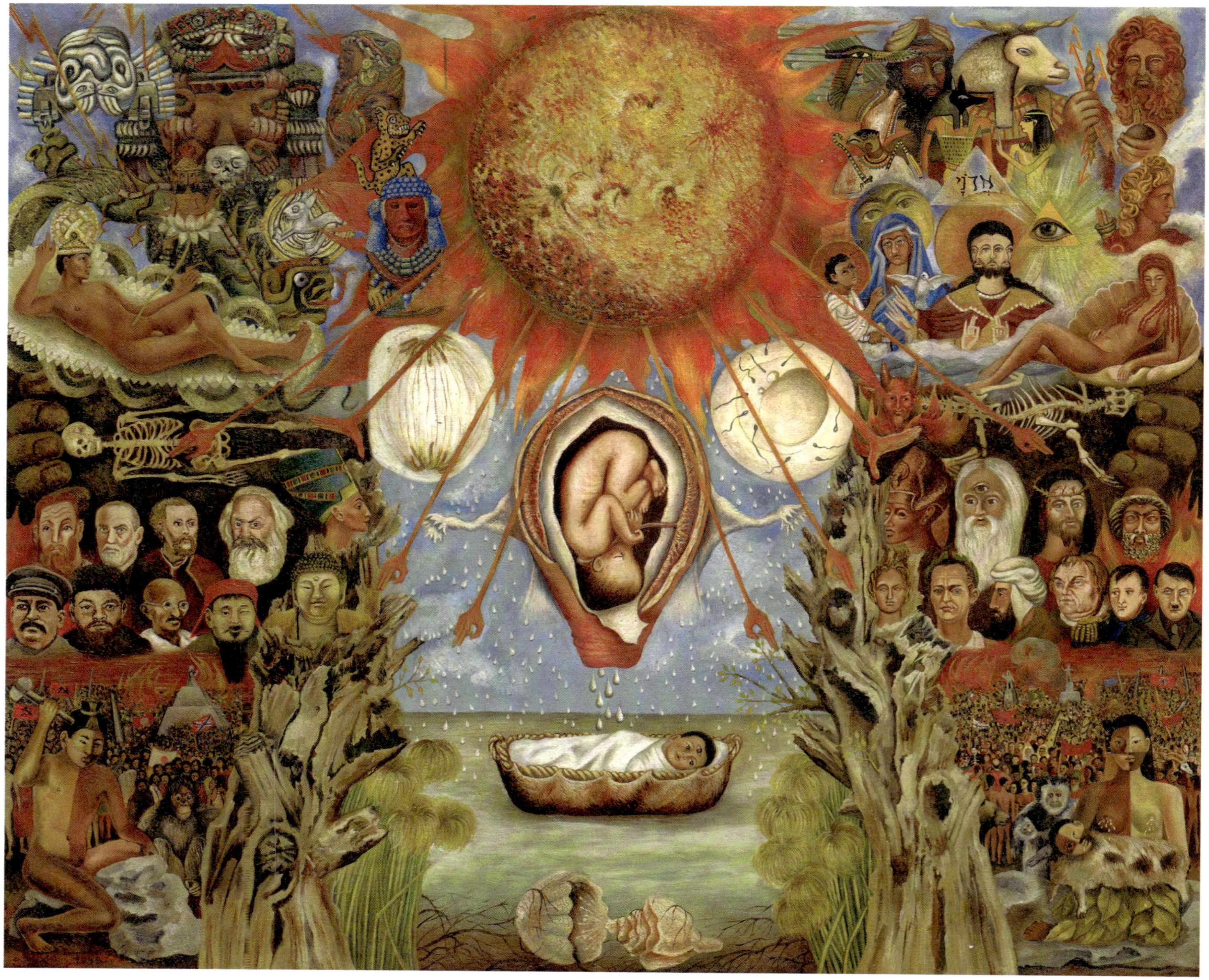

Plate 25
Frida Kahlo, Mexican, 1907-1954
Moses, 1945
Oil on Masonite
31 1/2 x 36 1/2 in. (80 x 92.7 cm)
Private collection

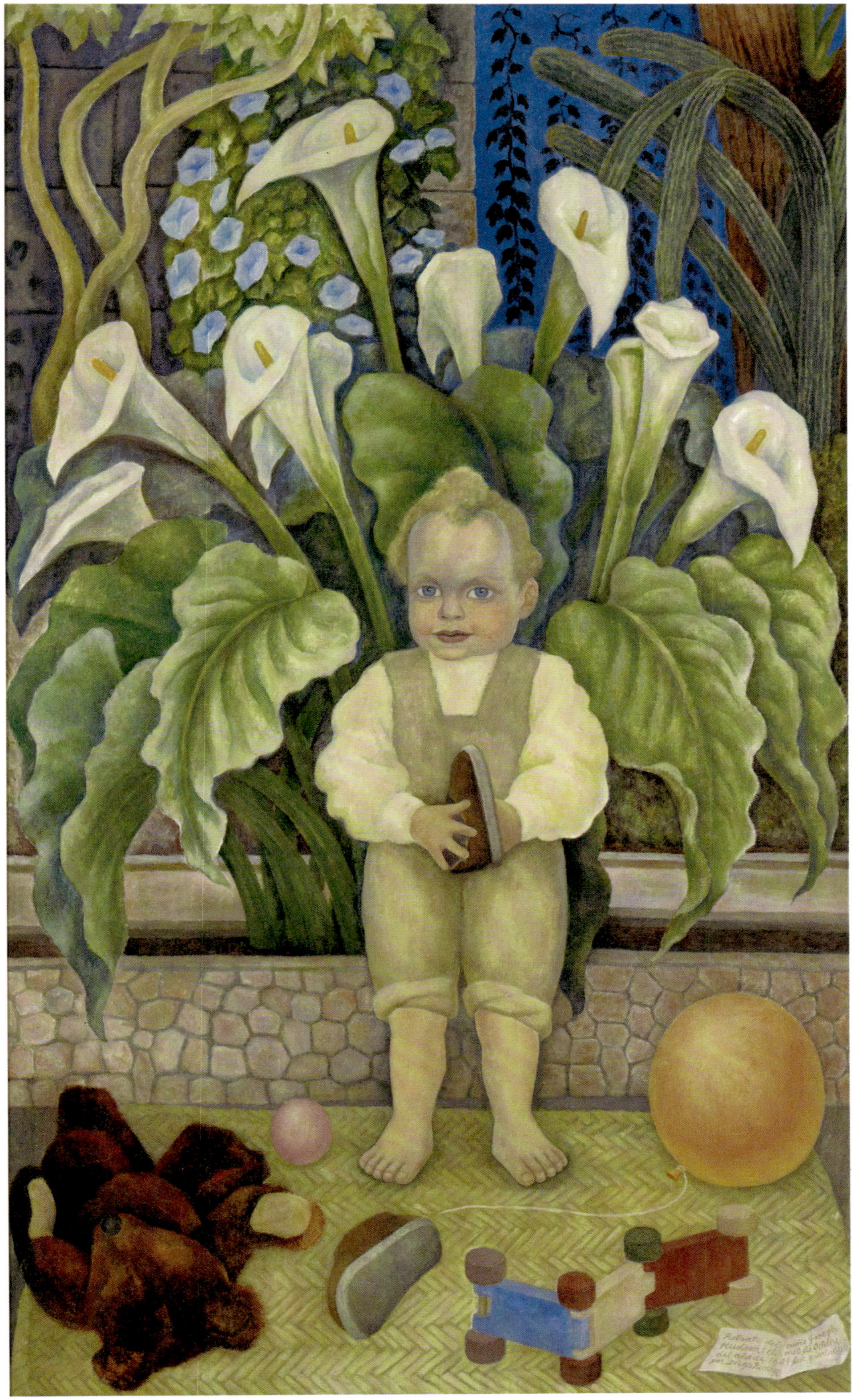

Plate 26
Diego Rivera, Mexican, 1886–1957
Jojo, 1955
Oil on canvas
68 x 42 in. (172.7 x 106.7 cm)
Private collection

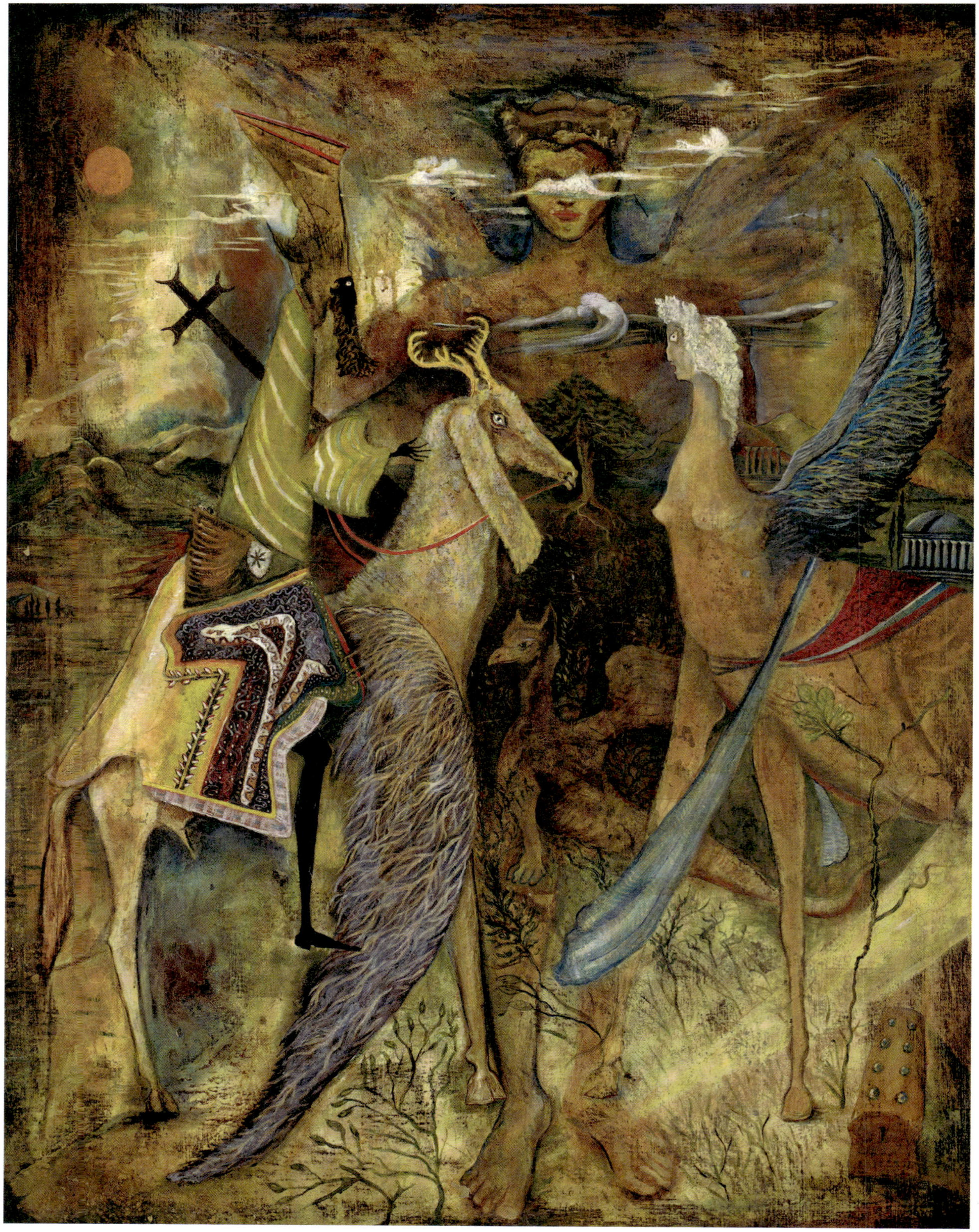

Plate 27
Leonora Carrington, British, born 1917;
Edward James, British, 1907-1984
The Journey of Prester John, 1953
Oil on canvas
39 3/8 x 31 11/16 in. (100 x 80.5 cm)
Collection of Mary and Roy Cullen

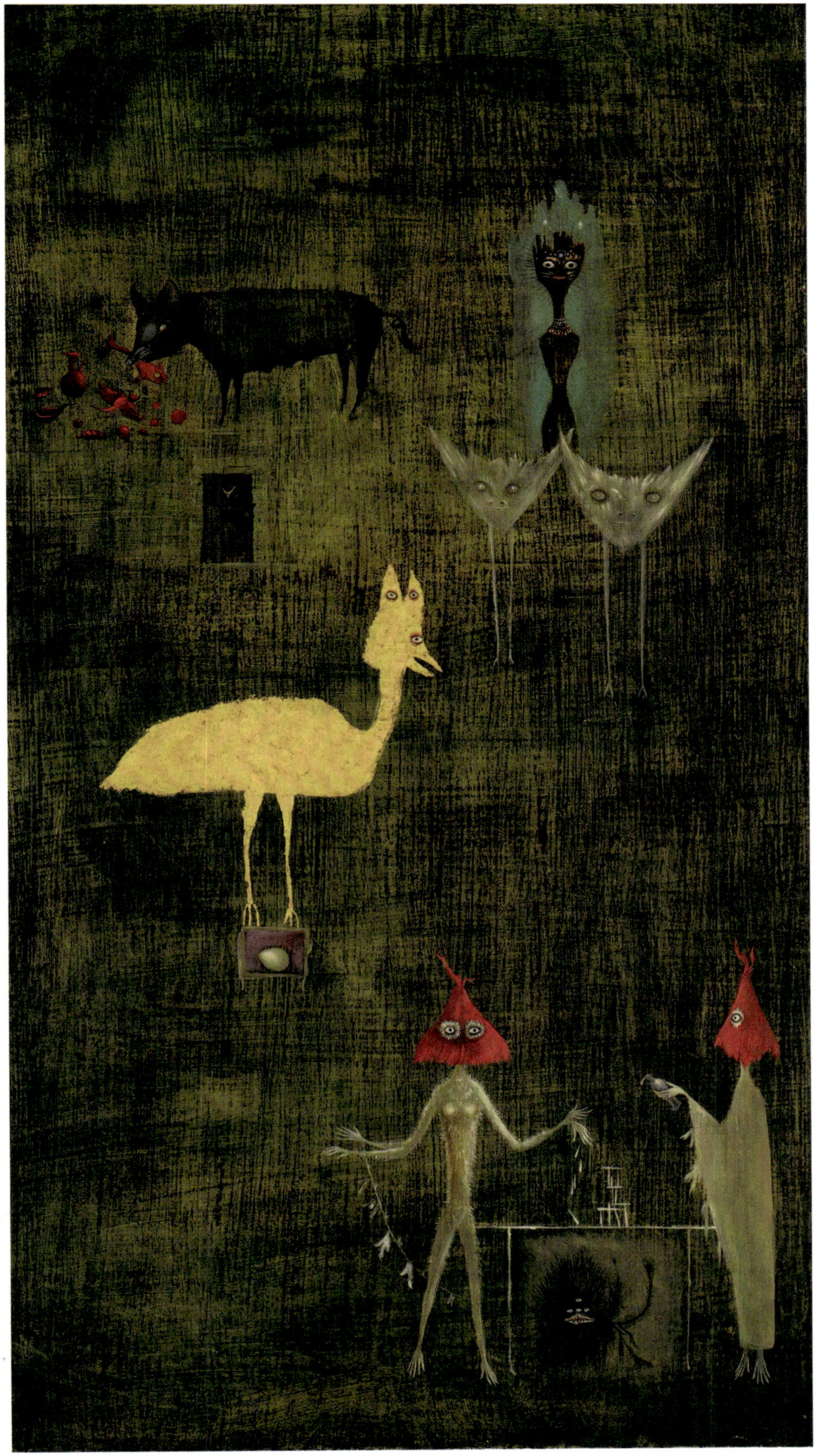

Plate 28
Leonora Carrington, British, born 1917
Casting the Runes, 1951
Mixed oil, tempera and gold leaf
30 3/8 x 17 3/8 in. (77.2 x 44.1 cm)
Collection of Charles W. and Judy Tate

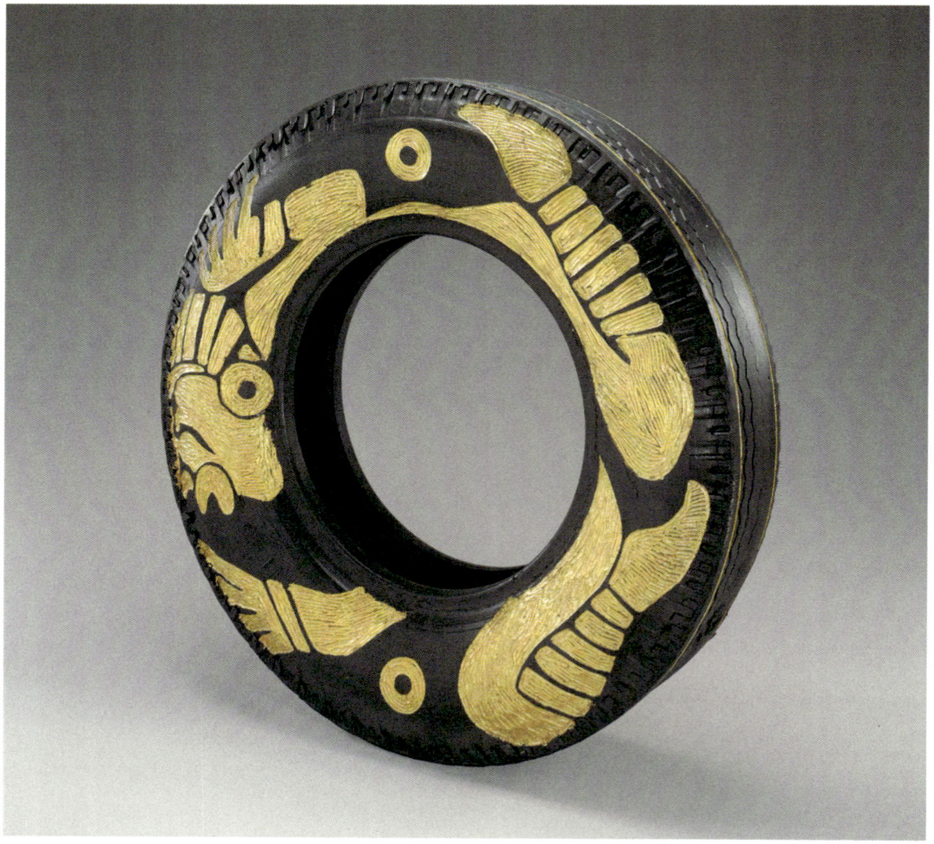

Plate 29
Betsabé Romero, Mexican, born 1963
Guerreros en cautiverio [Captive Warriors], 2006
Carved tire with gold leaf
9 7/16 x 40 3/16 dia. in. (24 x 102 dia. cm)
Collection of Gail and Louis Adler

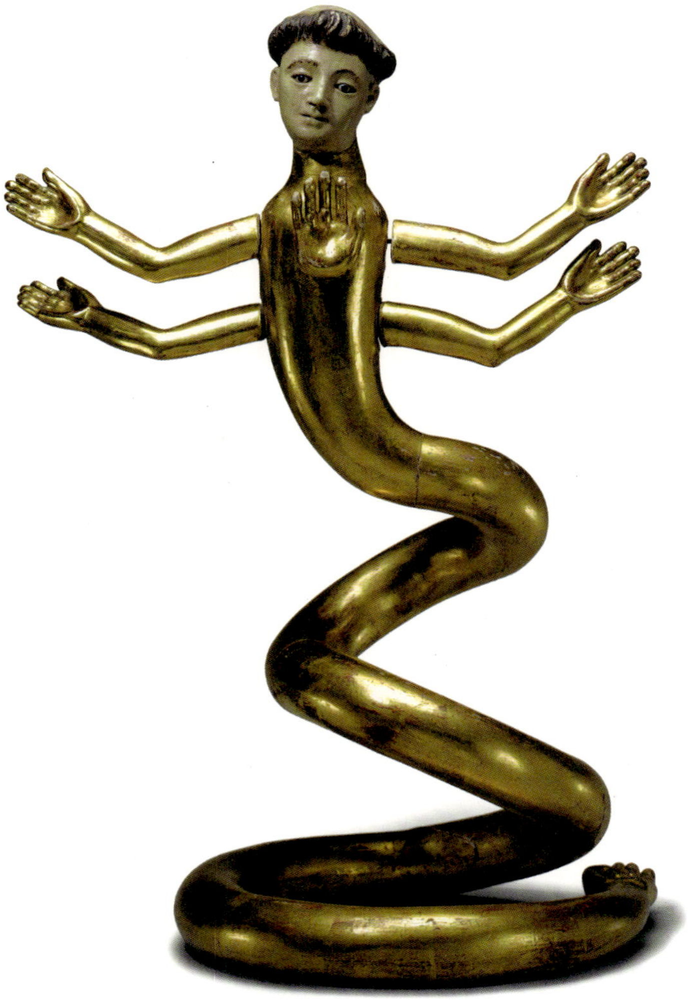

Plate 30
Pedro Friedeberg, Mexican, born 1936
Shiva-San Agustín [Shiva-St. Augustine], c. 1970
Gold leaf on wood with XVIII-century religious head
18 x 12 1/2 x 9 3/4 in. (45.7 x 31.8 x 24.8 cm)
Collection of Mary and Roy Cullen

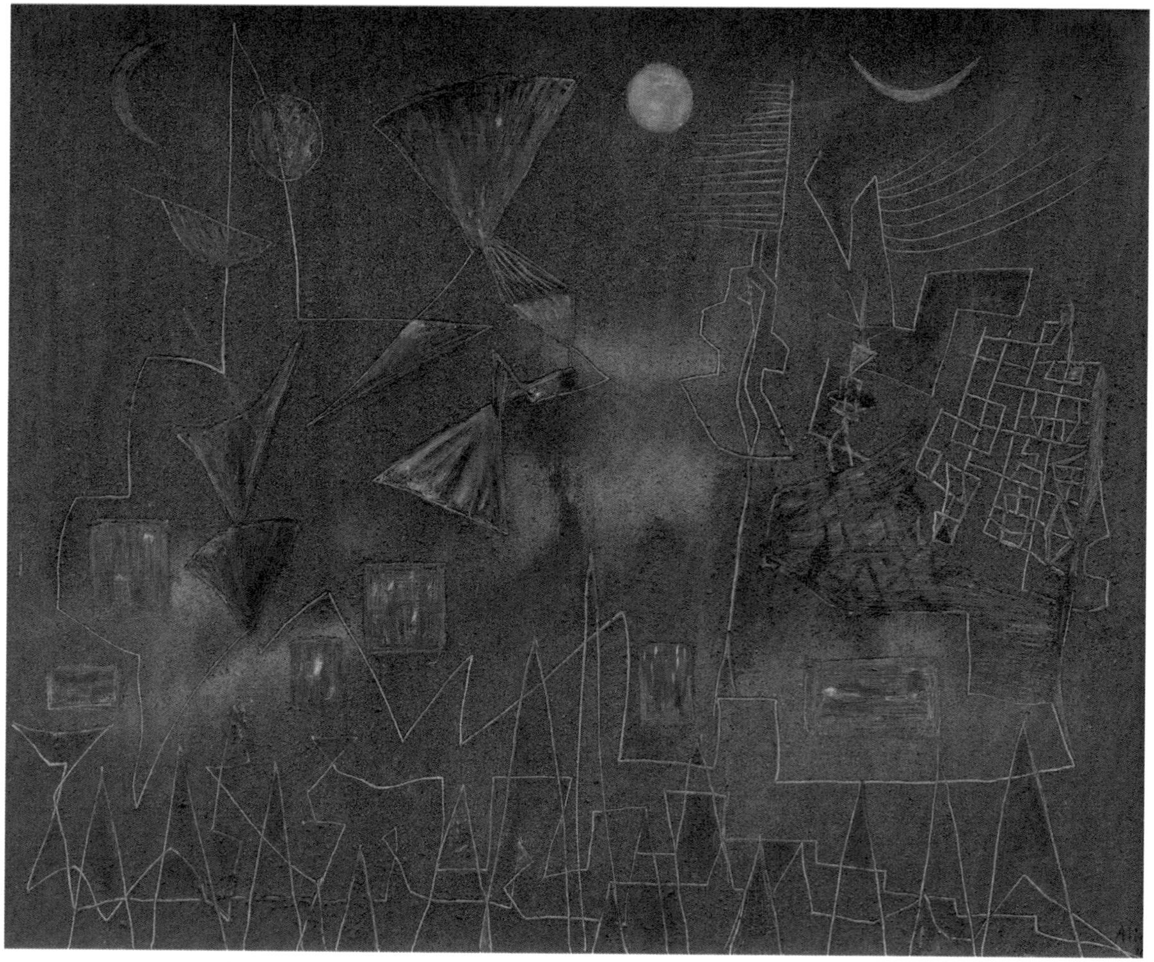

Plate 31
Alice Rahon, French, lived in Mexico, 1904-1987
The Sky above the City, 1945
Oil and sand on canvas
22 1/2 x 28 3/4 in. (57.2 x 73 cm)
Collection of Mary and Roy Cullen

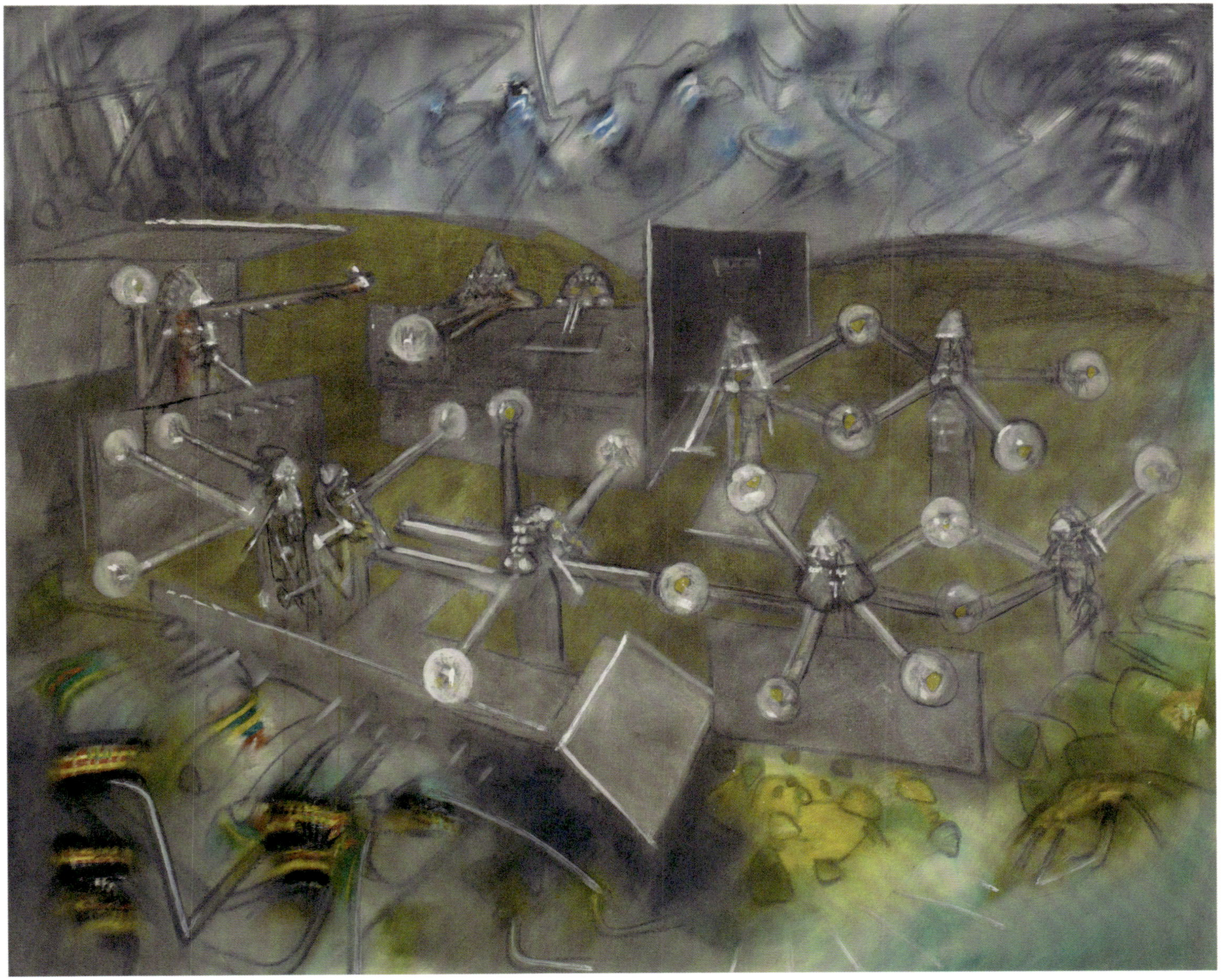

Plate 32
Roberto Matta, Chilean, 1911-2002
Sín titulo [Untitled], 1953
Oil on canvas
44 3/8 x 57 in. (111.8 x 143.5 cm)
Collection of Luis and Cecilia Campos

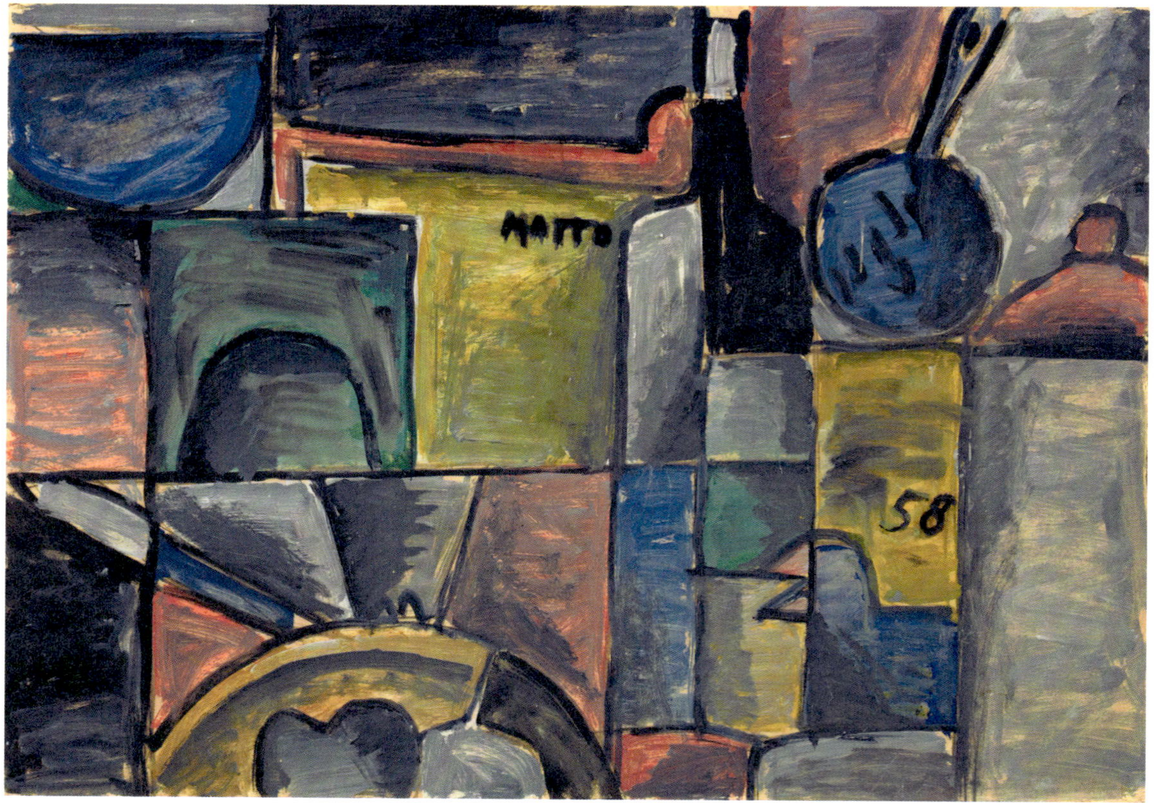

Plate 33
Francisco Matto, Uruguayan, 1911-1995
Planos constructivos [Constructivist Planes], 1958
Oil on board
17 x 14 in. (43.2 x 35.6 cm)
Private collection

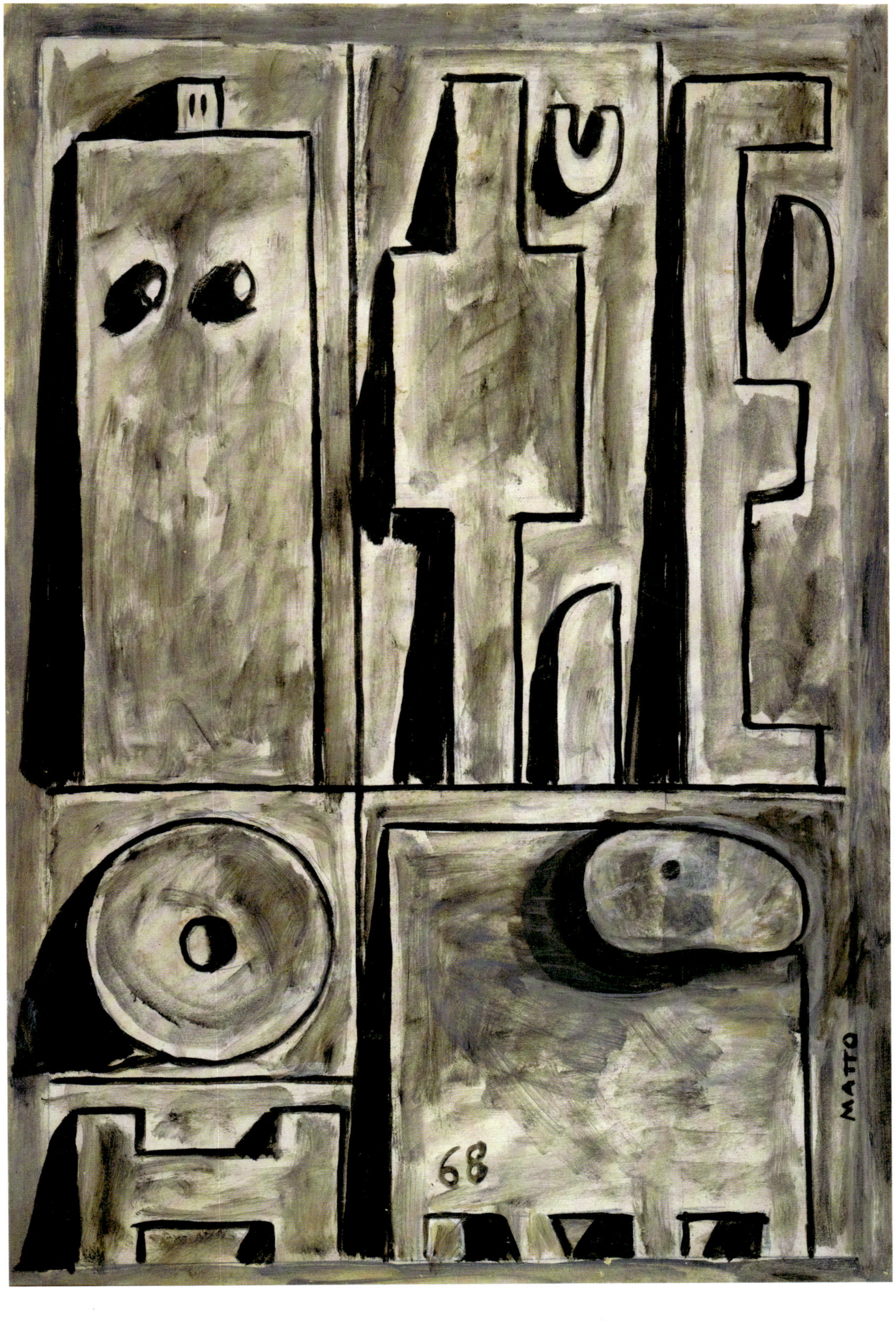

Plate 34
Francisco Matto, Uruguayan, 1911-1995
Ideas [Ideas], 1968
Oil on fiber board
40 x 28 in. (101.6 x 71.2 cm)
Collection of O. M. Jenney

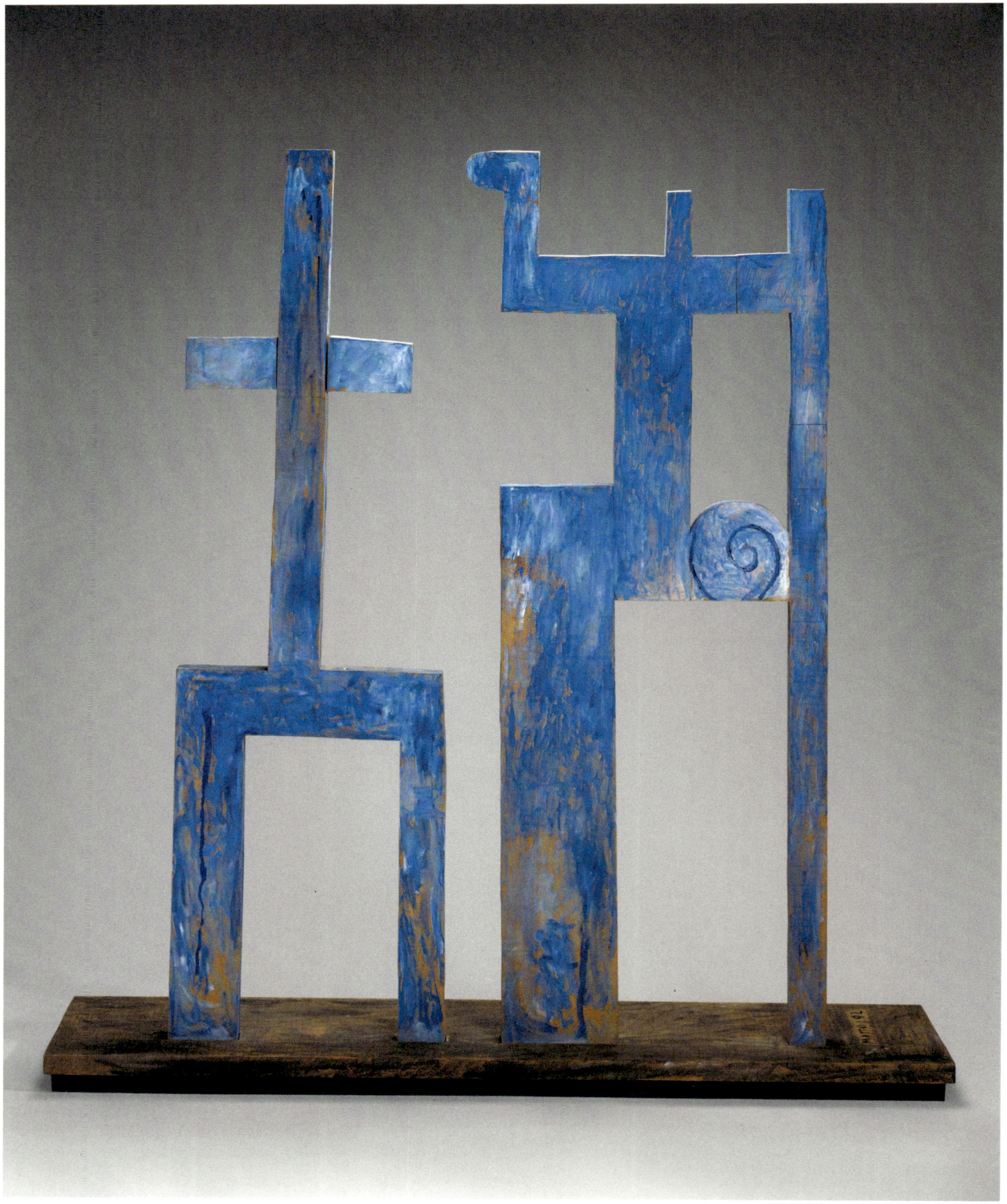

Plate 35
Francisco Matto, Uruguayan, 1911–1995
Monumento Azul [Blue Monument], 1992
Wood and paint
69 1/4 x 67 3/4 x 11 3/4 in.
(175.9 x 172.1 x 29.8 cm)
Estate of Frank Ribelin Collection,
Courtesy of McClain Gallery

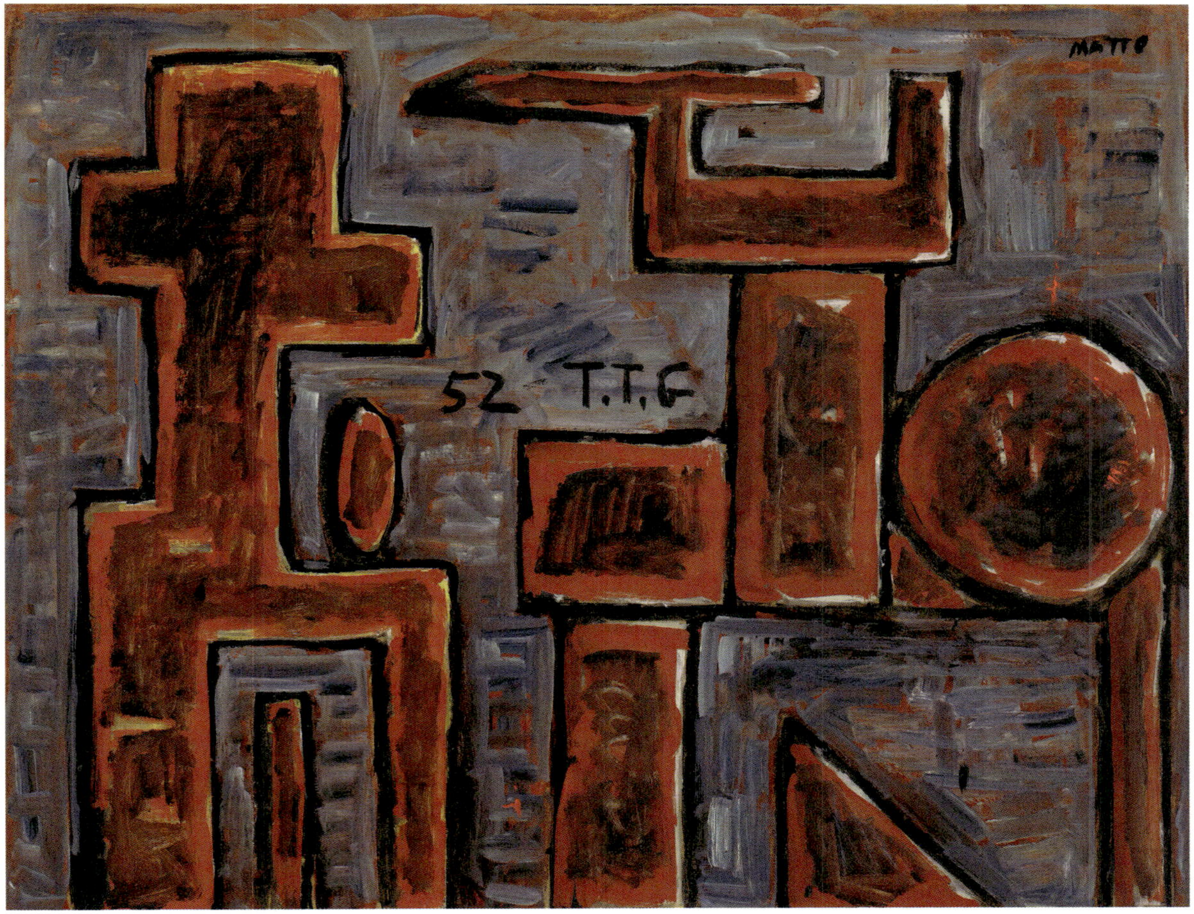

Plate 36
Francisco Matto, Uruguayan, 1911-1995
Estructuras en rojo [Structures in Red], 1952
Oil on board
29 1/4 x 36 in. (74.3 x 91.4 cm)
Private collection

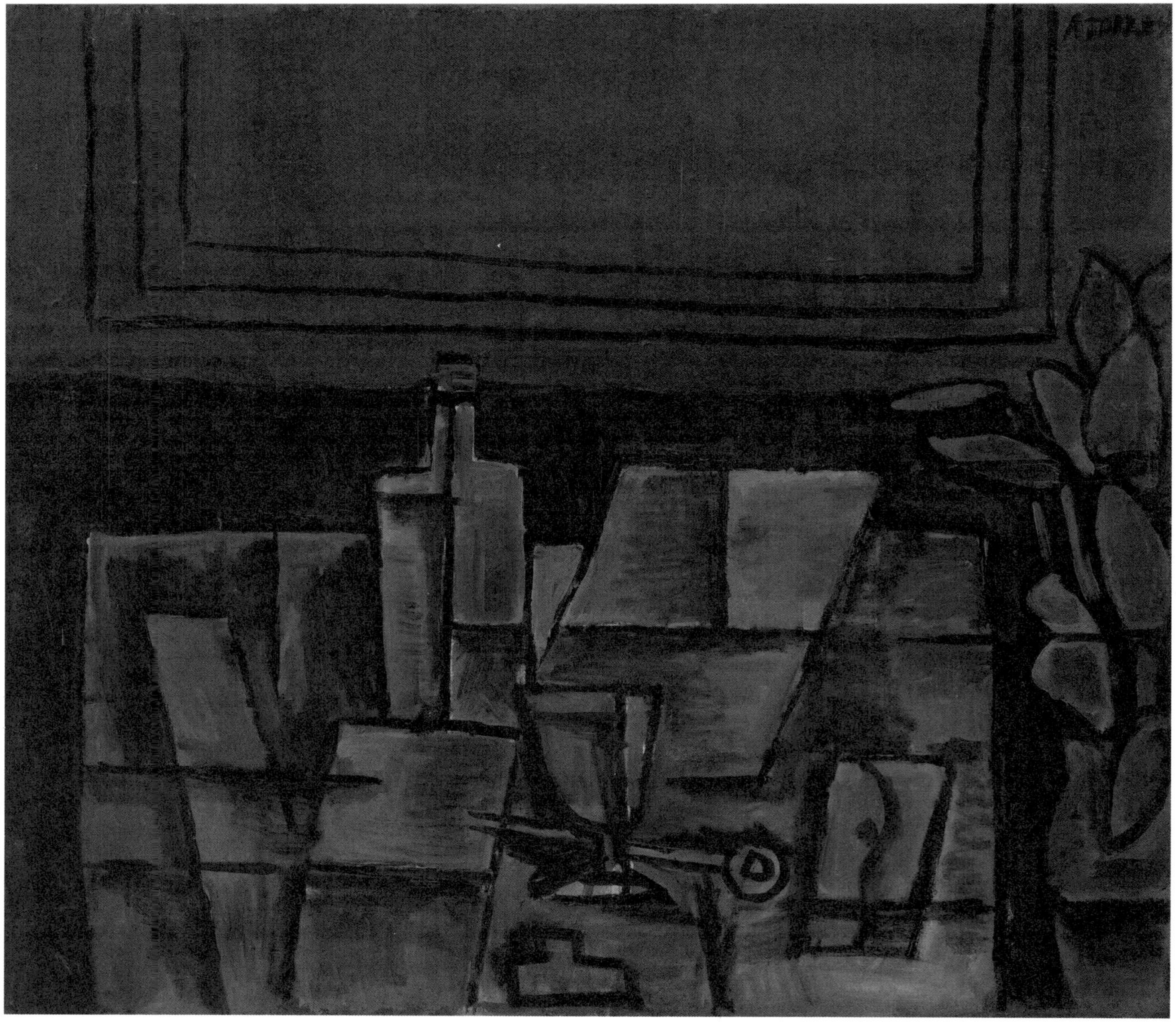

Plate 37
Augusto Torres, Spanish, 1913-1992
Naturaleza muerta [Still Life], 1962
Oil on canvas
25 7/8 x 30 in. (65.8 x 76.2 cm)
Private collection

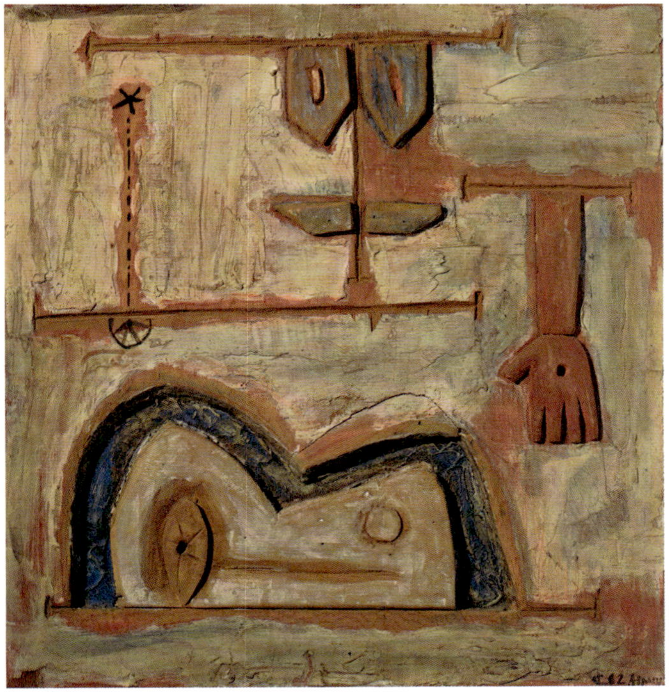

Plate 38
Julio Alpuy, Uruguayan, 1919-2009
Medida y naturaleza
[Measurement and Nature], 1962
Oil on wood
23 x 22 1/2 in. (58.4 x 57.2 cm)
Private collection

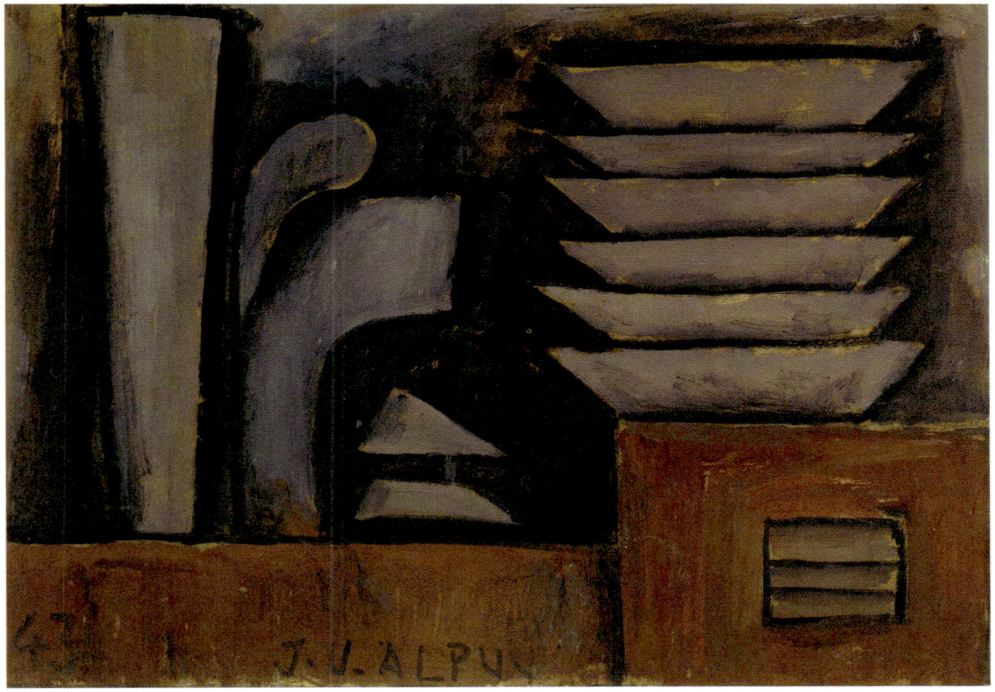

Plate 39
Julio Alpuy, Uruguayan, 1919-2009
Sin título [Untitled], 1943
Oil on cardboard
53 15/16 x 73 5/8 in. (137 x 187 cm)
Collection of Frances and Donald Baxter

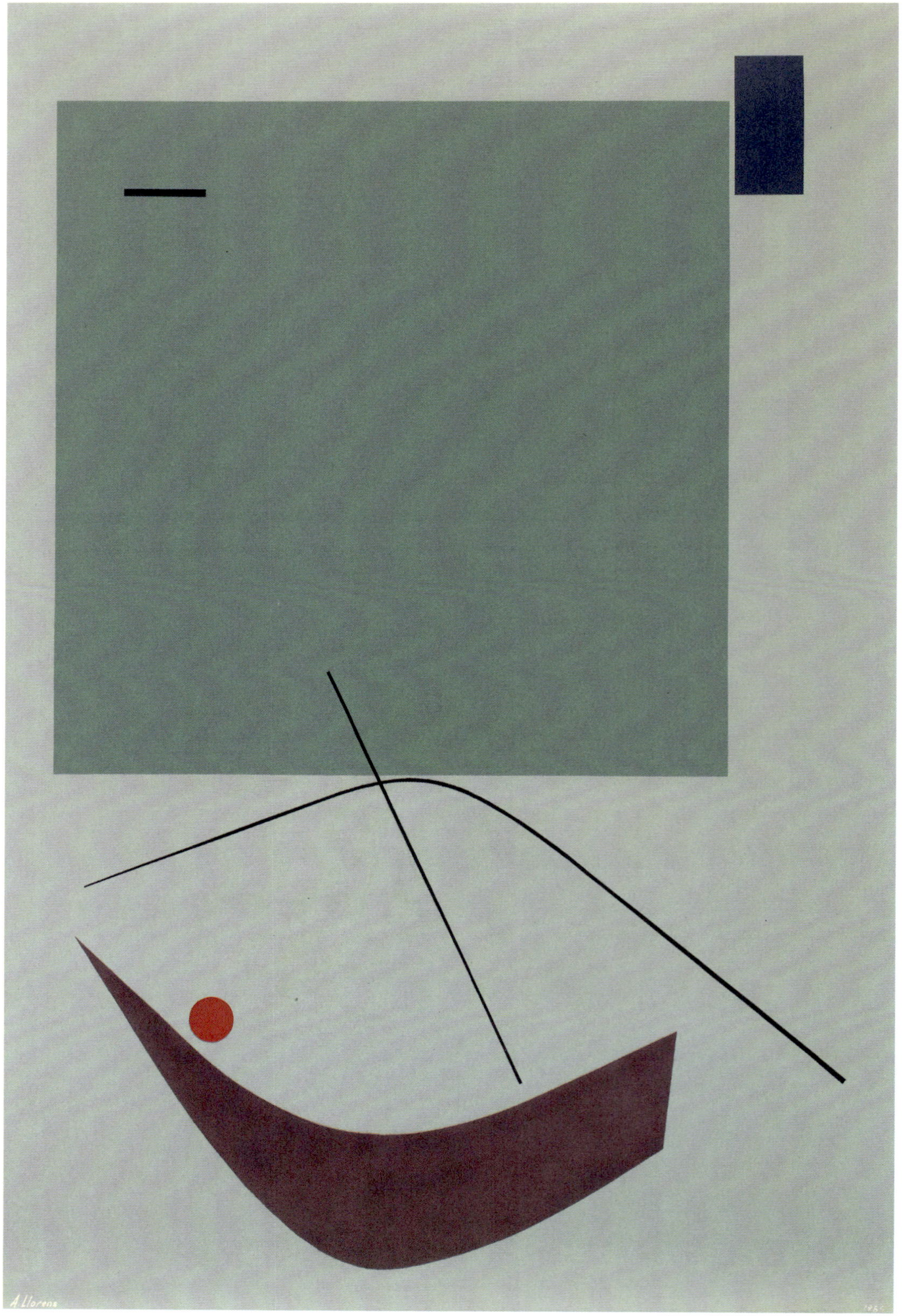

Plate 40
Antonio Llorens, Uruguayan, 1920–1995
Geométrico con cuadrado
[Geometric with Square], 1952
Oil on wood
48 1/16 x 39 in. (122 x 99 cm)
Collection of Mary and Roy Cullen

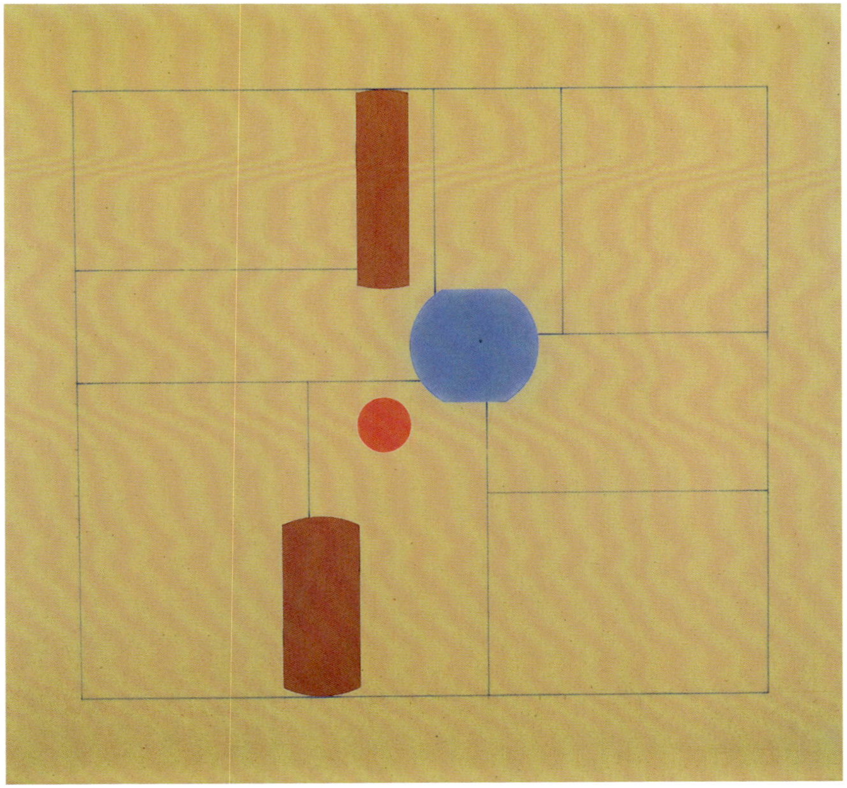

Plate 41
Hélio Oiticica, Brazilian, 1937-1980
Sêco # 15, 1955
Gouache on paper
15 3/8 x 16 15/16 in. (39 x 43 cm)
Collection of Mary and Roy Cullen

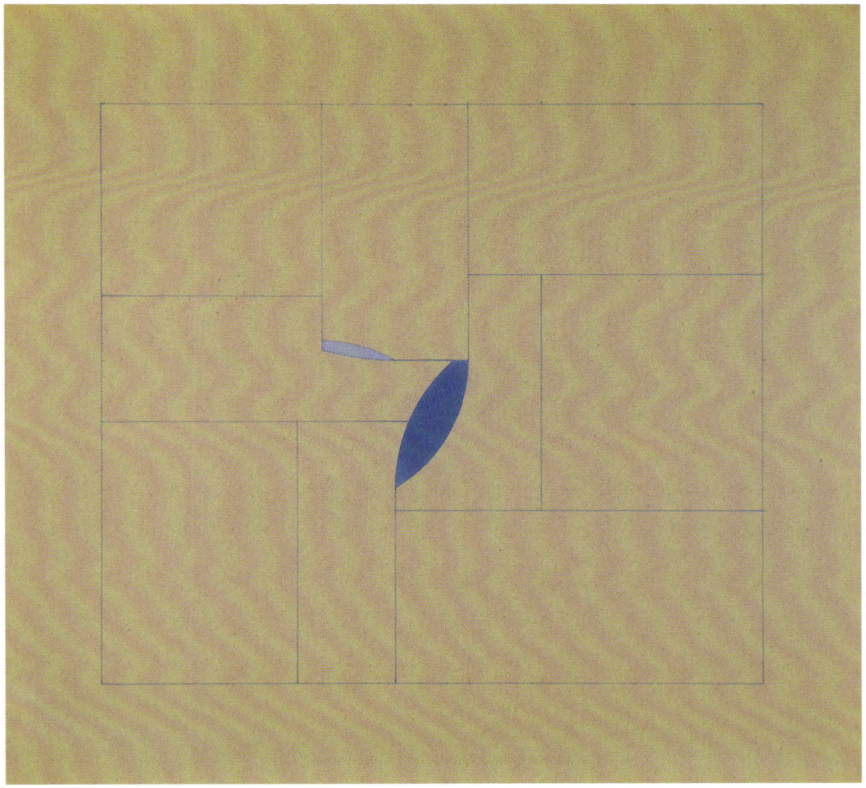

Plate 42
Hélio Oiticica, Brazilian, 1937-1980
Sêco # 9, 1956
Gouache on paper
15 x 16 1/2 in. (38.1 x 6.5 cm)
Collection of Leslie and Brad Bucher

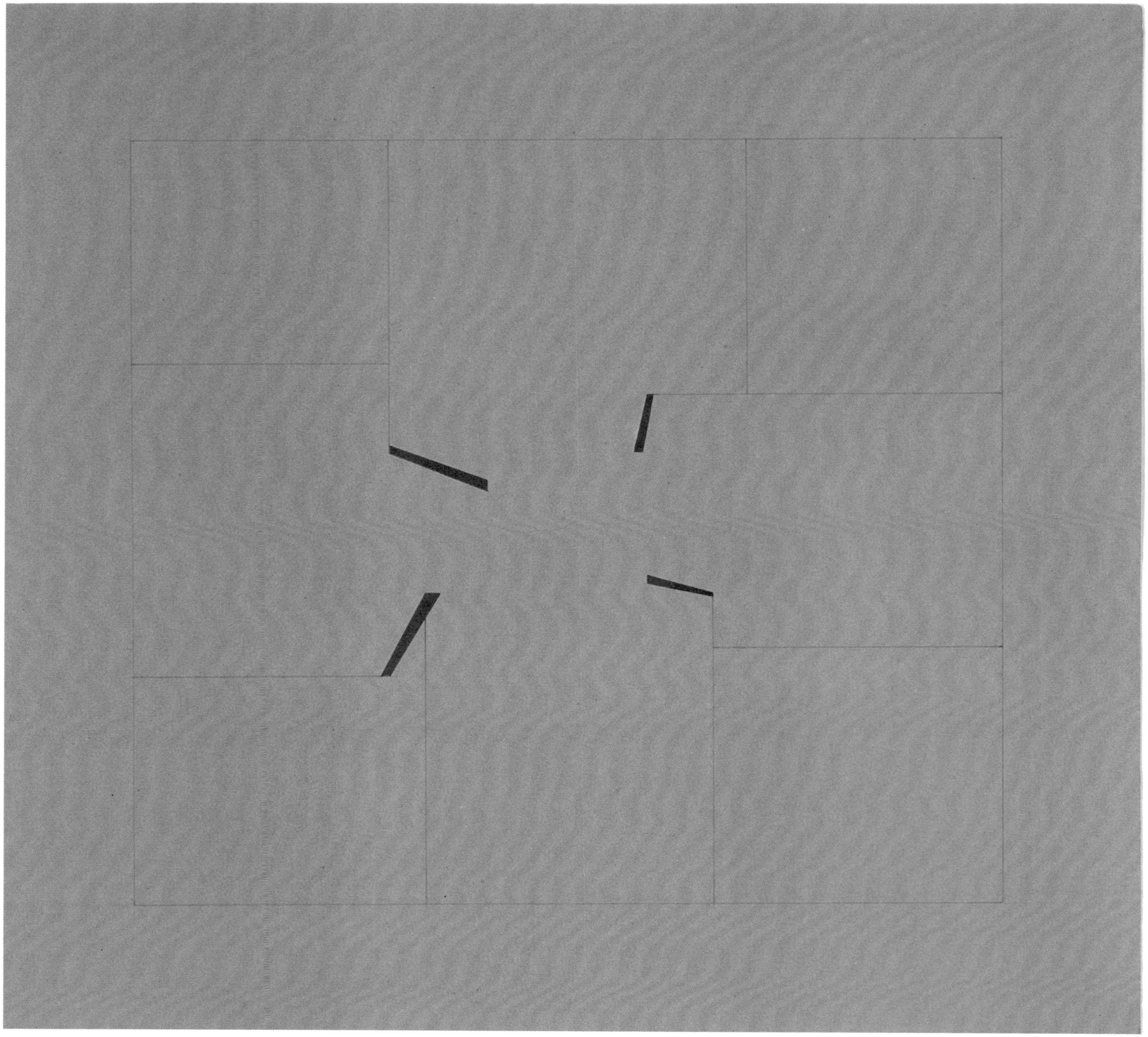

Plate 43
Hélio Oiticica, Brazilian, 1937–1980
Sêco # 16, 1957
Gouache on paper
43 x 39 in. (109.2 x 99.1 cm)
Collection of Charles W. and Judy Tate

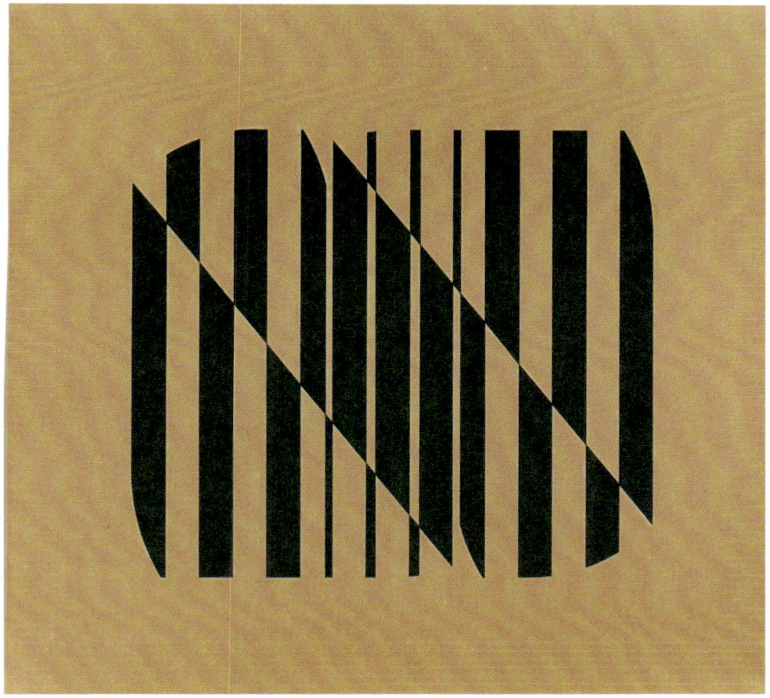

Plate 44
Hélio Oiticica, Brazilian, 1937-1980
Metaesquema, 1957
Gouache on cardboard
16 1/2 x 18 1/8 in. (41.9 x 46.1 cm)
Estate of Frank Ribelin Collection,
Courtesy of McClain Gallery

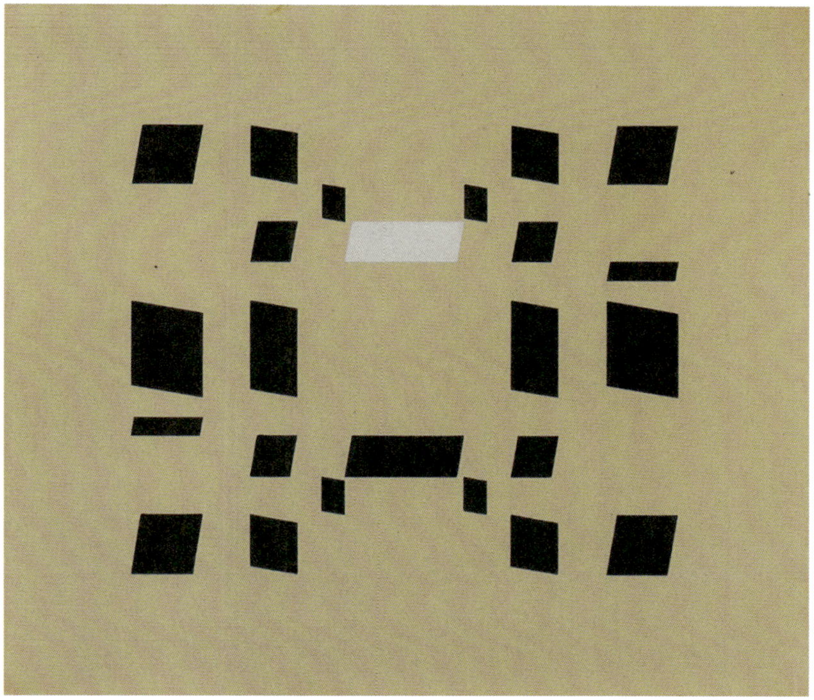

Plate 45
Hélio Oiticica, Brazilian, 1937-1980
Metaesquema, c. 1956-57
Gouache on cardboard
19 3/4 x 22 3/4 in. (50.2 x 57.8 cm)
Collection of Luis and Cecilia Campos

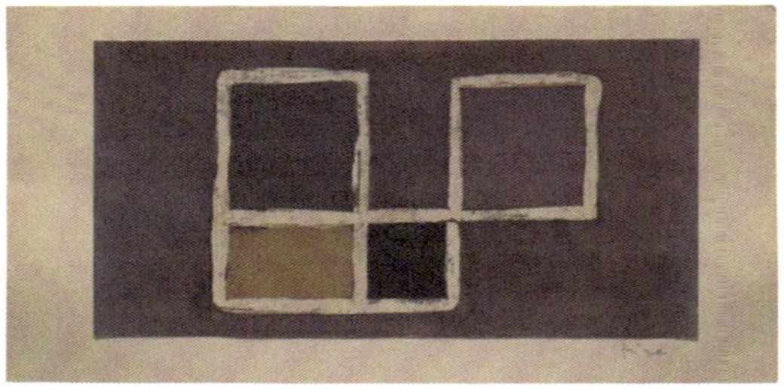
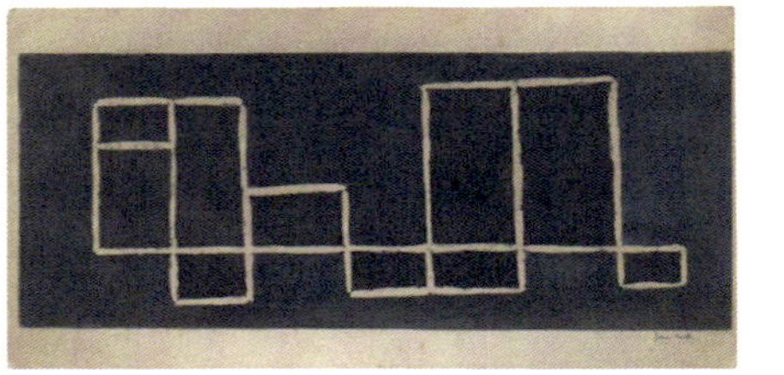
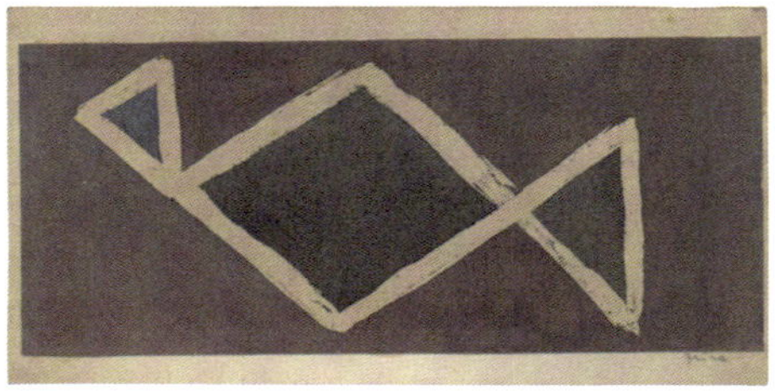
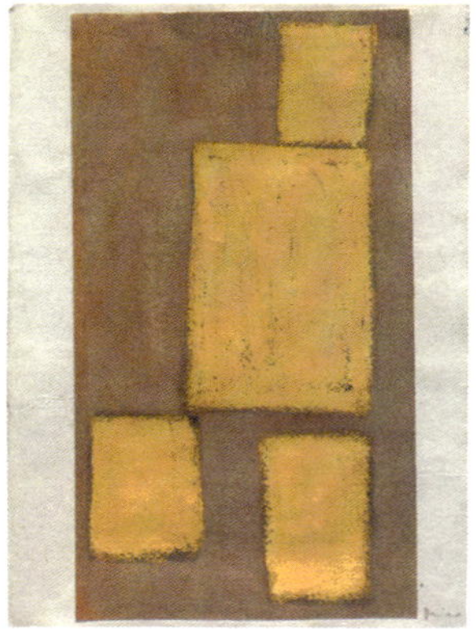
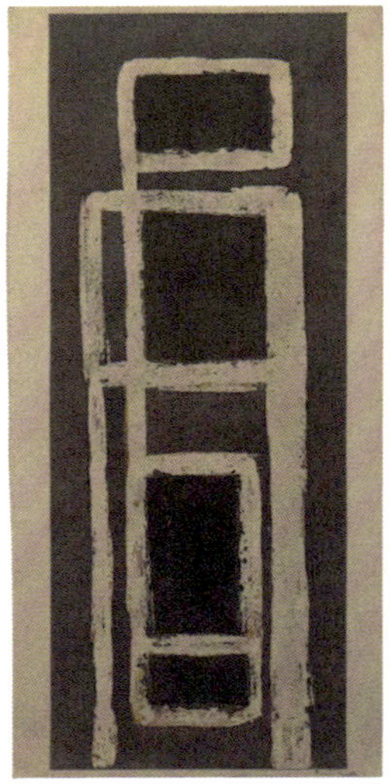
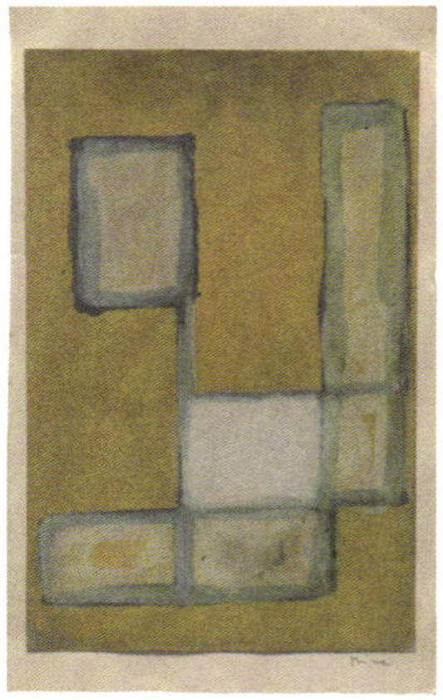
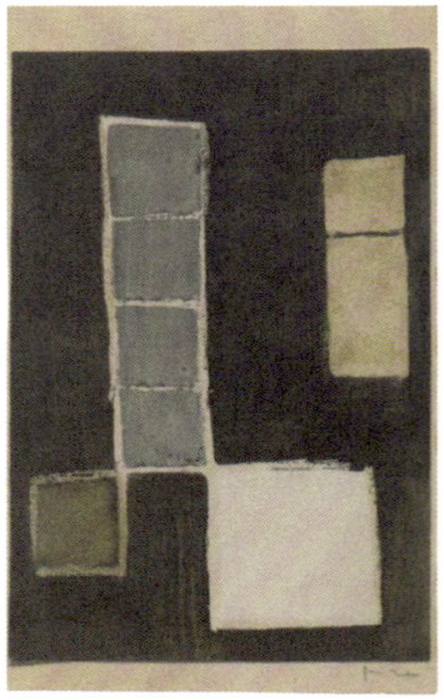

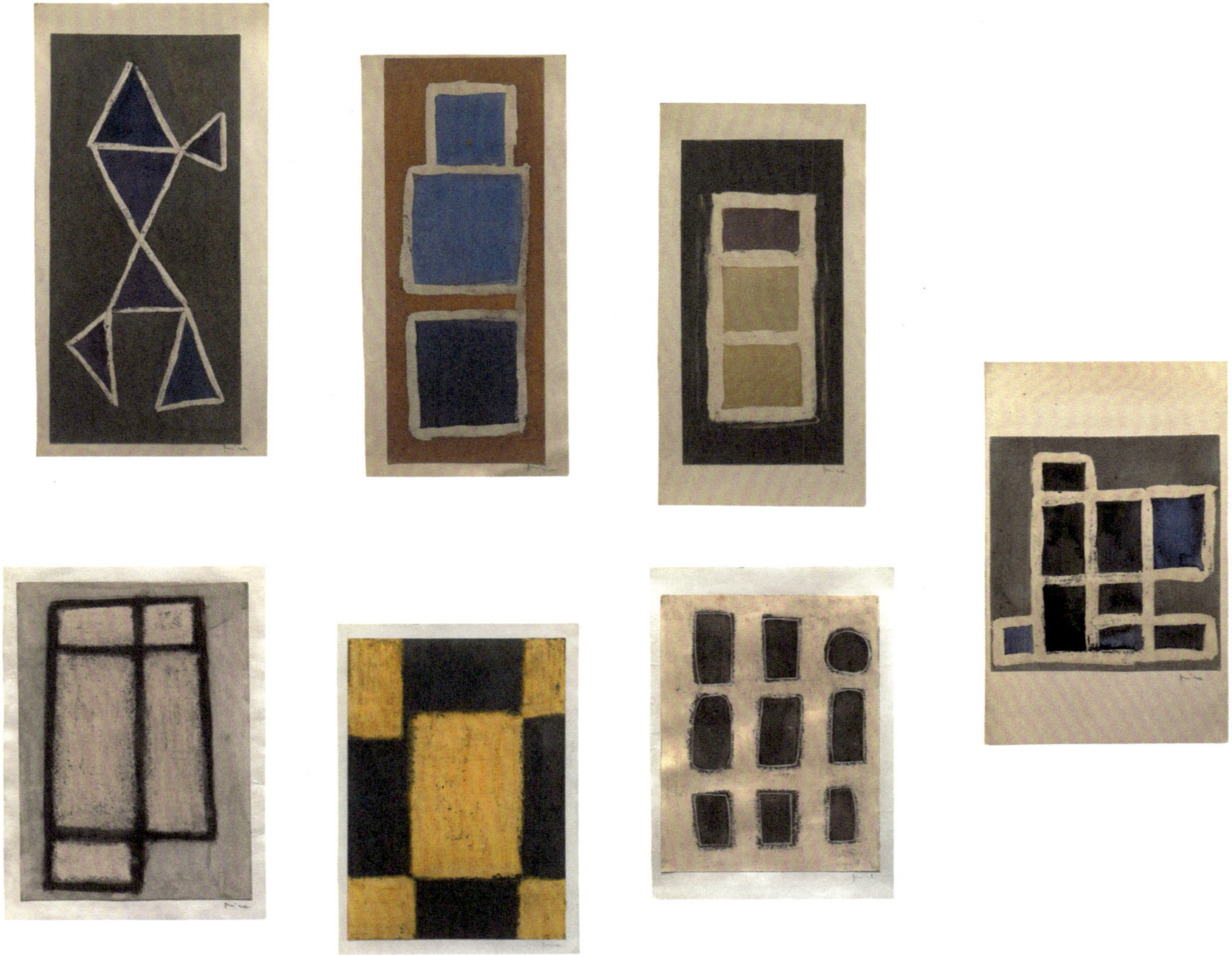

Plate 46
Mira Schendel, Brazilian, 1919-1988
Sín titulo [Untitled], c. 1960
Mixed media on paper
Each approximately 7 1/2 x 5 1/2 in. (19 x 14 cm)
Mixed media on paper
Collection of Luis and Cecilia Campos

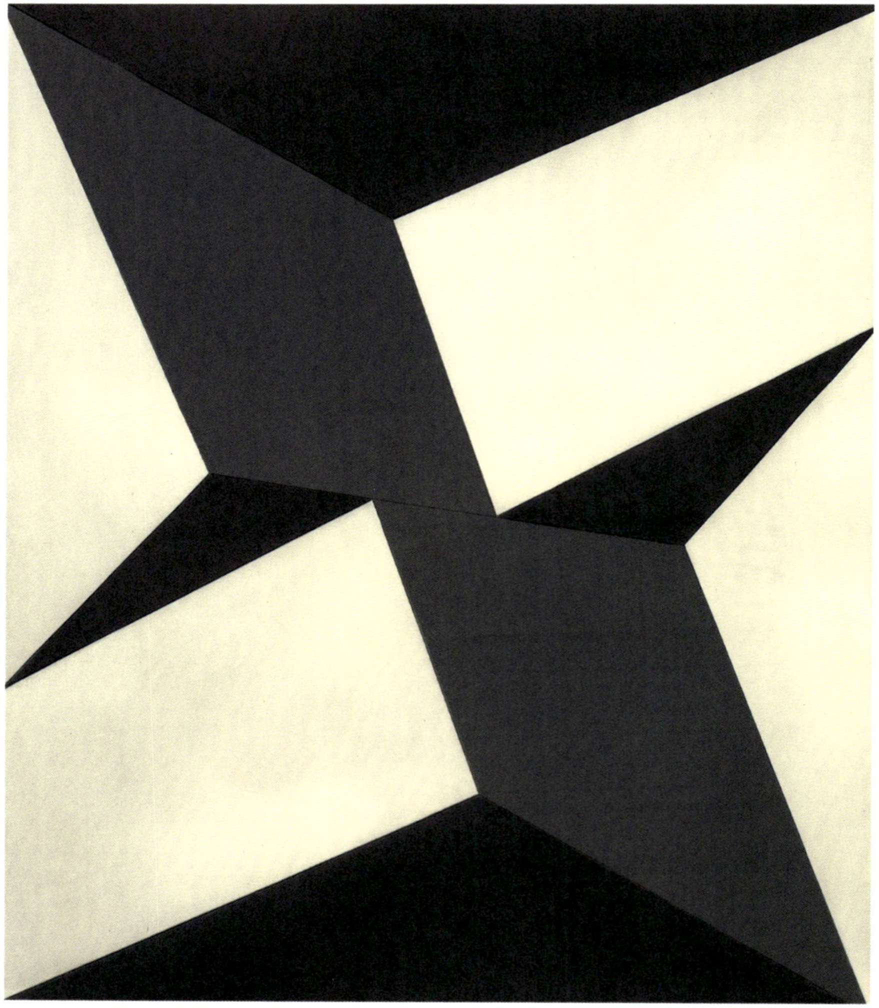

Plate 47
Lygia Clark, Brazilian, 1920-1988
Planos em superfície modulada no. 5
[Planes on modulated surface no. 5], 1957
Alkyd and nitrocellulose paint on plywood
31 3/8 x 27 9/16 in. (79.8 x 70 cm)
The Adolpho Leirner Collection of Brazilian Constructive Art,
museum purchase with funds provided by the
Caroline Wiess Law Accessions Endowment Fund

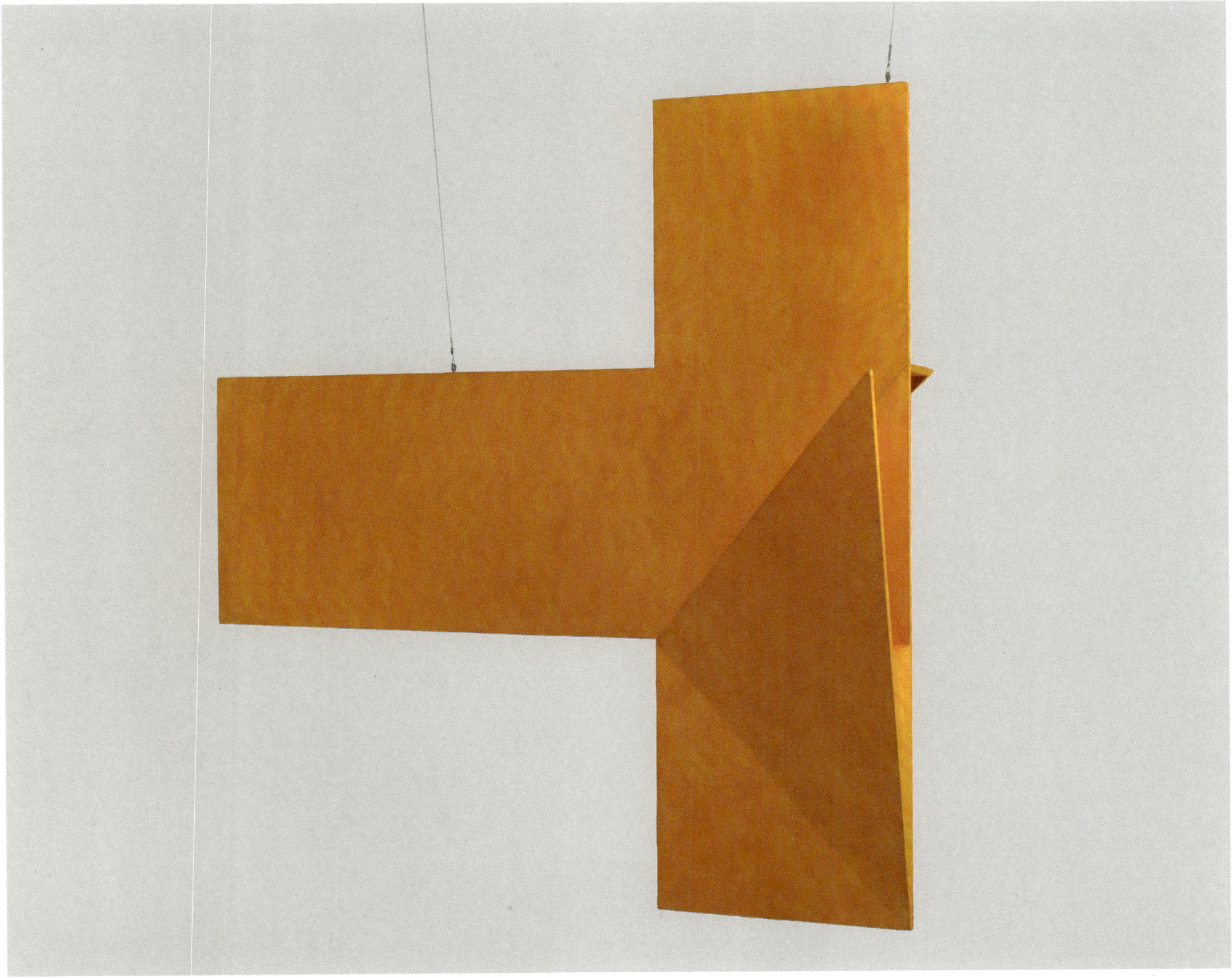

Plate 48
Hélio Oiticica, Brazilian, 1937–1980
Relevo espacial [Spatial Relief], c. 1960
Paint on cutout wood
45 x 45 x 10 in. (114.3 x 114.3 x 25.4 cm)
The Adolpho Leirner Collection of Brazilian Constructive Art,
gift of the Caroline Wiess Law Foundation

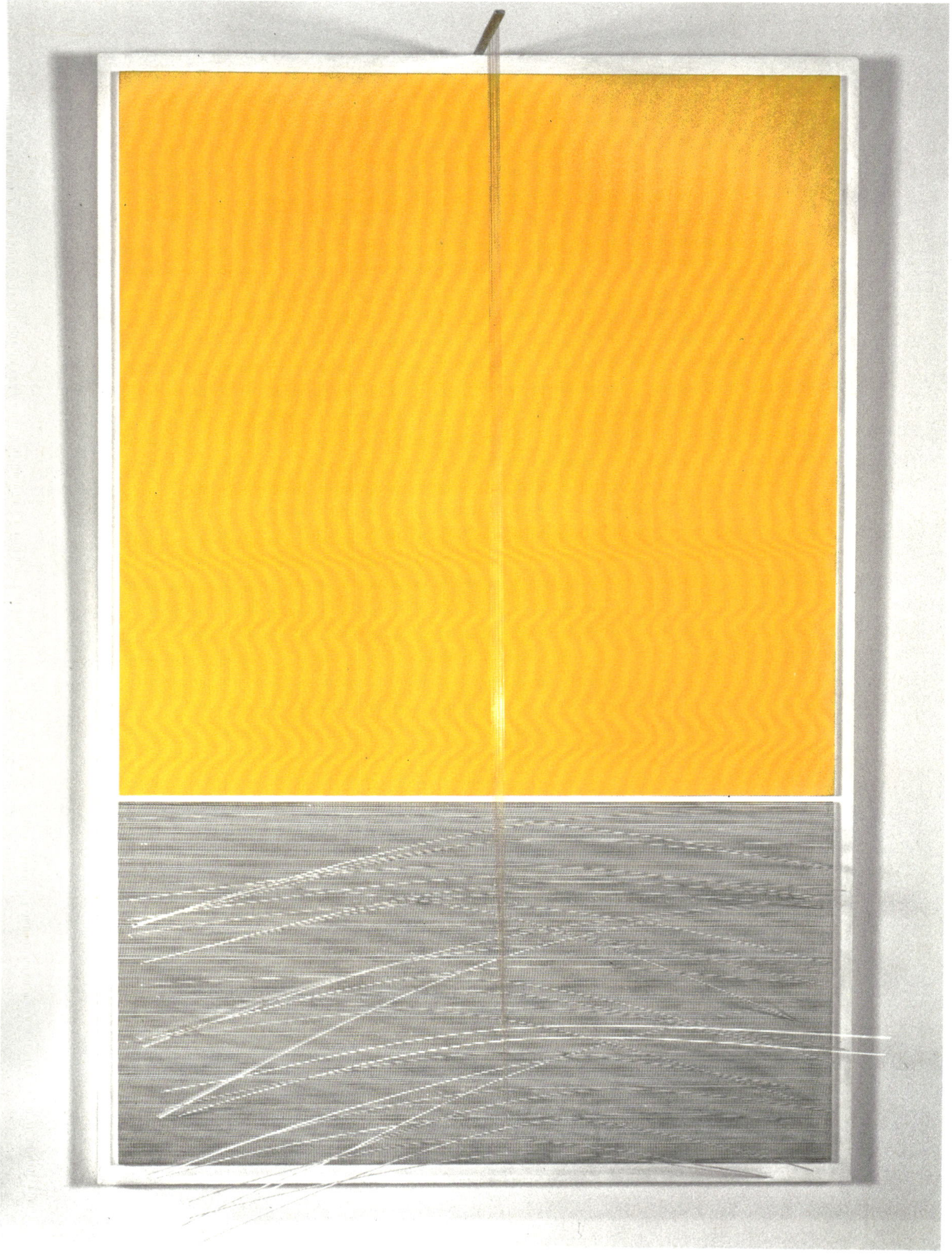

Plate 49
Jesús Rafael Soto, Venezuelan, 1923-2005
Sin título [Untitled], 1965
Wood, paint, and metal
61 3/4 x 42 1/2 x 11 3/4 in.
(156.8 x 108 x 29.8 cm)
Collection of Diane and Bruce Halle

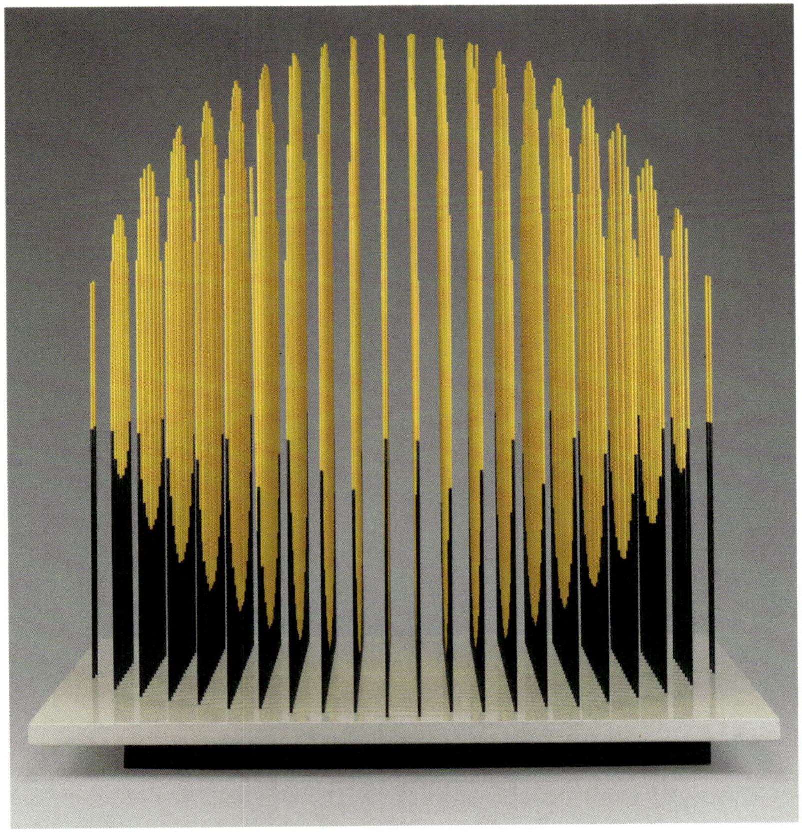

Plate 50
Jesús Rafael Soto, Venezuelan, 1923-2005
Sphere de Bale [Sphere for Basel], 1997
Paint on metal
43 1/2 x 45 1/2 x 45 1/4 in. (110.5 x 115.6 x 114.9 cm)
Collection of John and Carola Herrin

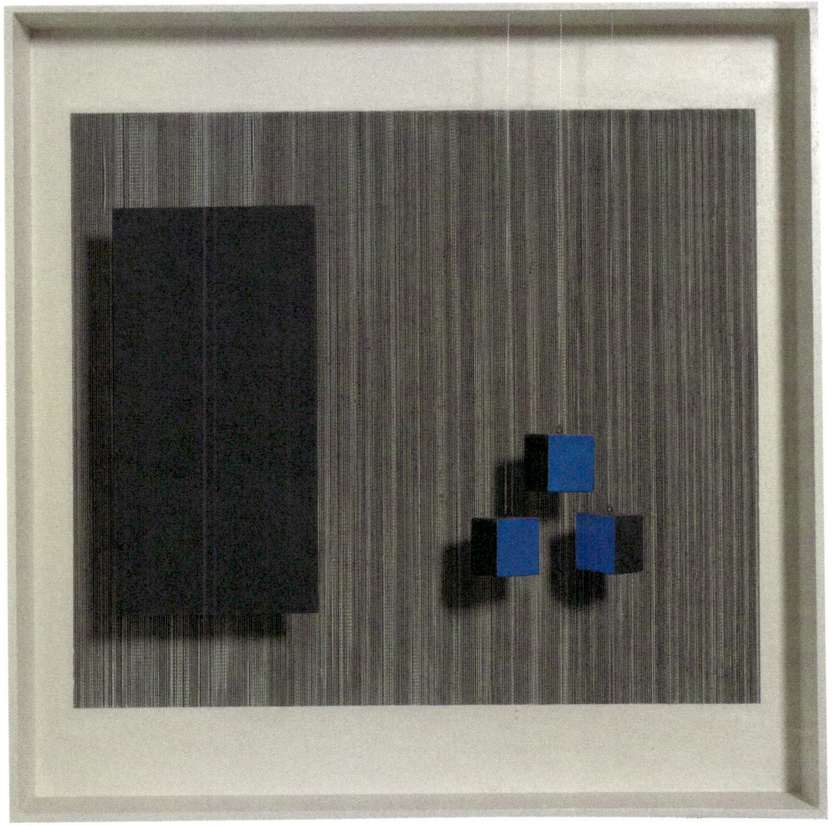

Plate 51
Jesús Rafael Soto, Venezuelan, 1923-2005
Les Trois Cube Bleus [The Three Blue Cubes], 1962
Paint on wood and metal with nylon filament
39 1/2 x 39 1/2 x 5 1/2 in.
(100.3 x 100.3 x 14 cm)
Collection of María Cristina and Pablo Henning

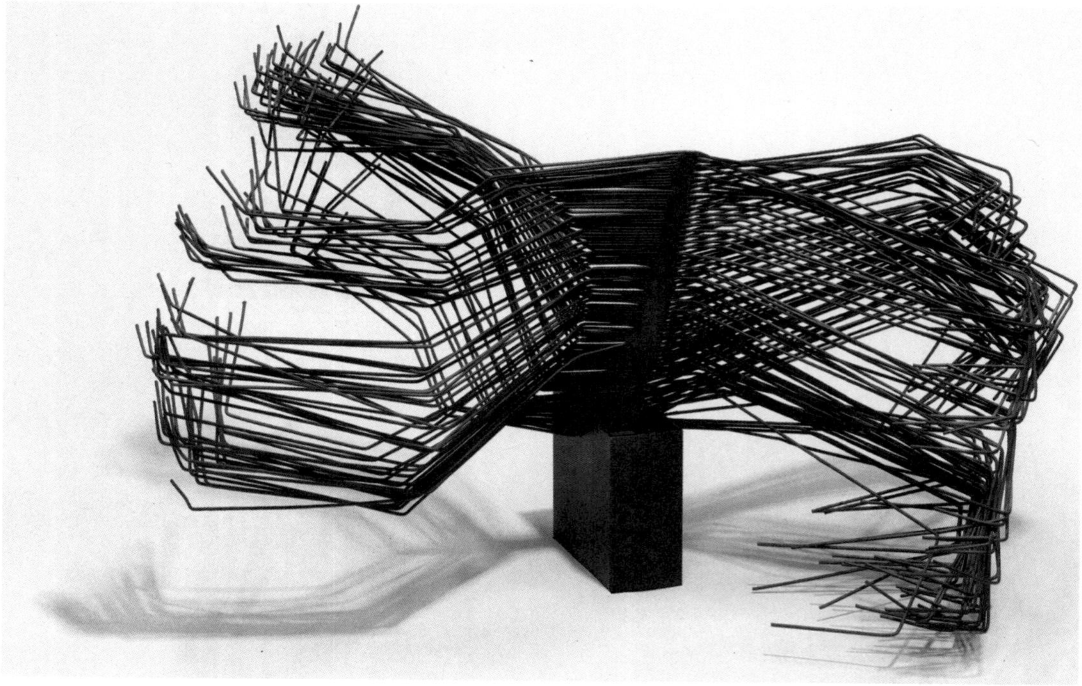

Plate 52
Gego (Gertrud Goldschmidt), Venezuelan,
born Germany, 1912-1994
Una de cinco variantes
[One of Five Variants], 1967
Painted iron wire with metal base
8 5/8 x 13 3/4 x 25 5/8 in. (21.9 x 34.9 x 65.1 cm)
Collection of John and Carola Herrin

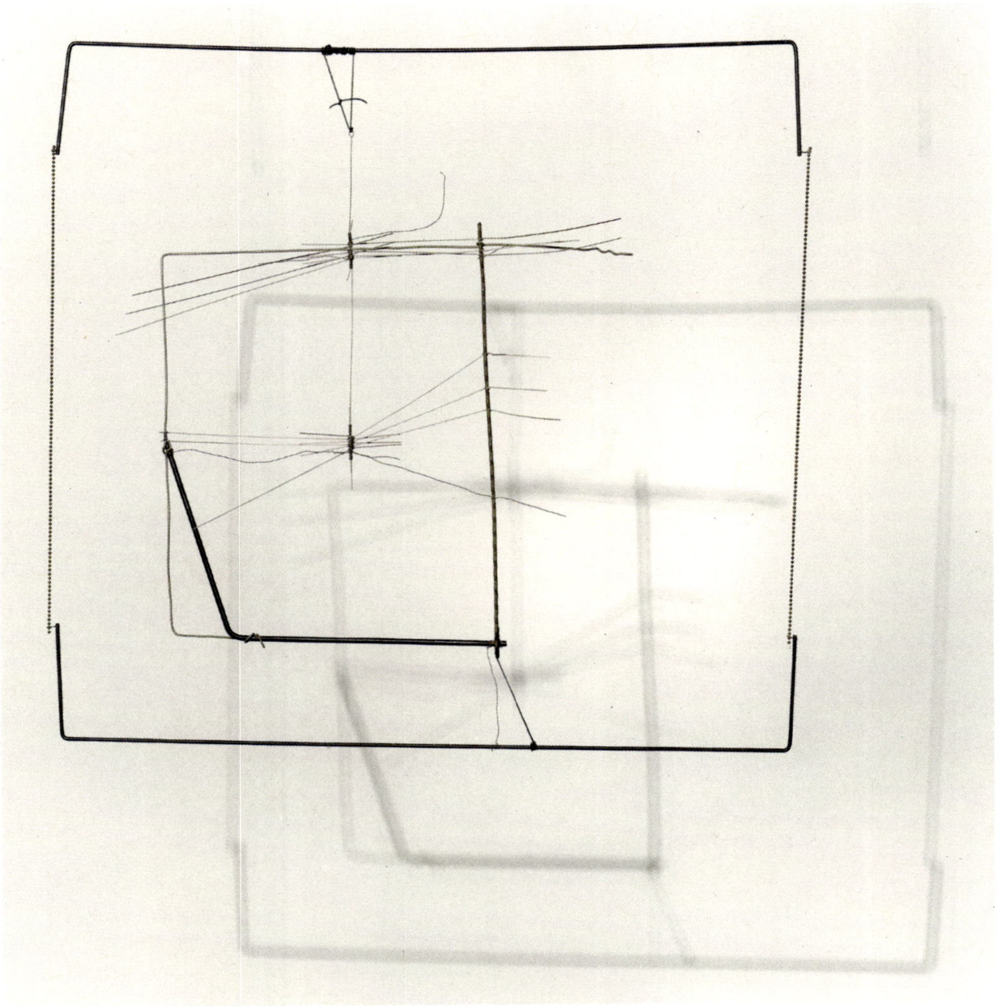

Plate 53A
Gego (Gertrud Goldschmidt), Venezuelan,
born Germany, 1912-1994
Dibujo sin papel, 85/18 [Drawing without Paper, 85/18], 1985
Wire and metal objects
43 5/16 x 30 1/2 in. (110 x 77.5 cm)
Collection of María Cristina and Pablo Henning

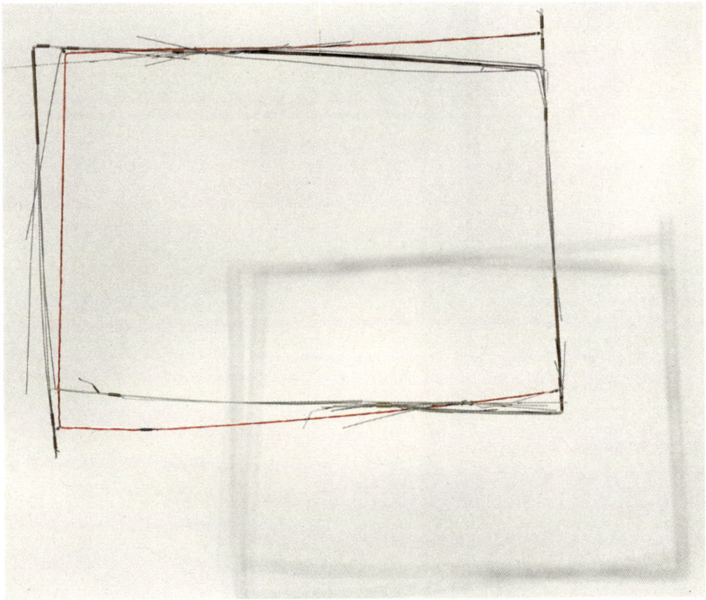

Plate 53B
Gego (Gertrud Goldschmidt), Venezuelan,
born Germany, 1912-1994
Dibujo sin papel 79/19
[Drawing without Paper], 1979
Stainless steel, bronze, thread
17 1/3 x 23 x 1 1/5 in. (44 x 58.5 x 3 cm)
Collection of Peter and Linda Zweig

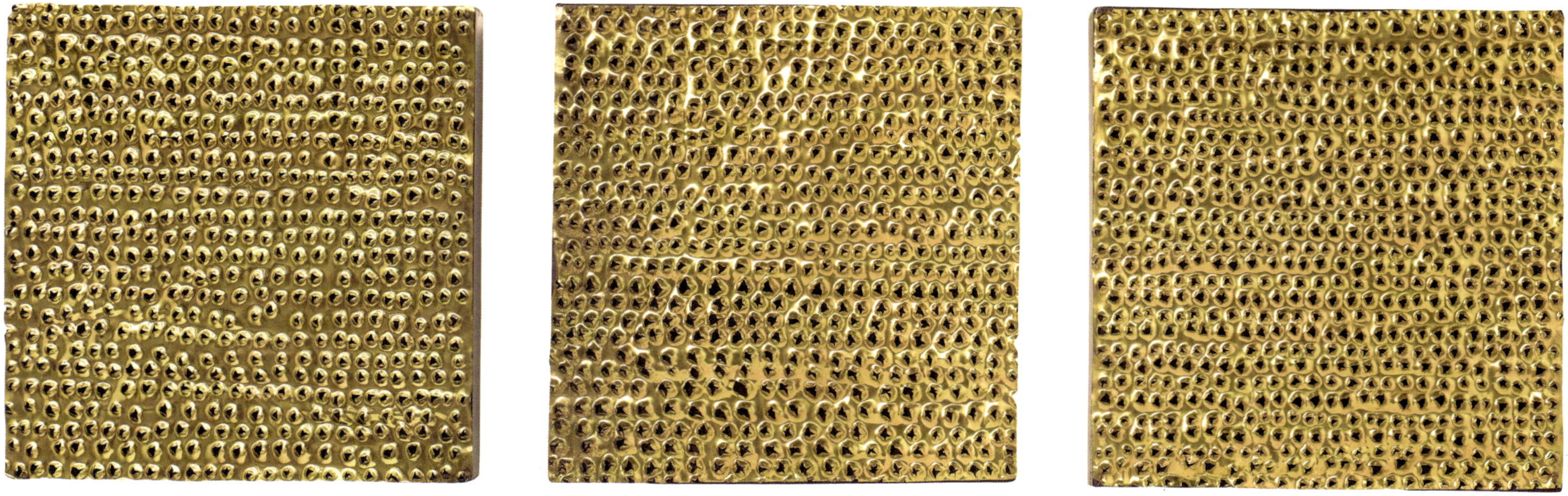

Plate 54
Mathias Goeritz, Mexican, born Germany, 1915–1990
Tres láminas perforadas y doradas
[3 Perforated Golden Sheets], c. 1960s
Brass, metal sheets
Each 8 1/8 x 8 x 2 in. (21.4 x 20.3 x 5.1 cm)
Collection of Luis and Cecilia Campos

Plate 55
Mathias Goeritz, Mexican, born Germany, 1915–1990
Mensaje [Message], c. 1960s
Gold leaf on wood
31 1/2 x 29 1/4 in. (80 x 74.3 cm)
Collection of Mary and Roy Cullen

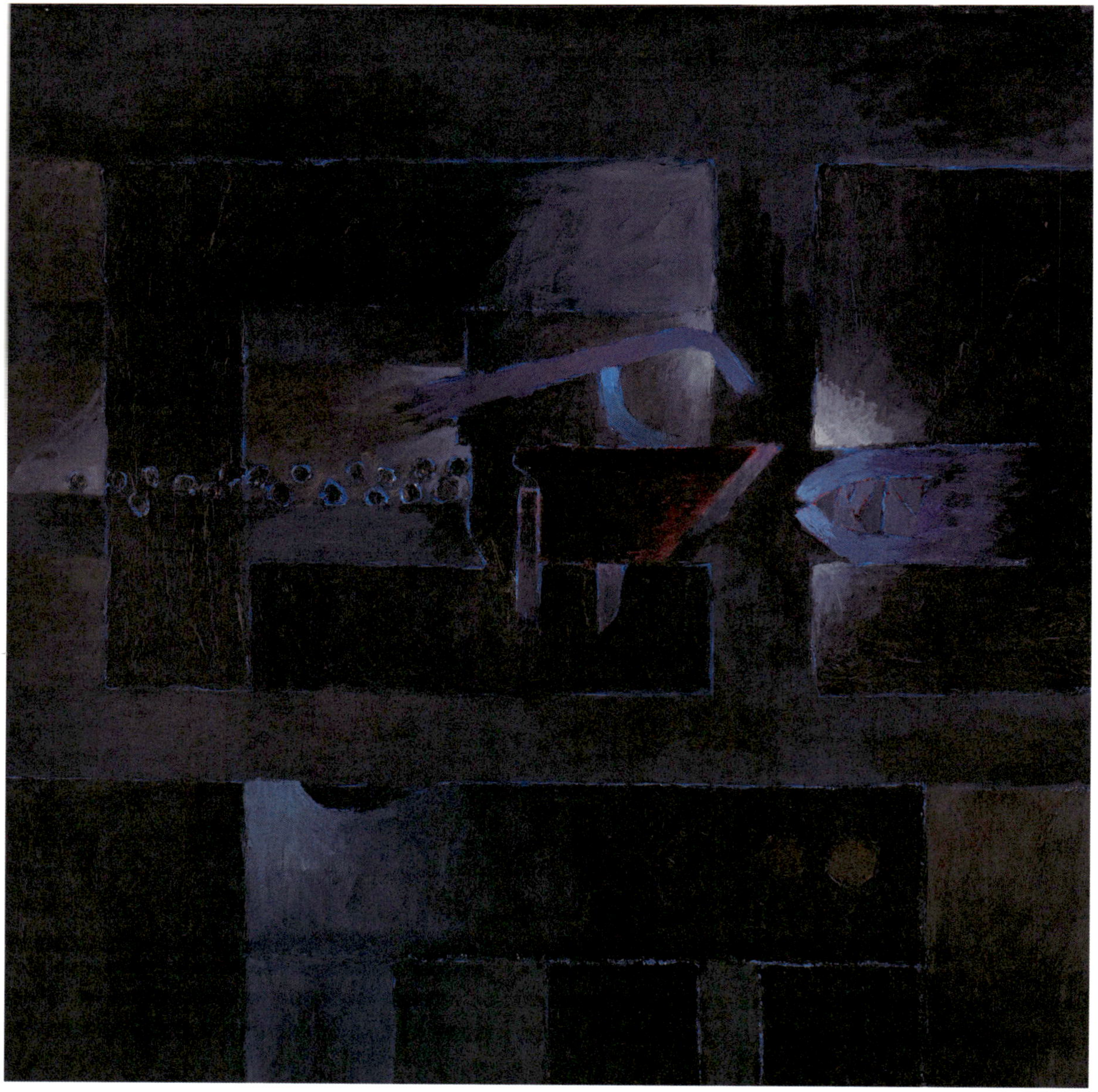

Plate 56
Fernando de Szyszlo, Peruvian, born 1925
Sol Negro, 19 [Black Sun, 19], 2008
Acrylic on canvas
48 x 48 in. (121.9 x 121.9 cm)
Collection of Juan Carlos Uriarte

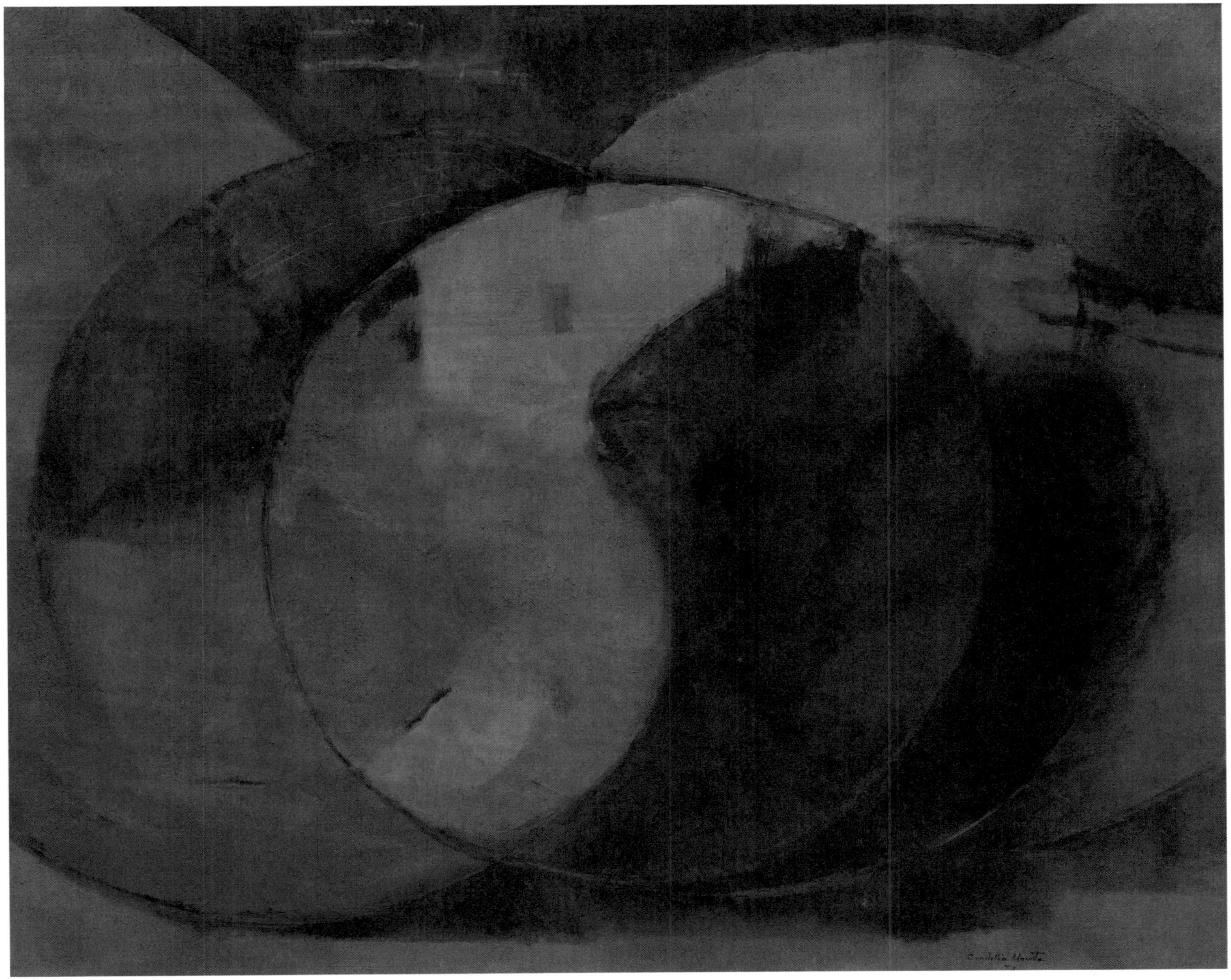

Plate 57
Cordelia Urueta, Mexican, born 1908
Tiempo estacionado [Time at a Standstill], 1968
Oil on canvas
44 x 56 in. (111.8 x 142.2 cm)
Collection of Mr. and Mrs. Richard Wortham III

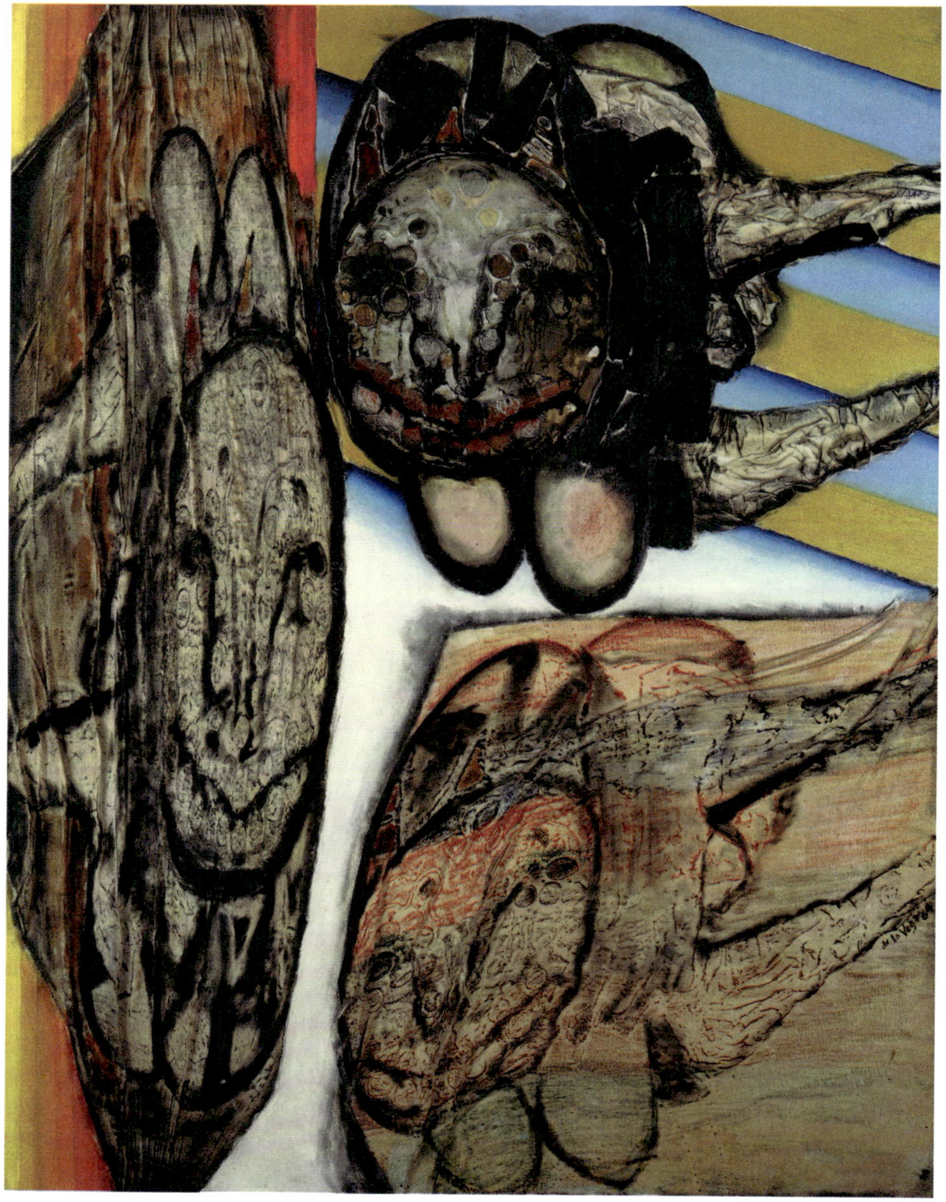

Plate 58
Jorge de la Vega, Argentinean, 1930–1971
Conflicto anamórfico, No. 5: El Agua
[Anamorphic Conflict, No. 5: Water], 2002
Oil and collage on canvas
57 1/2 x 44 7/8 in. (146 x 114 cm)
Private collection

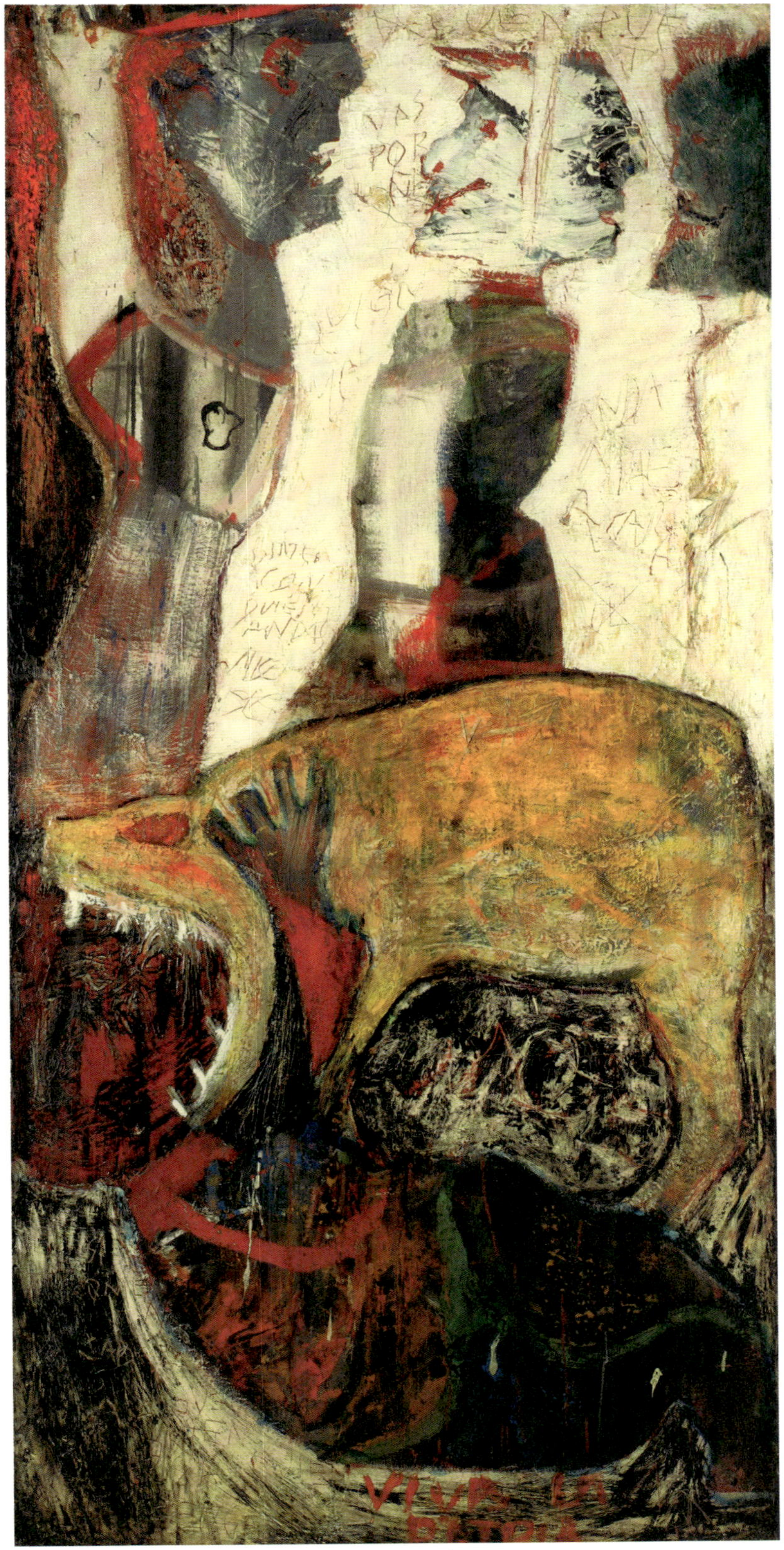

Plate 59
Luis Felipe Noé, Argentinean, born 1933
Alias el chancho [Alias the Pig], 1962
76 3/8 x 37 13/16 in. (194 x 96 cm)
Private collection

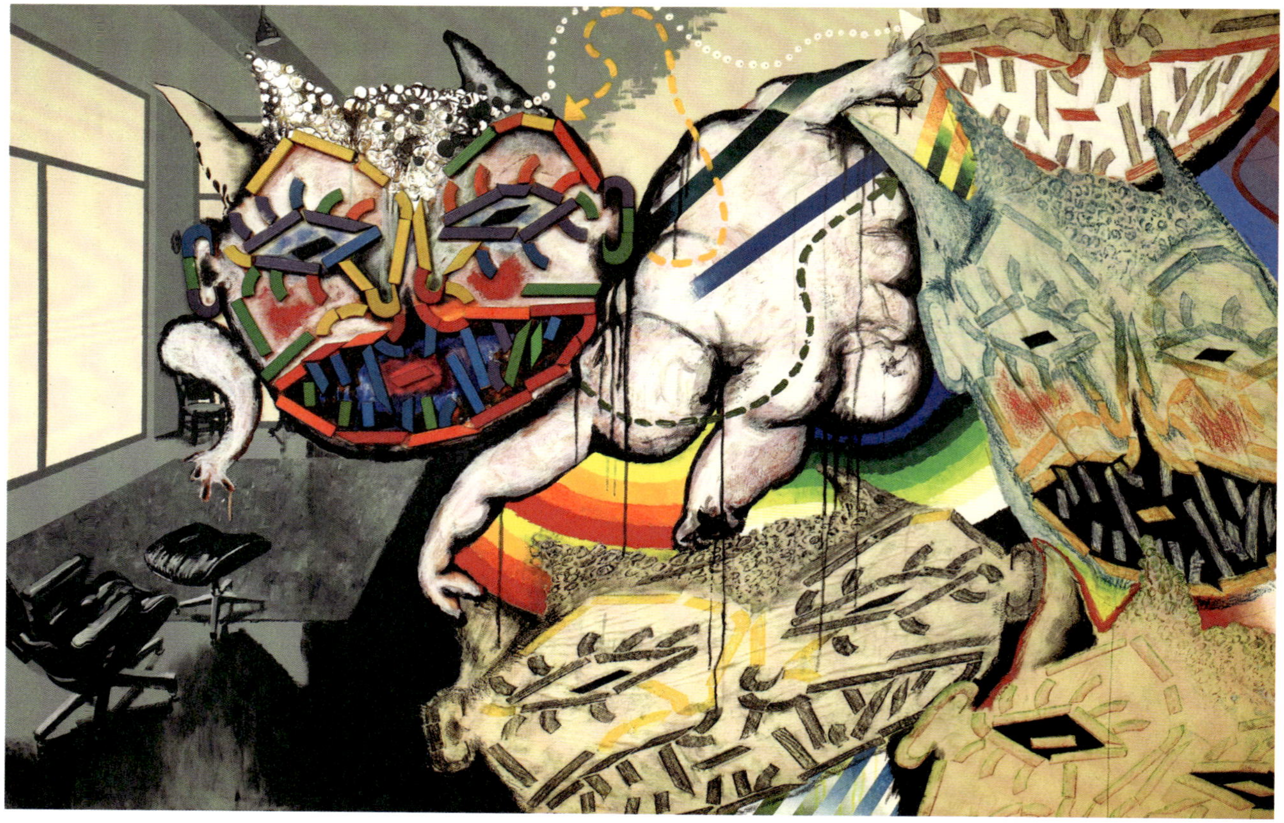

Plate 60
Jorge de la Vega, Argentinean, 1930–1971
And Even in the Office, 1965
Oil and collage on canvas
51 3/16 x 79 1/2 in. (130 x 202 cm)
Private collection

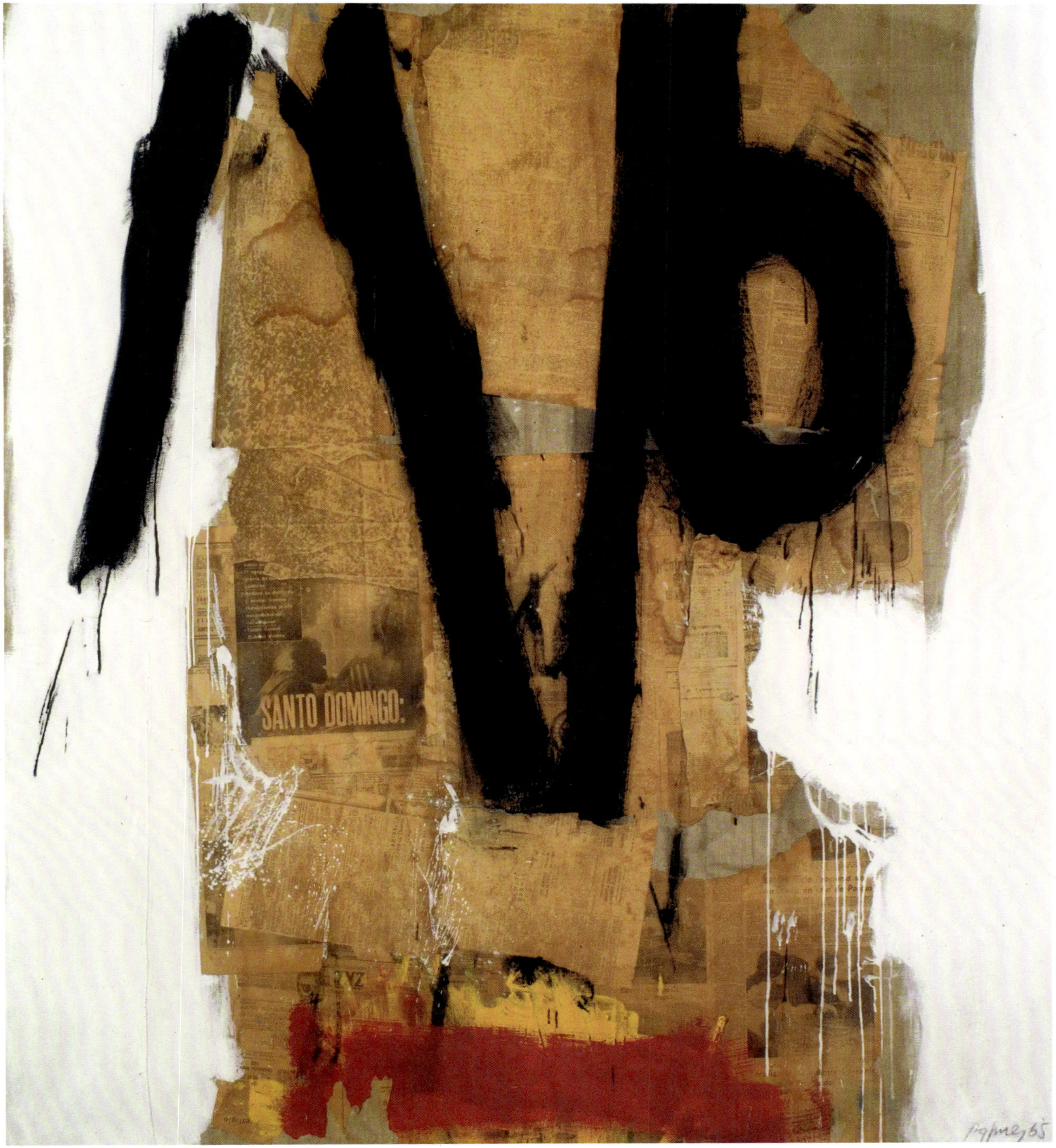

Plate 61
José Balmes, Spanish, active Chile, born 1927
No (from the Santo Domingo series), 1965
Acrylic and collage on canvas
63 x 59 1/16 in. (160 x 150 cm)
Collection of Carlos Cruz Puga, Santiago, Chile

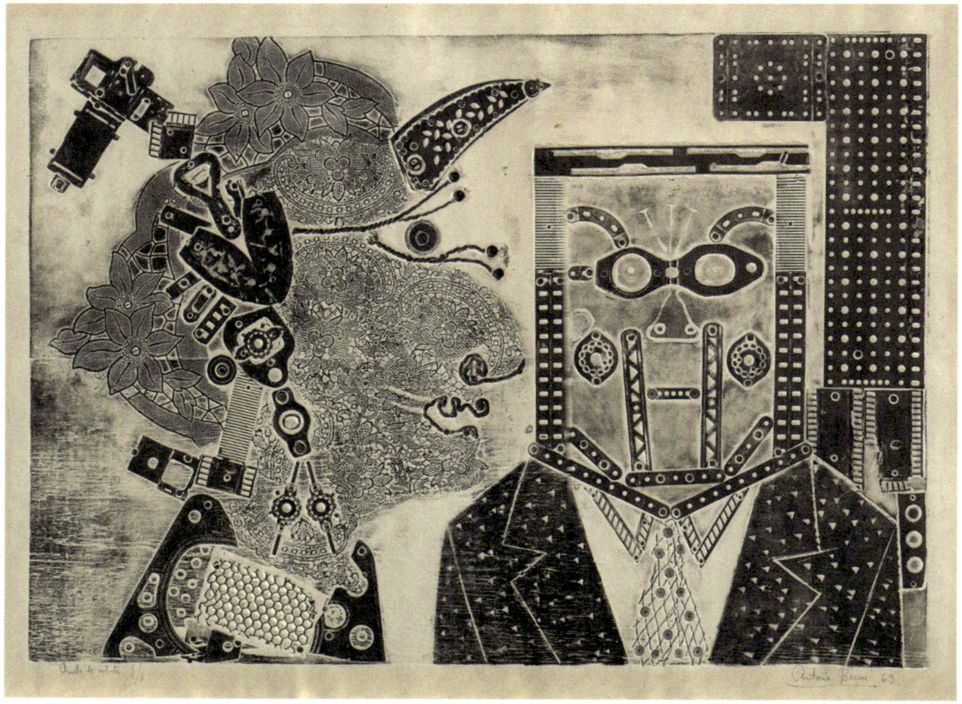

Plate 62
Antonio Berni, Argentinean, 1905-1981
El señor y la señora Pérez [Mr. and Mrs. Pérez], 1963
Xilocollage relief, 8/8
25 1/8 x 37 1/4 in. (63.5 x 95 cm)
Collection of Gail and Louis Adler

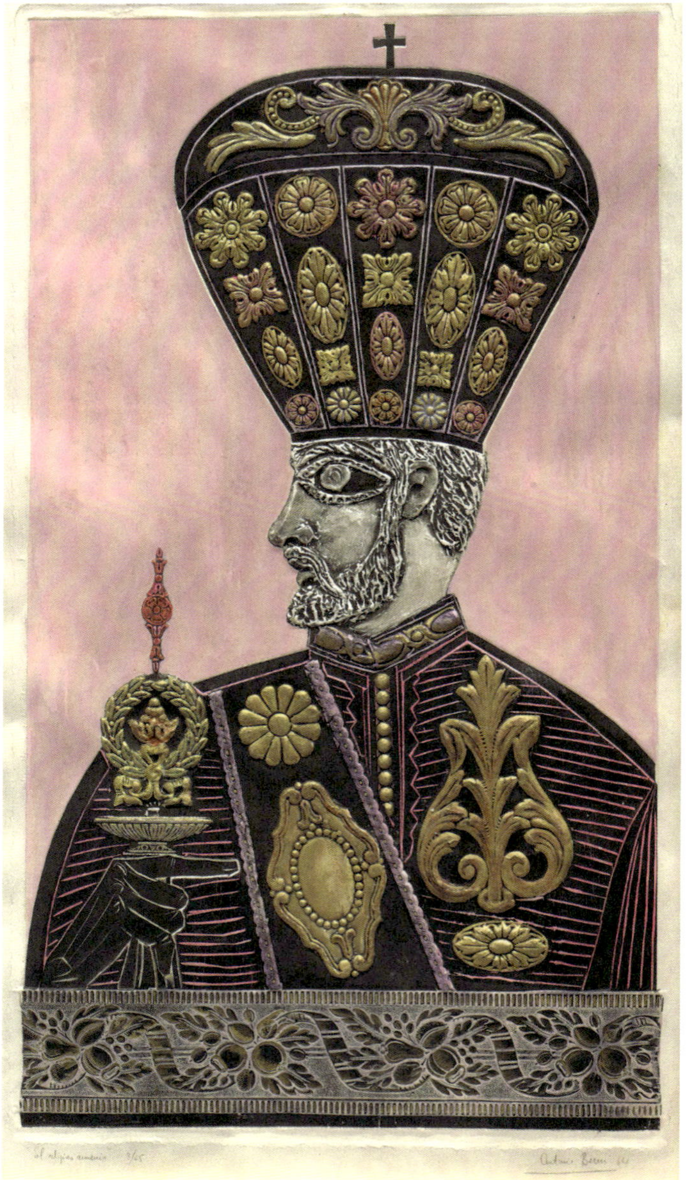

Plate 63
Antonio Berni, Argentinean 1905-1981
El religioso Armenia [The Religious One Armenia], 1964
Xilocollage relief, 3/25
41 x 26 1/2 in. (104 x 67.25 cm)
Collection of Gail and Louis Adler

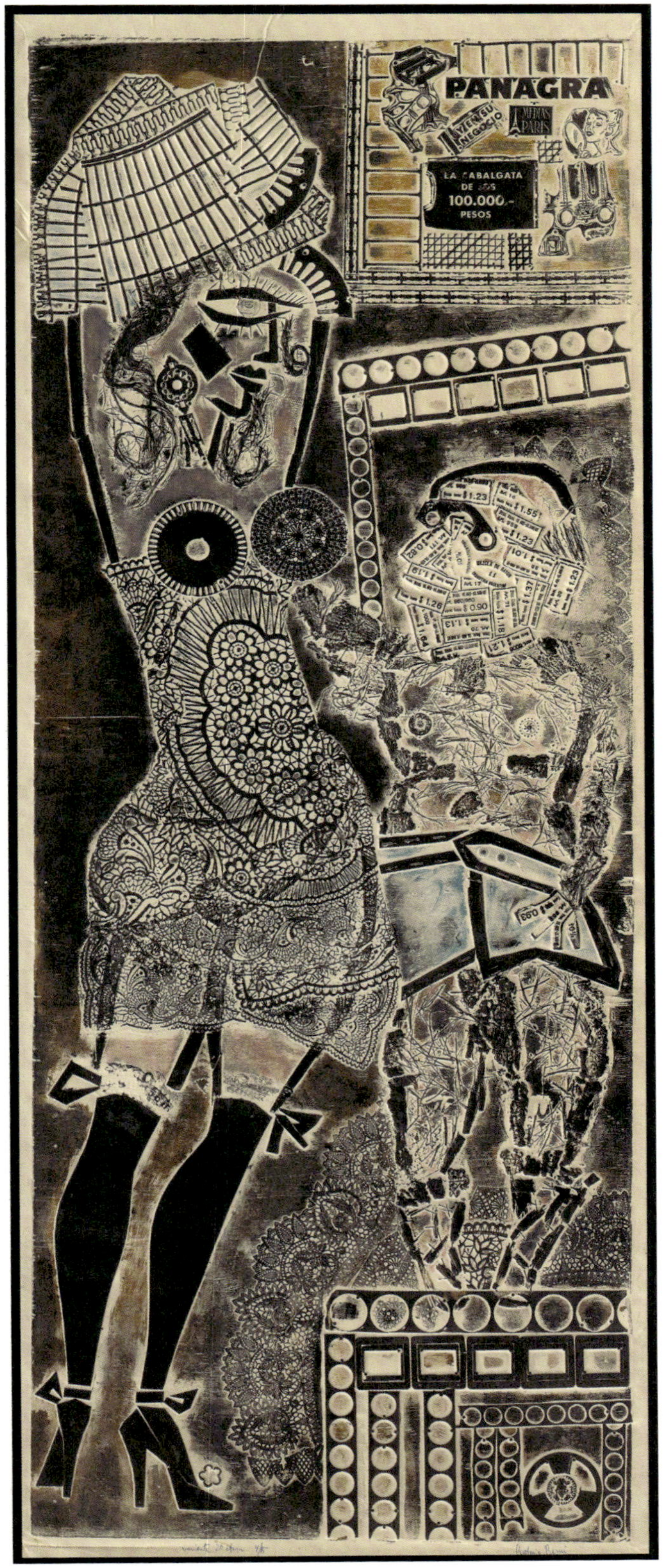

Plate 64
Antonio Berni, Argentinean, 1905-1981
Ramona uy el Viejo [Ramona and the Old Man], 1962
Xilocollage relief, 4/15
60 3/4 x 28 1/2 in. (154 x 72 cm)
Collection of Gail and Louis Adler

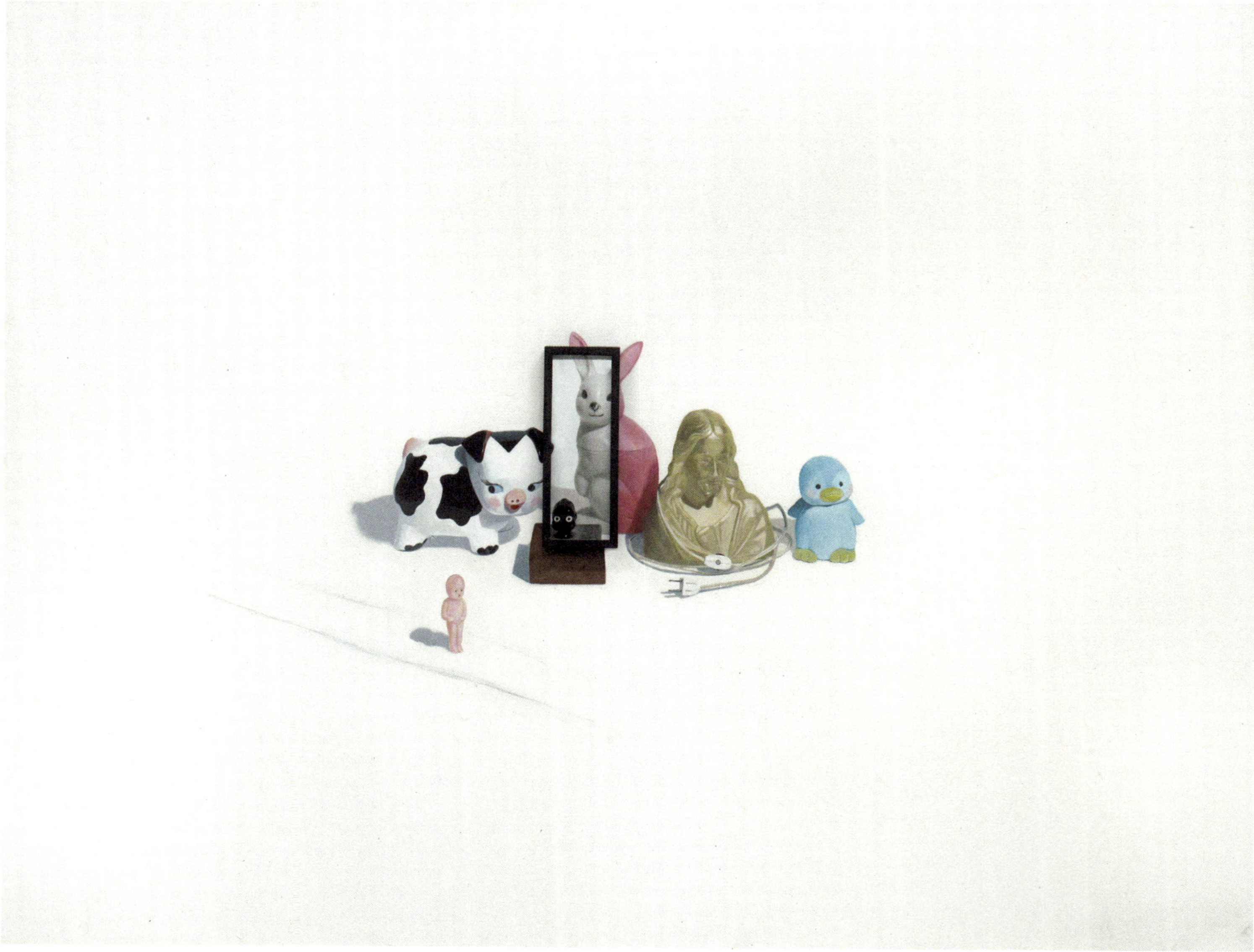

Plate 65
Liliana Porter, Argentinean, born 1941
Them, 1996
Acrylic, black-and-white photograph, and wooden frame on canvas
60 x 80 3/8 x 2 in. (152.4 x 203.2 x 5.1 cm)
Literal Collection

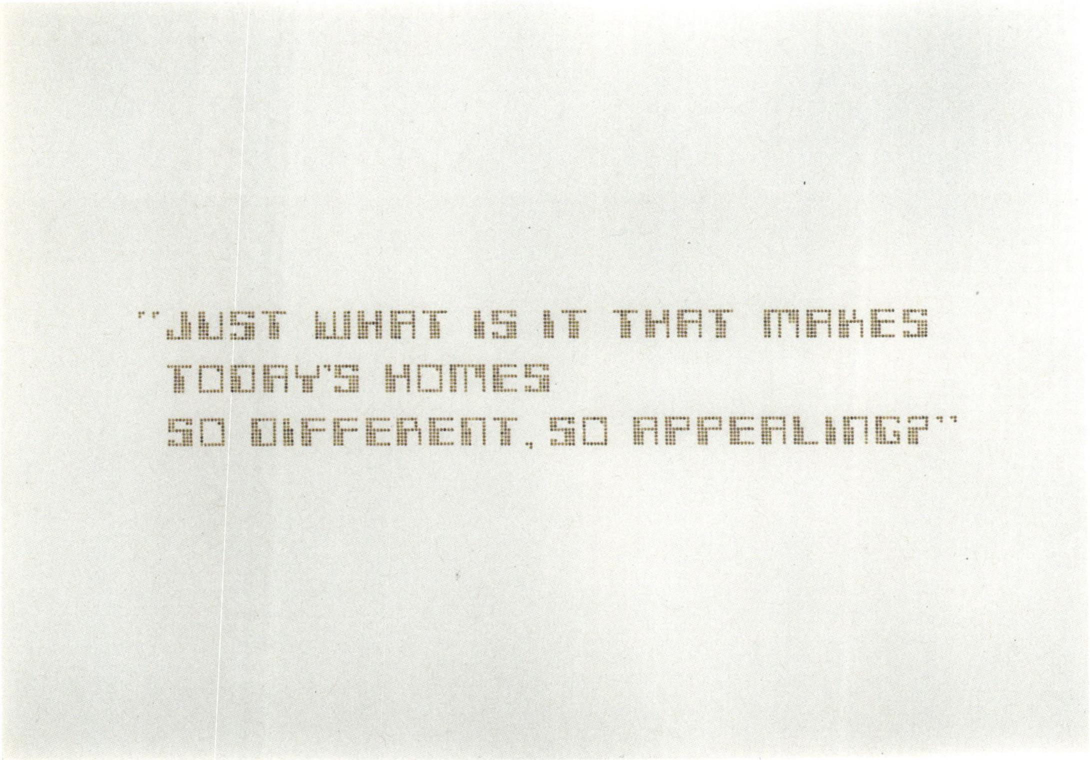

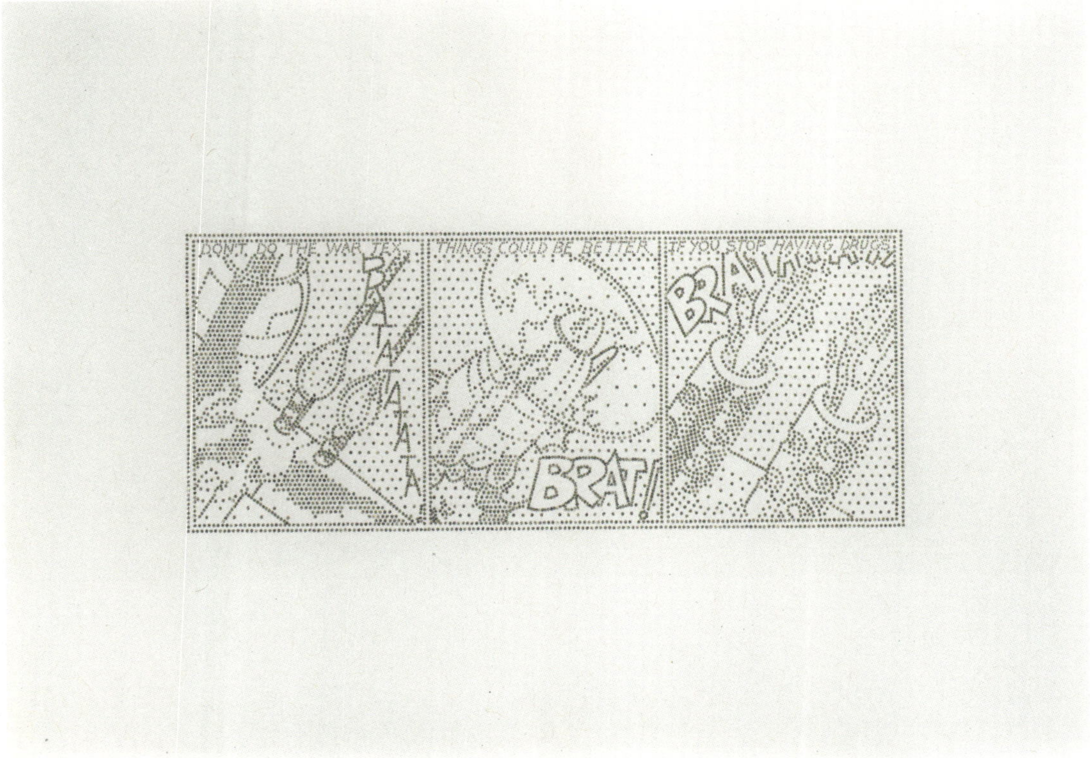

Plate 66
Miguel Ángel Rojas, Colombian, born 1946
Nowadays, 2005
Coca leaves on paper
38 1/2 x 52 3/4 in. (97.8 x 134 cm)
Bratatata, 2005
United States dollar bills on paper
38 1/2 x 52 3/4 in. (97.8 x 134 cm)
Collection of Sofía Adrogué and Sten Gustafson

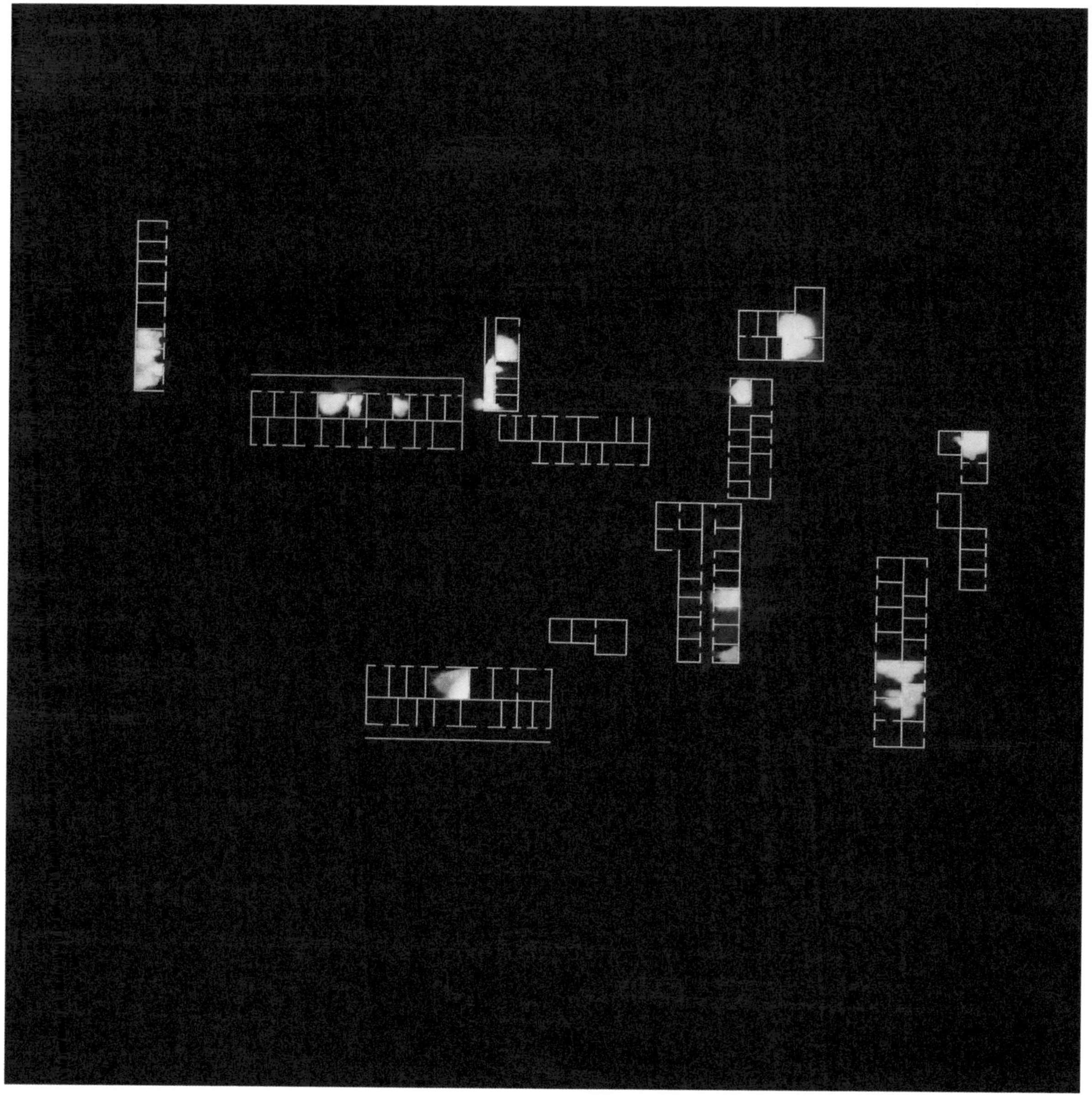

Plate 67
Guillermo Kuitca, Argentinean, born 1961
Sín titulo [Untitled], 1998
Oil on canvas
78 1/2 x 78 1/2 in. (199.4 x 199.4 cm)
Collection of Leslie and Brad Bucher

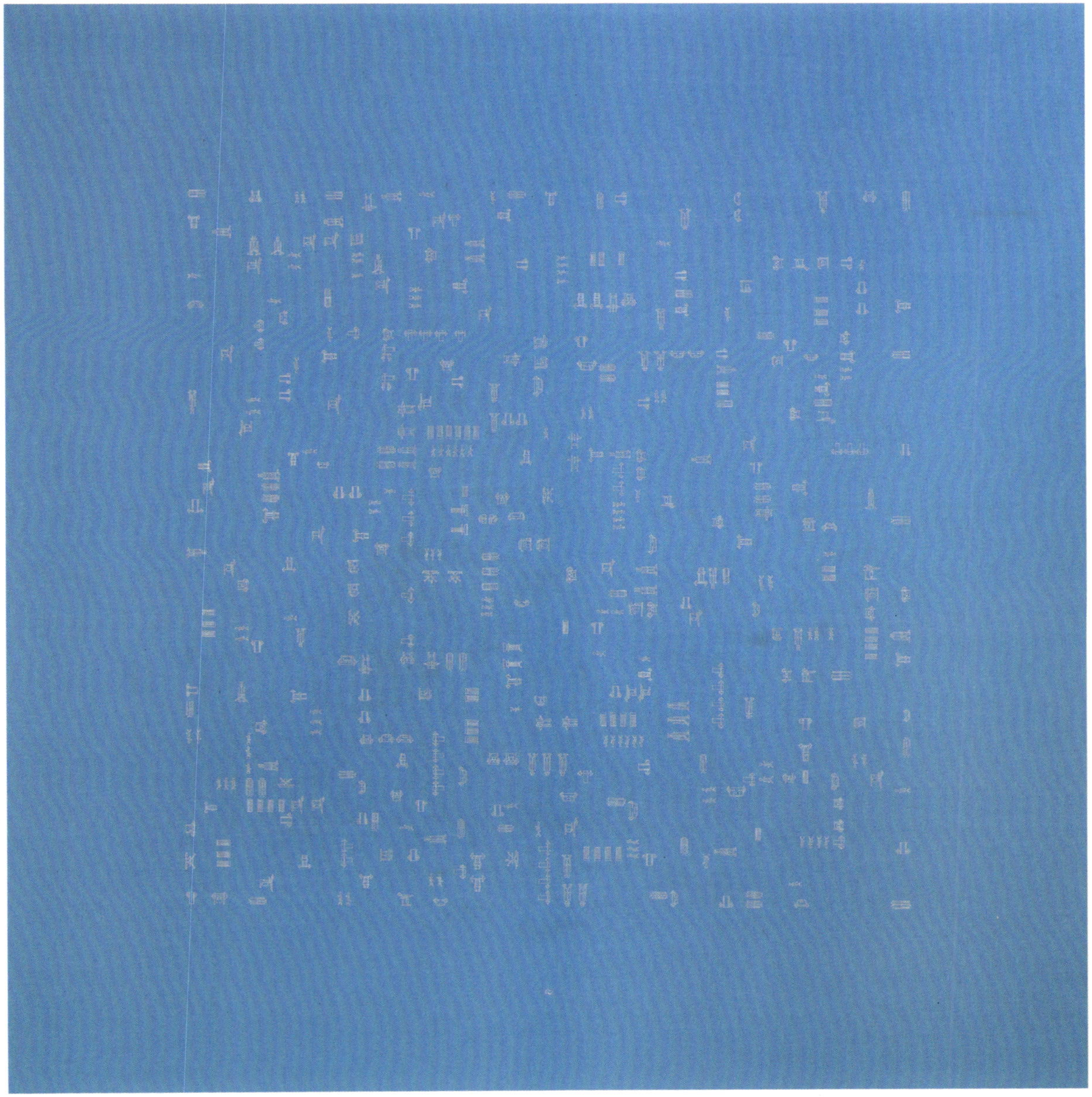

Plate 68
Guillermo Kuitca, Argentinean, born 1961
Neufert Suite: (Workout Equipment), 1998-99
Oil and colored pencil on linen
78 3/4 x 78 3/4 in. (200 x 200 cm)
Private collection

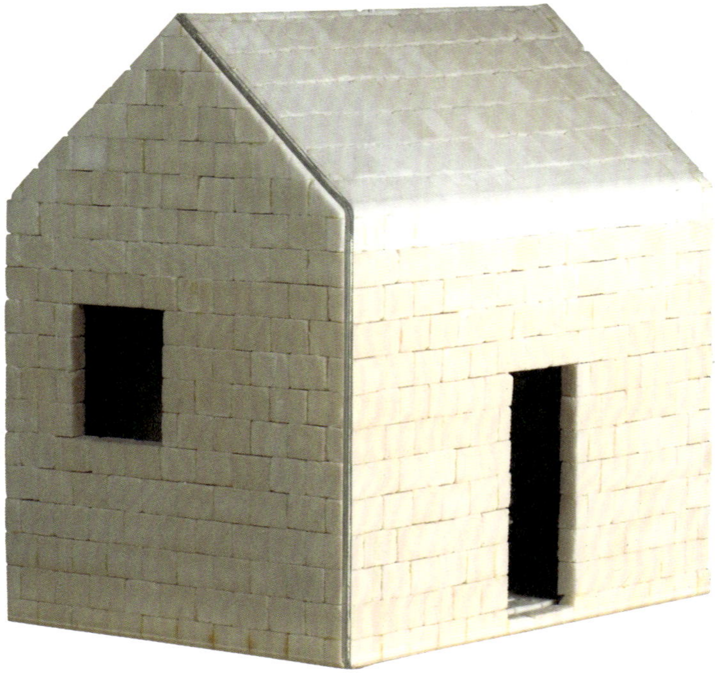

Plate 69
Luis F. Benedit, Argentinean, born 1937
Rancho de azúcar [Sugar Barn], 1990
Plexiglas, wood, and sugar
18 1/2 x 17 1/8 x 13 3/8 in. (47 x 43.5 x 34 cm)
Private collection

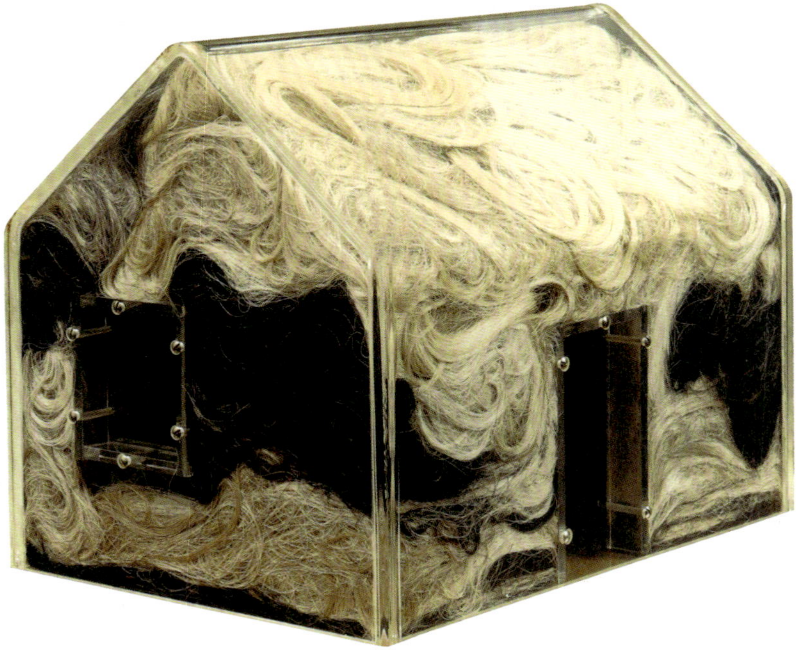

Plate 70
Luis F. Benedit, Argentinean, born 1937
Rancho de crín [Horsehair Barn], 1991
Plexiglas, wood, and horsehair
18 1/2 x 17 5/16 x 13 3/8 in. (47 x 44 x 34 cm)
Private collection

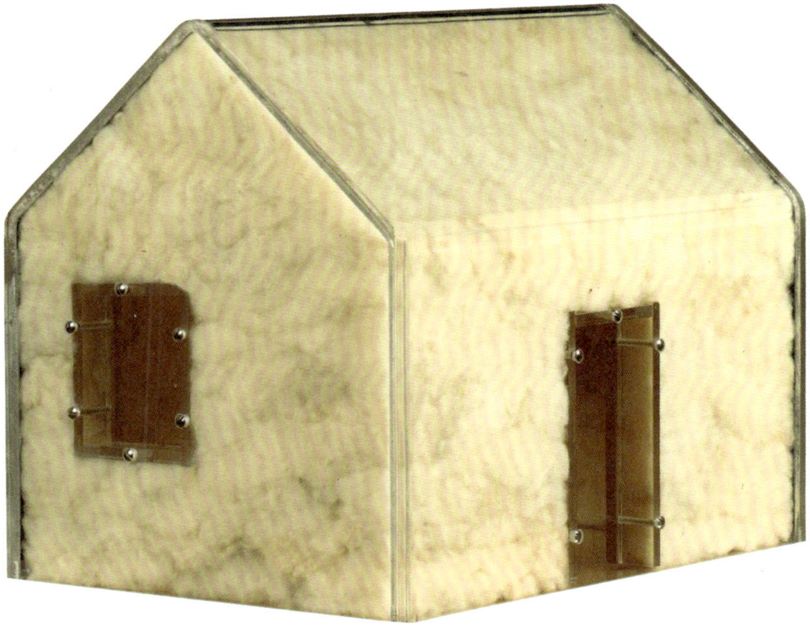

Plate 71
Luis F. Benedit, Argentinean, born 1937
Rancho de lana [Wool Barn], 1991
Plexiglass, wood, and wool
18 1/2 x 17 5/16 x 13 3/8 in. (47 x 44 x 34 cm)
Private collection

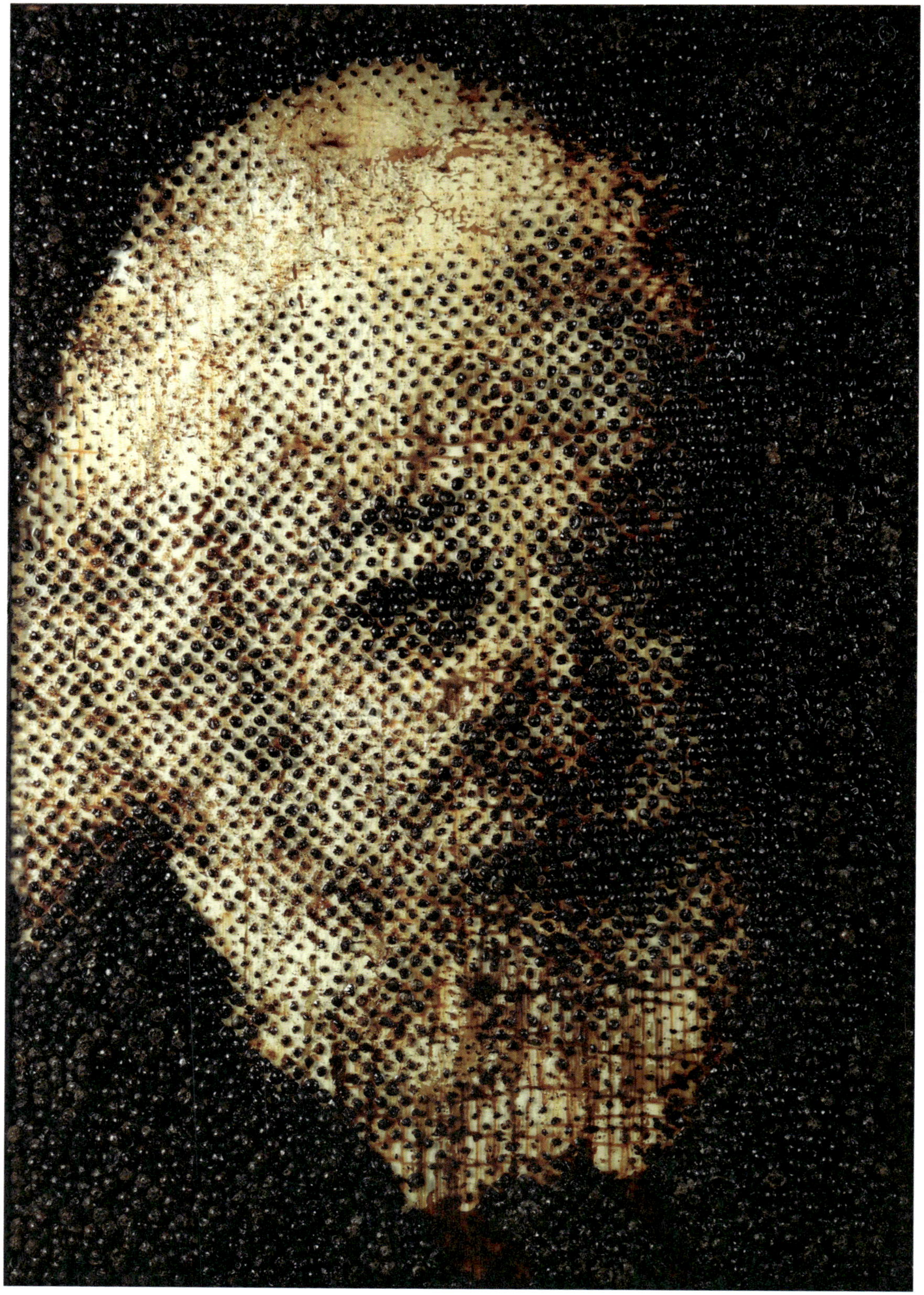

Plate 72
Mondongo (Agustina Picasso, b. 1977;
Juliana Laffitte, b. 1974; and
Manuel Mendanha, b. 1976), Argentinean
Jorge Glusberg, 2001
4,233 "*Media Hora*" candies over canvas
73 5/8 x 53 15/16 in. (187 x 137 cm)
Collection of Gabriel Werthein

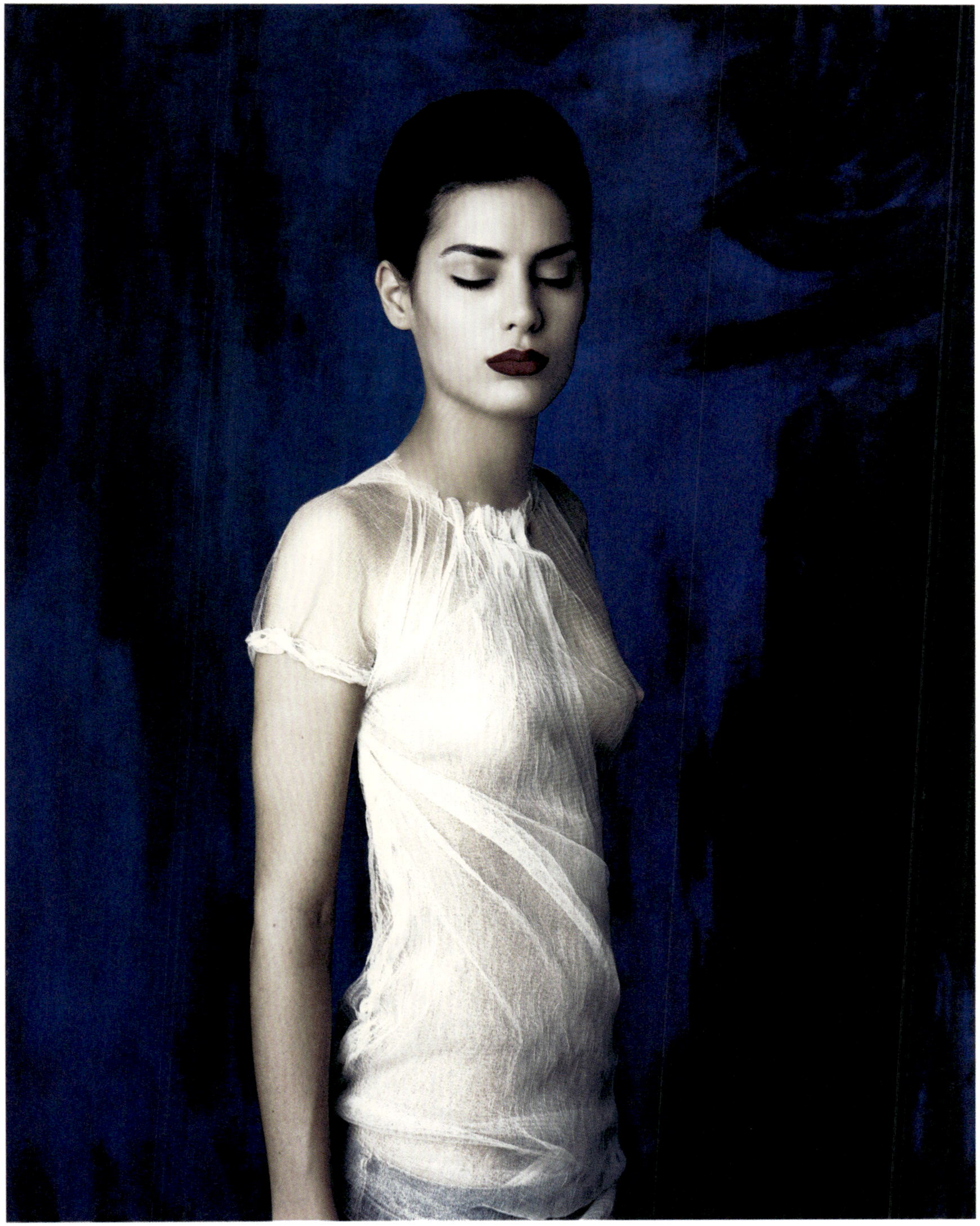

Plate 73
res, Argentinean, born 1957
Chica azul (from the series Conatus), 2006
Chromogenic print
62 5/8 x 50 in. (159 x 127 cm)
Collection of Gail and Louis Adler

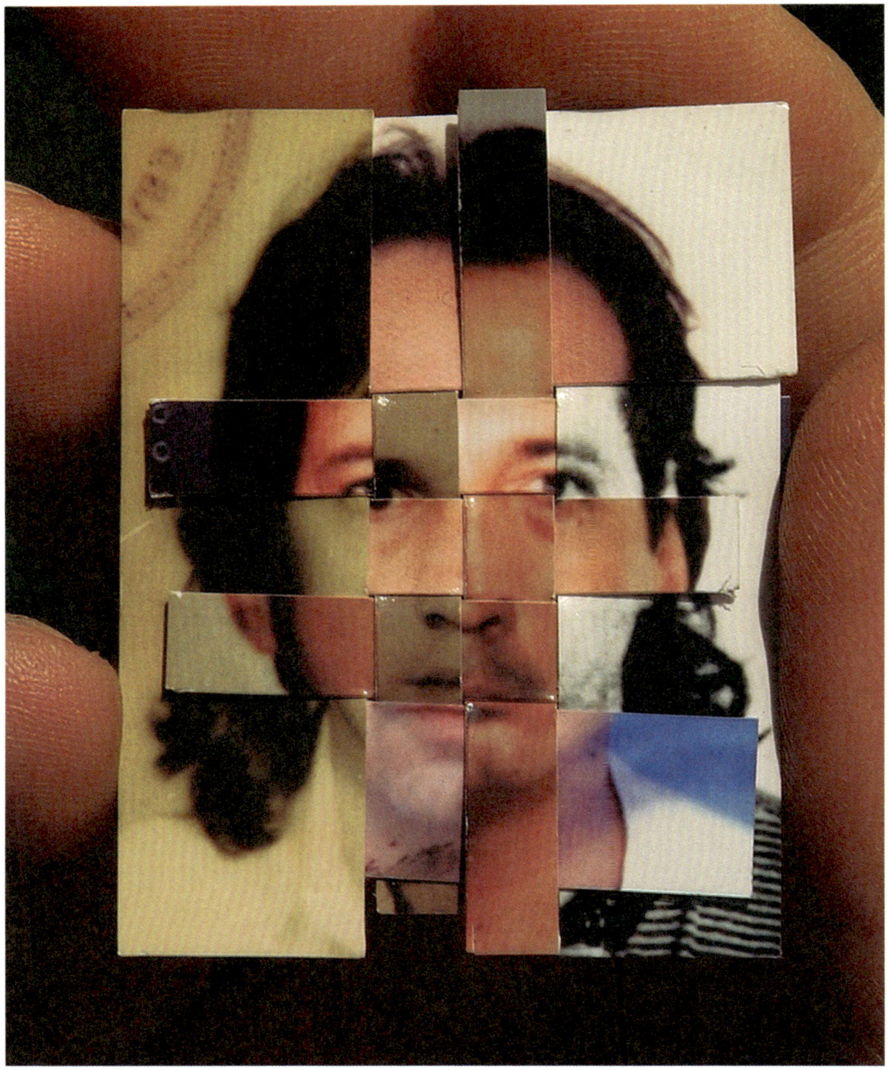

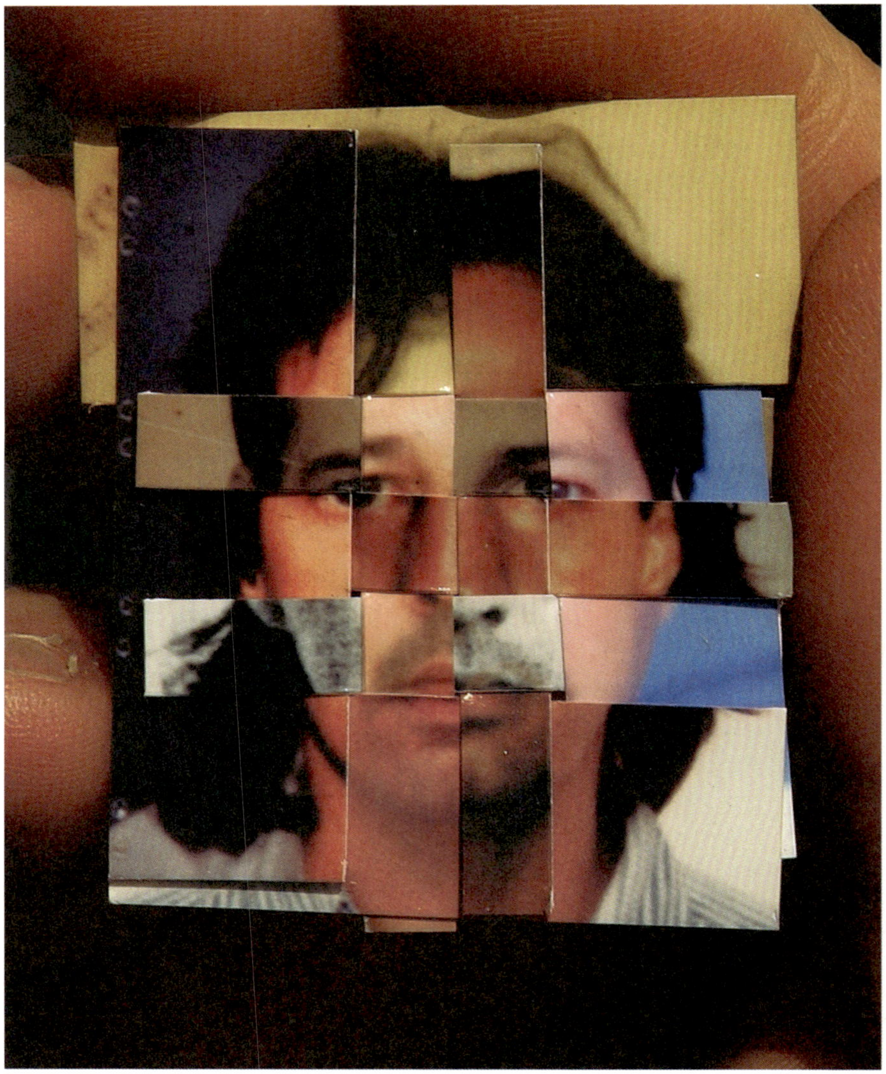

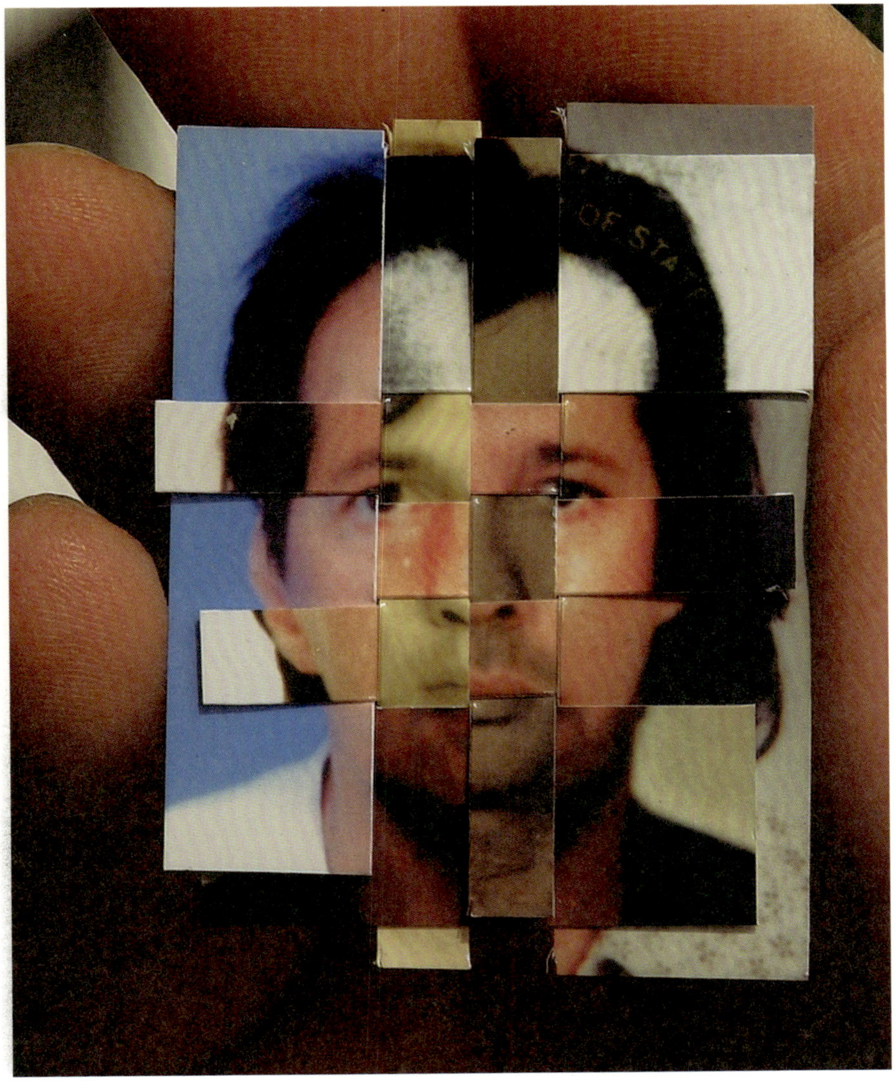

Plate 74
Oscar Muñoz, Colombian, born 1951
El juego de las probabilidades [The Game of Probabilities]
Ed: AP 1
Chromogenic print, printed 2008
Image (each): 19 1/2 x 15 1/2 in. (49.5 x 39.4 cm)
Collection of Renée Wallace

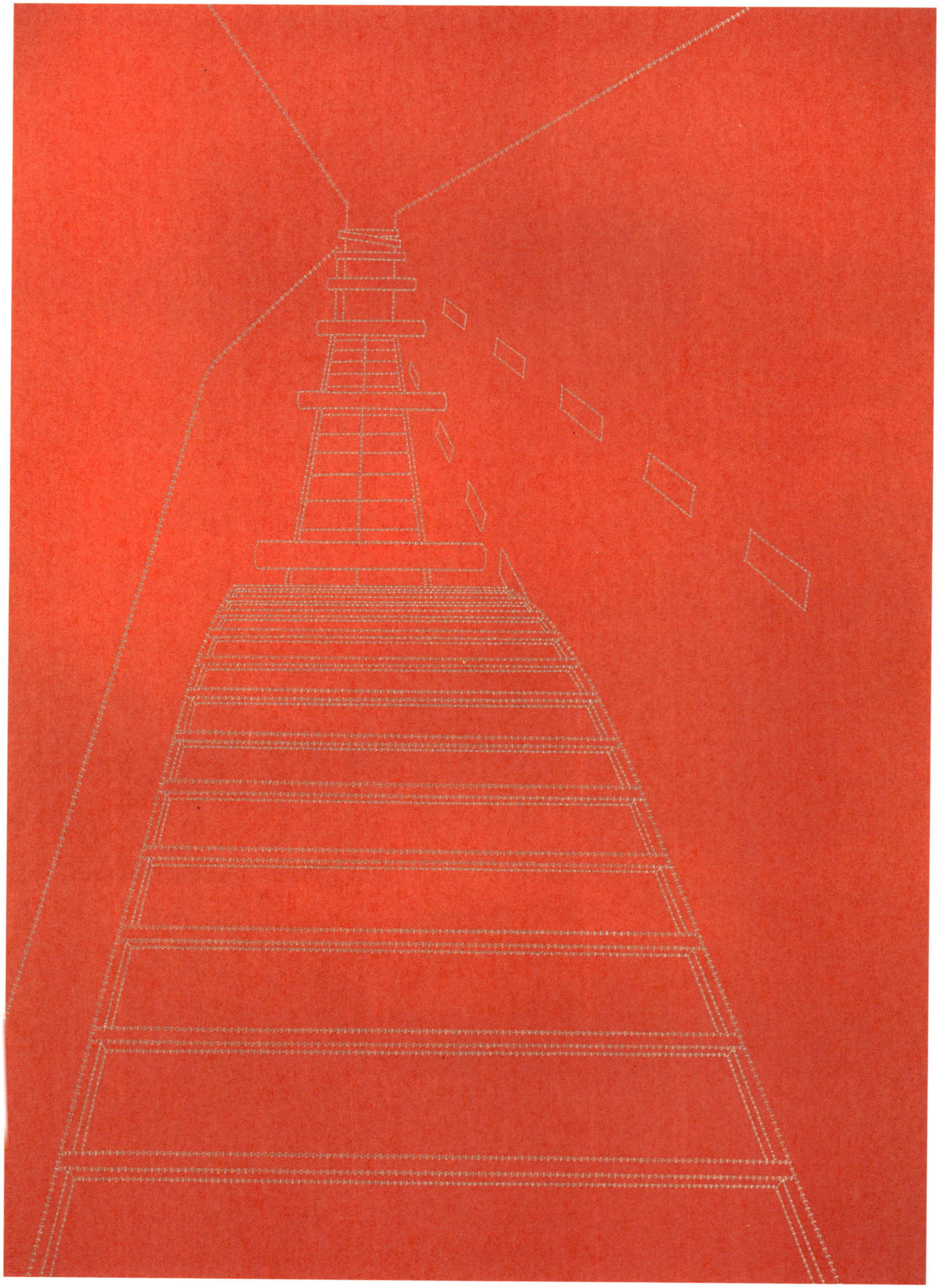

Plate 75
Paulo Climachauska, Brazilian, born 1962
MAMSP (Museum of Modern Art, São Paulo), 2006
India ink and acrylic on canvas
73 5/8 x 53 15/16 in. (187 x 137 cm)
Collection of Carolina and Sergio G. Weitzman

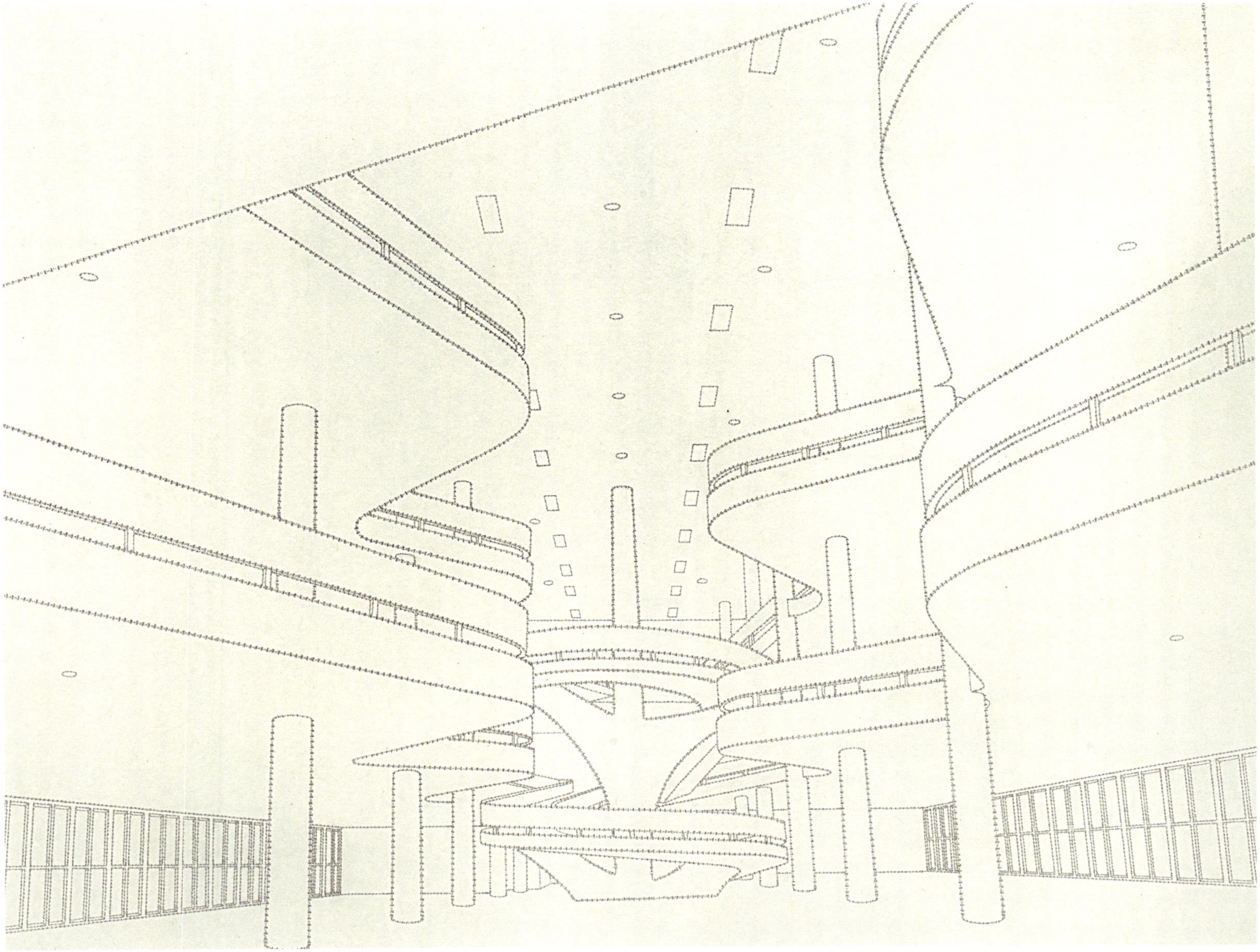

Plate 76
Paulo Climachauska, Brazilian, born 1962
Biennale [Biennial], 2004
Ink on MDF
72 13/16 x 53 15/16 in. (185 x 137 cm)
Collection of Gail and Louis Adler

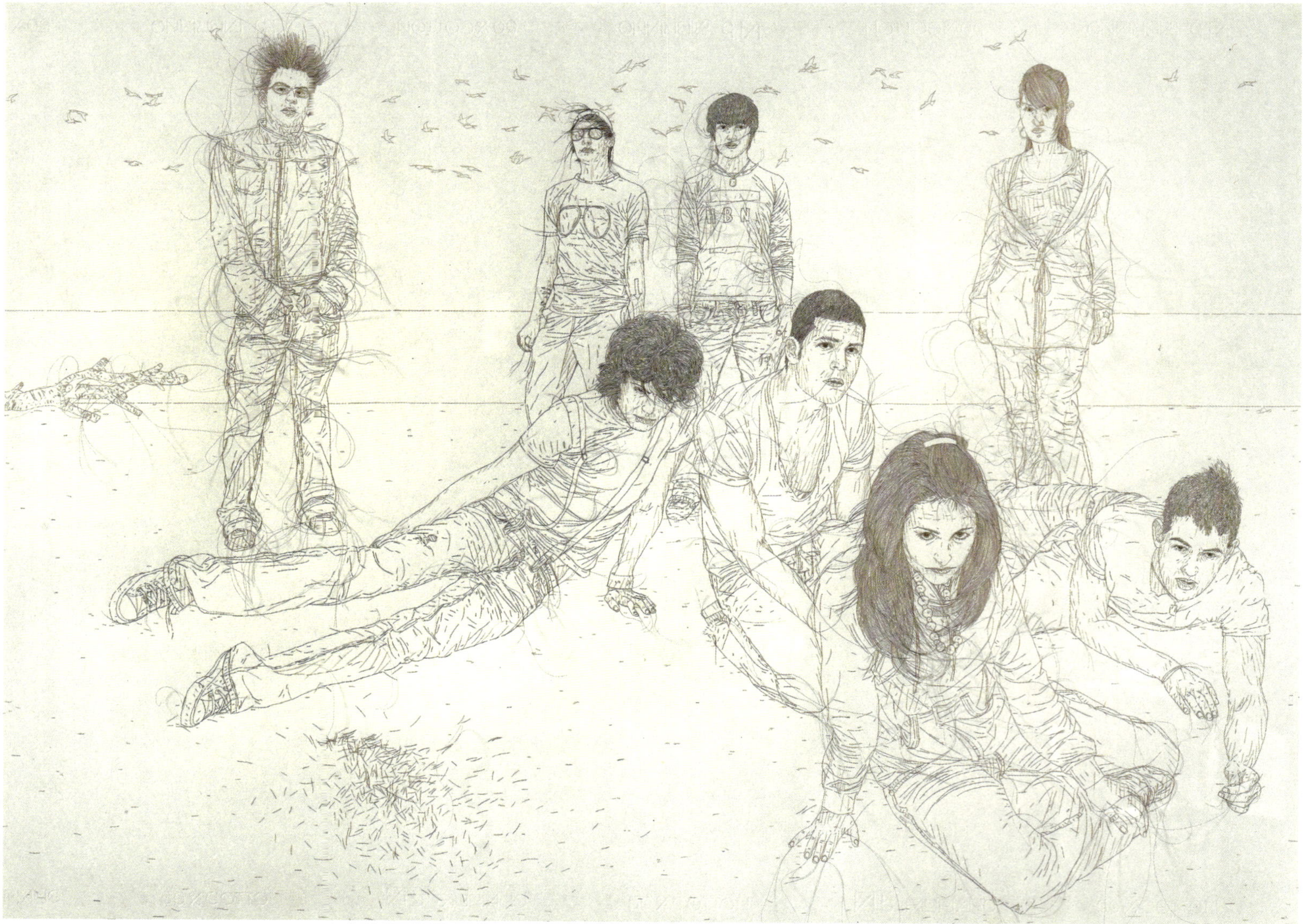

Plate 77
Gabriel de la Mora, Mexican, born 1968
E.P.R.B.A.X.L.J., 2007
Human hair on paper
27 1/2 x 39 1/2 in. (69.9 x 100.3 cm)
Collection of Leslie and Brad Bucher

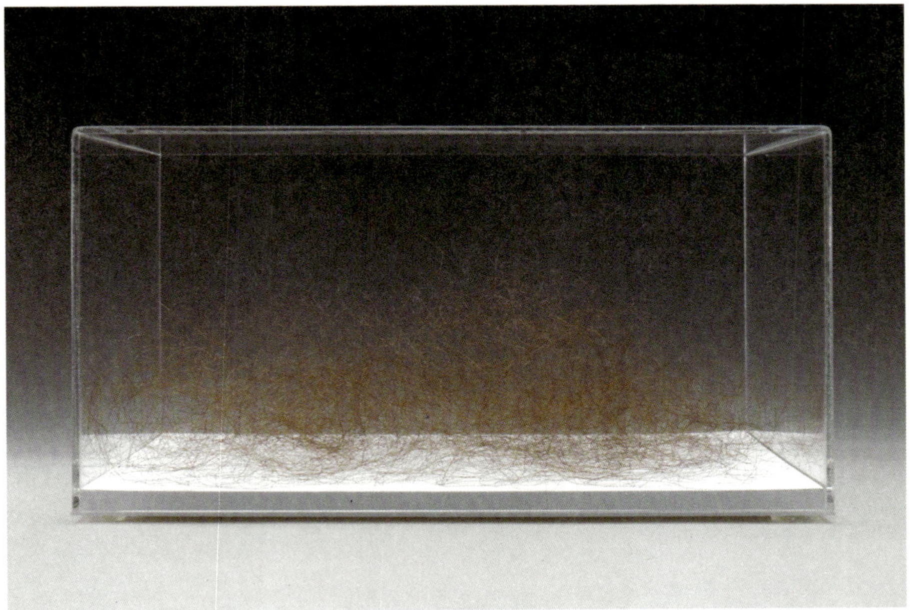

Plate 78
Gabriel de la Mora, Mexican, born 1968
M.E.A.I., 2008
Tied human hair on paper in acrylic box
6 1/4 x 11 x 11 in. (15.9 x 27.9 x 27.9 cm)
Collection of María Inés Sicardi, promised gift to
the Museum of Fine Arts, Houston

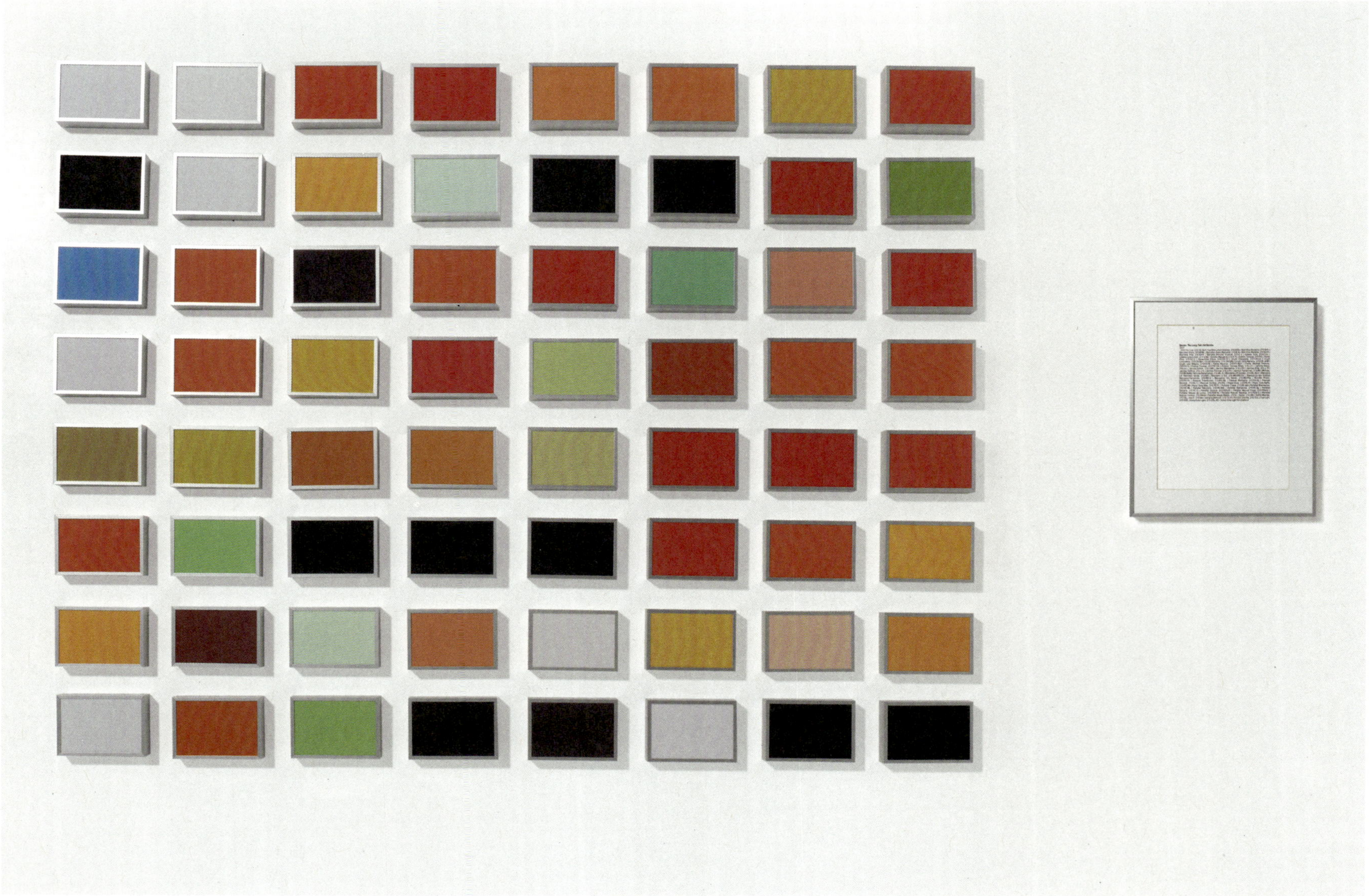

Plate 79
Emilio Chapela Pérez, Mexican, born 1978
The Long Tail (64 drinks), 2007
Chromogenic prints
41 x 53 in. (104.1 x 134.6 cm)
Collection of Rebecca Elizabeth Leach

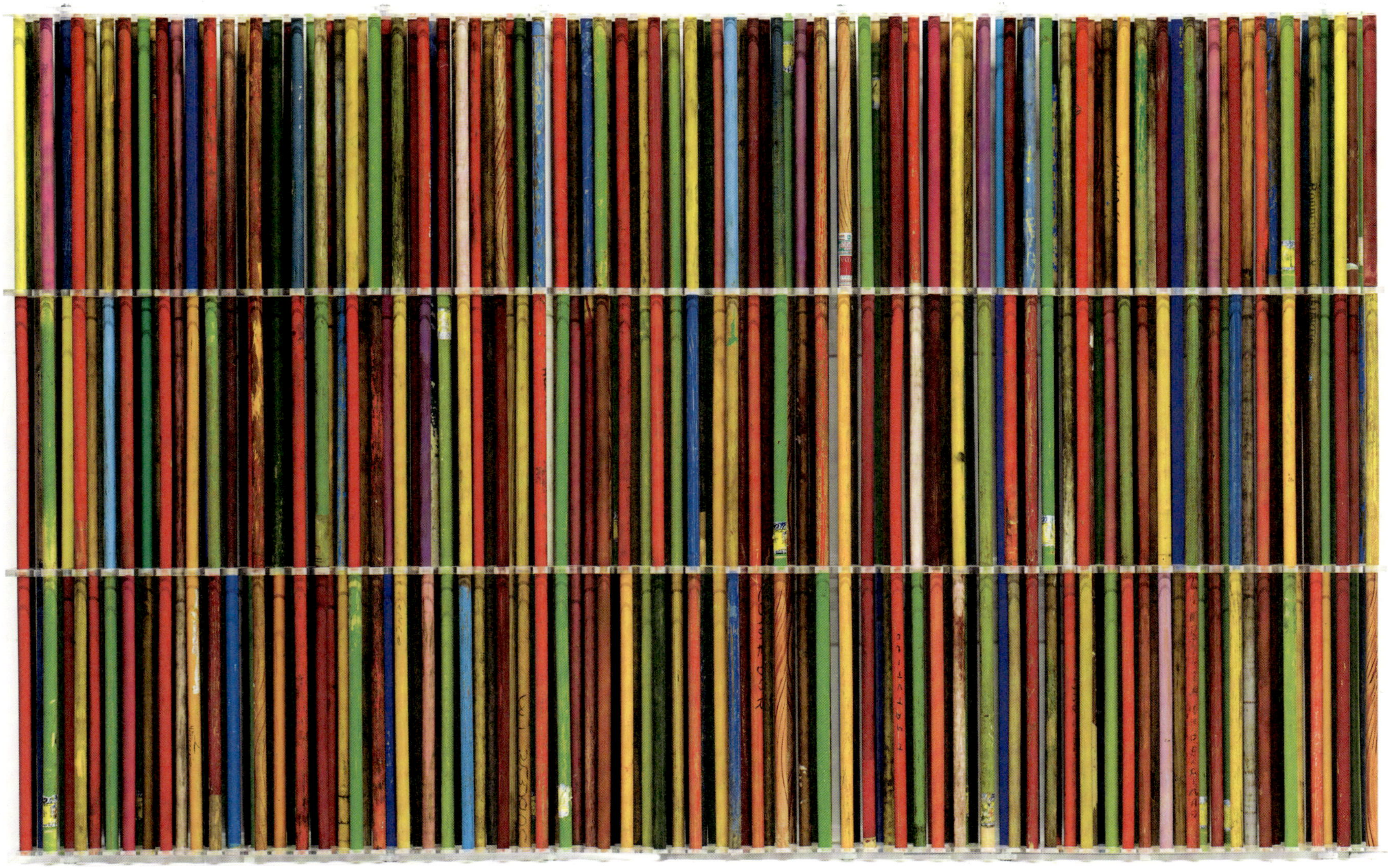

Plate 80
Thomas Glassford, American,
living in Mexico, born 1963
She Didn't Realize I was Watching/Half-Stick Medley, 2010
Broomsticks, metal, and Plexiglas
60 5/8 x 97 5/8 x 5 7/8 in. (154 x 248 x 15 cm)
Collection of David and Allison Ayers

Plate 81
Gerd Leufert, Venezuelan, born Prussia, 1914–1998
Pampatar, 1968
Oil on canvas
61 7/16 x 31 1/2 in. (156 x 80 cm)
Private collection

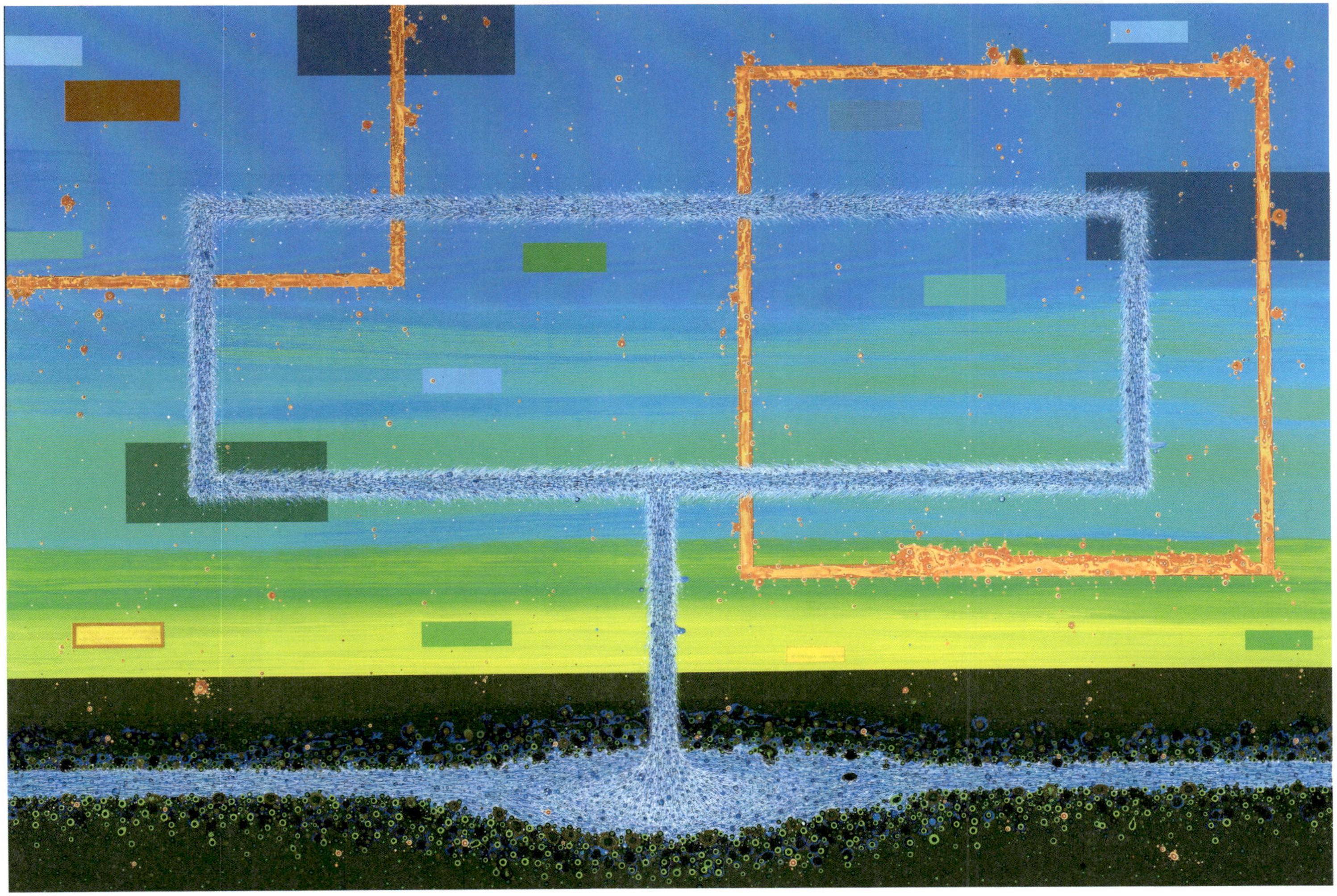

Plate 82
Marcelo Pombo, Argentinean, born 1959
Atardecer junto al arroyo [Sunset by the Stream], 2001
Enamel on wood panel
39 5/16 x 59 x 1 7/8 in. (99.9 x 149.9 x 4.8 cm)
Collection of Gail and Louis Adler

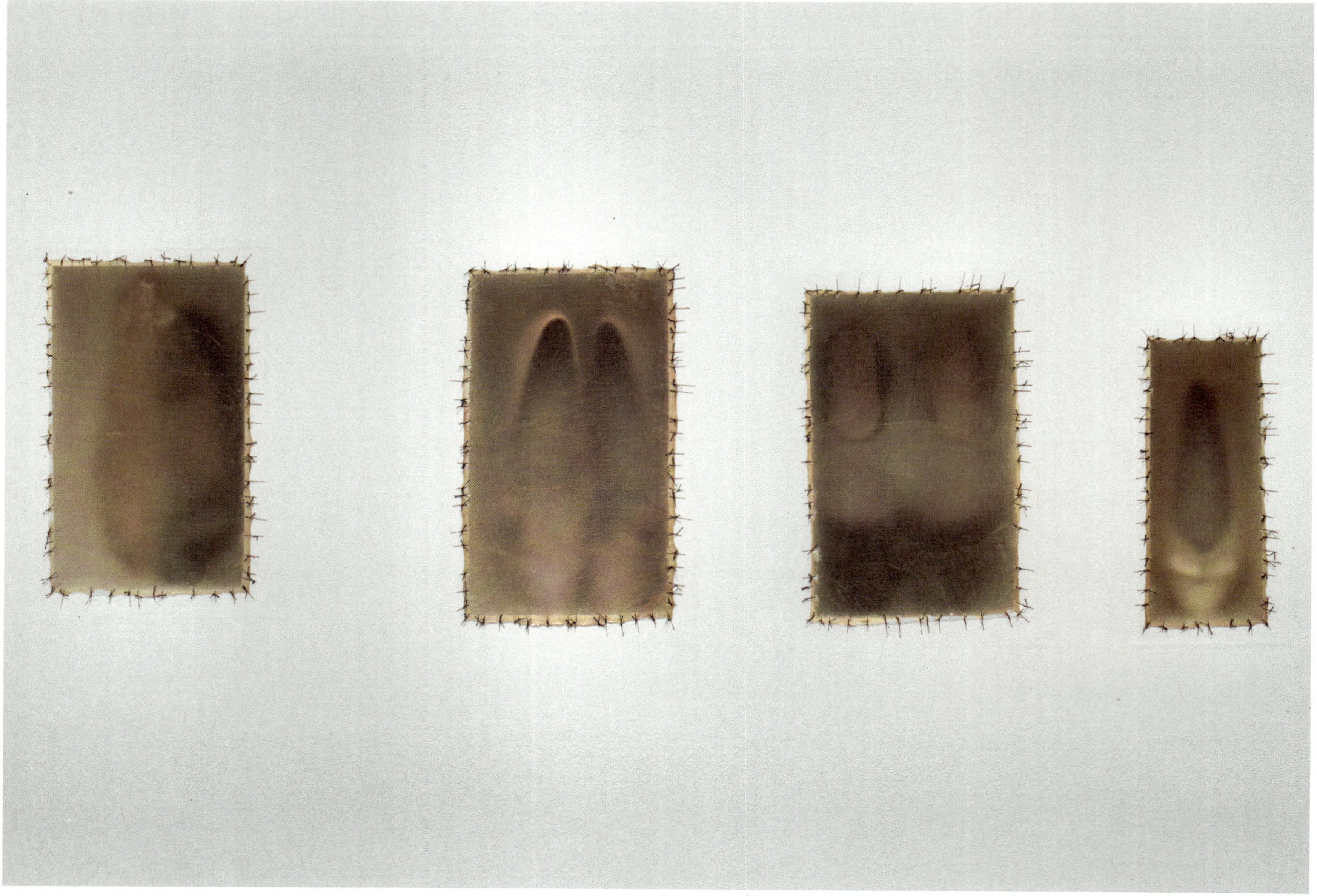

Plate 83
Doris Salcedo, Colombian, born 1958
Atrabiliarios [Defiant], 1992-93
Drywall, shoes, cow bladder, and surgical thread
35 3/4 x 48 x 5 in. (90.8 x 121.9 x 12.7 cm)
Collection of Diane and Bruce Halle

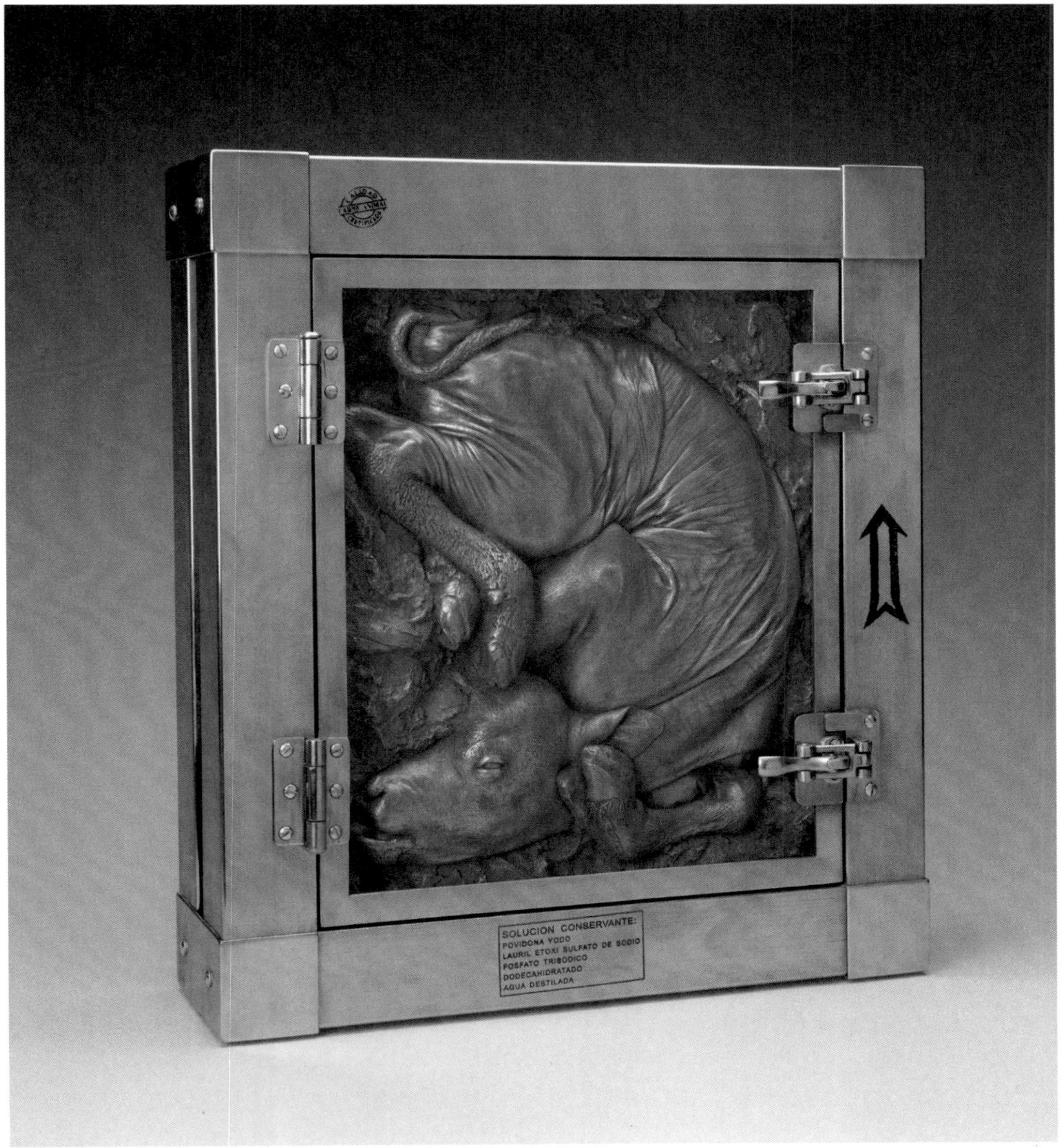

Plate 84
Nicola Costantino, Argentinean, born 1964
Box-Number 6, 2005
Chromed iron, aluminum and resin
Edition of six , 21 x 19 x 5 3/4 in. (53 x 48.3 x 14.6 cm)
Collection of Gail and Louis Adler

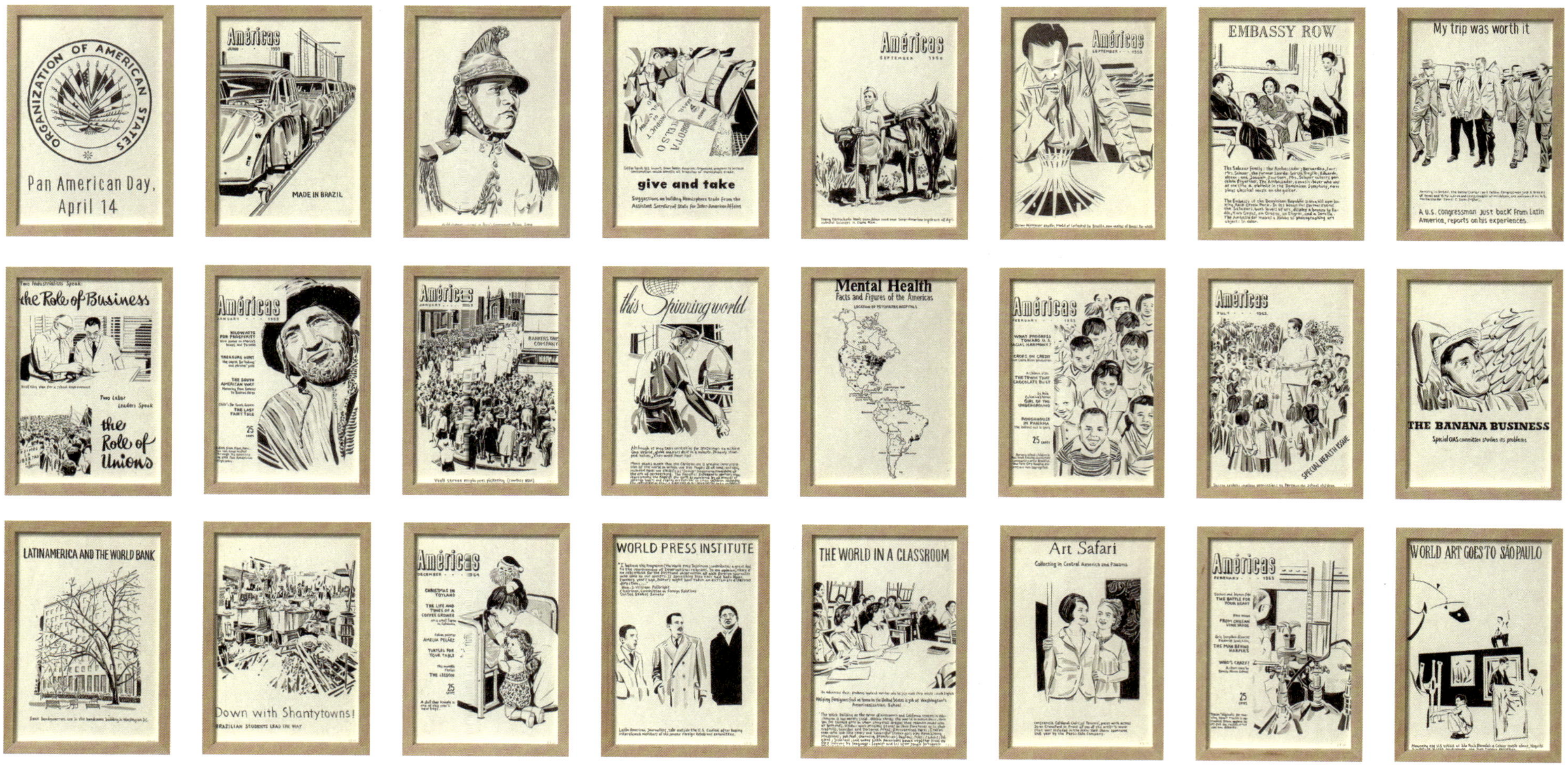

ORGANIZATION OF AMERICAN STATES
Pan American Day, April 14
Américas
MADE IN BRAZIL
give and take
Américas
Américas
EMBASSY ROW
My trip was worth it
A U.S. congressman just back from Latin America, reports on his experiences.
the Role of Business
the Role of Unions
Américas
Américas
this Spinning world
Mental Health
Facts and Figures of the Americas
Américas
Américas
SPECIAL HEALTH ISSUE
THE BANANA BUSINESS
Special OAS committee studies its problems
LATIN AMERICA AND THE WORLD BANK
Down with Shantytowns!
BRAZILIAN STUDENTS LEAD THE WAY
Américas
WORLD PRESS INSTITUTE
THE WORLD IN A CLASSROOM
Art Safari
Américas
WORLD ART GOES TO SÃO PAULO

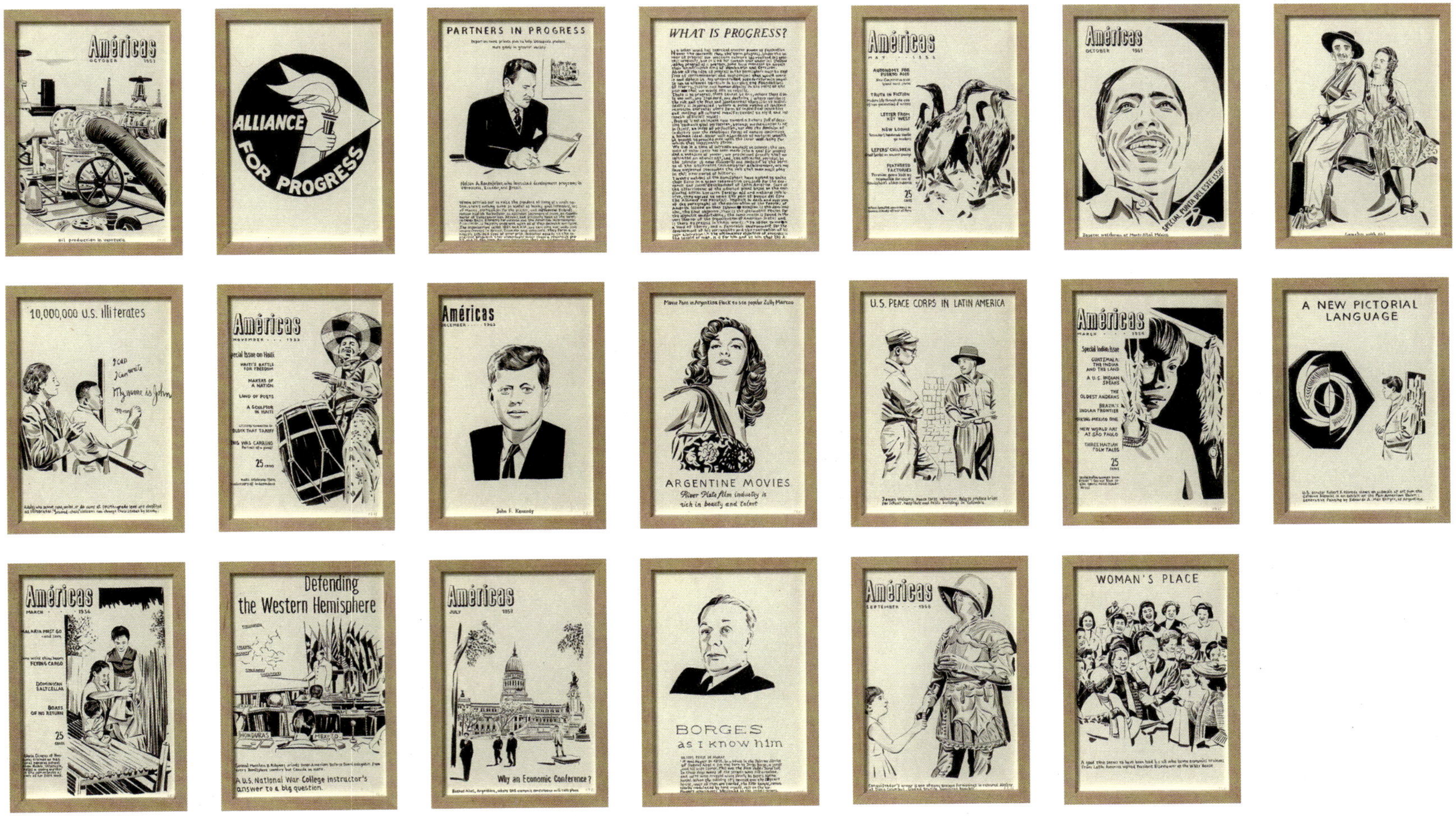

Plate 85
Fernando Bryce, Peruvian, born 1965
Américas series, 2005
Ink on paper
Each 11 13/16 x 10 1/16 in. (30 x 25.5 cm)
Collection of María Cristina and Pablo Henning

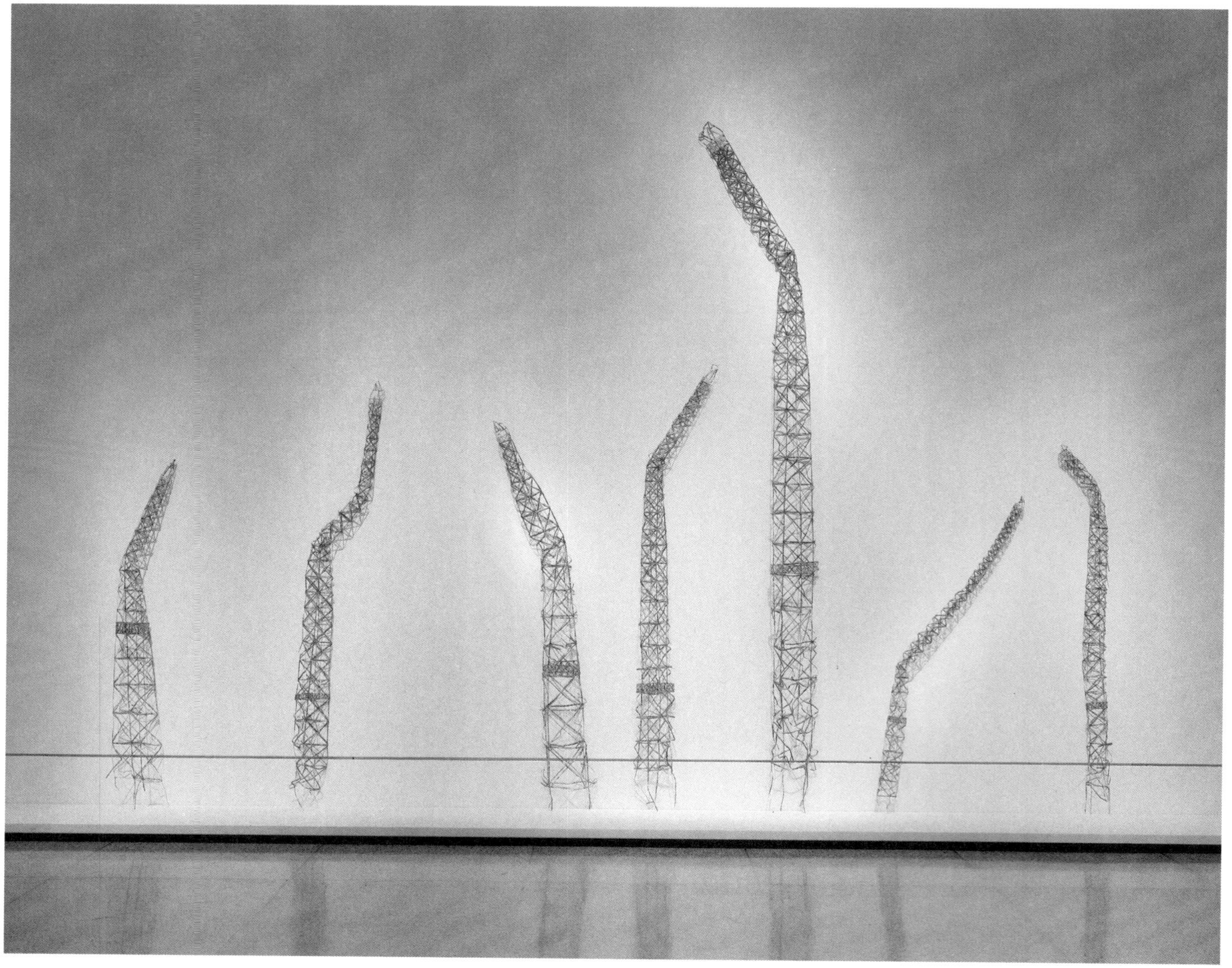

Plate 86
Máximo González, Argentinean,
lives in Mexico, born 1971
Oil Drills, 2006 Cut paper (Mexican pesos,
currency out of circulation)
Dimensions variable
Collection of Sara and Bill Morgan
Collection of Roy and Mary Cullen
Collection of Ron Garcia

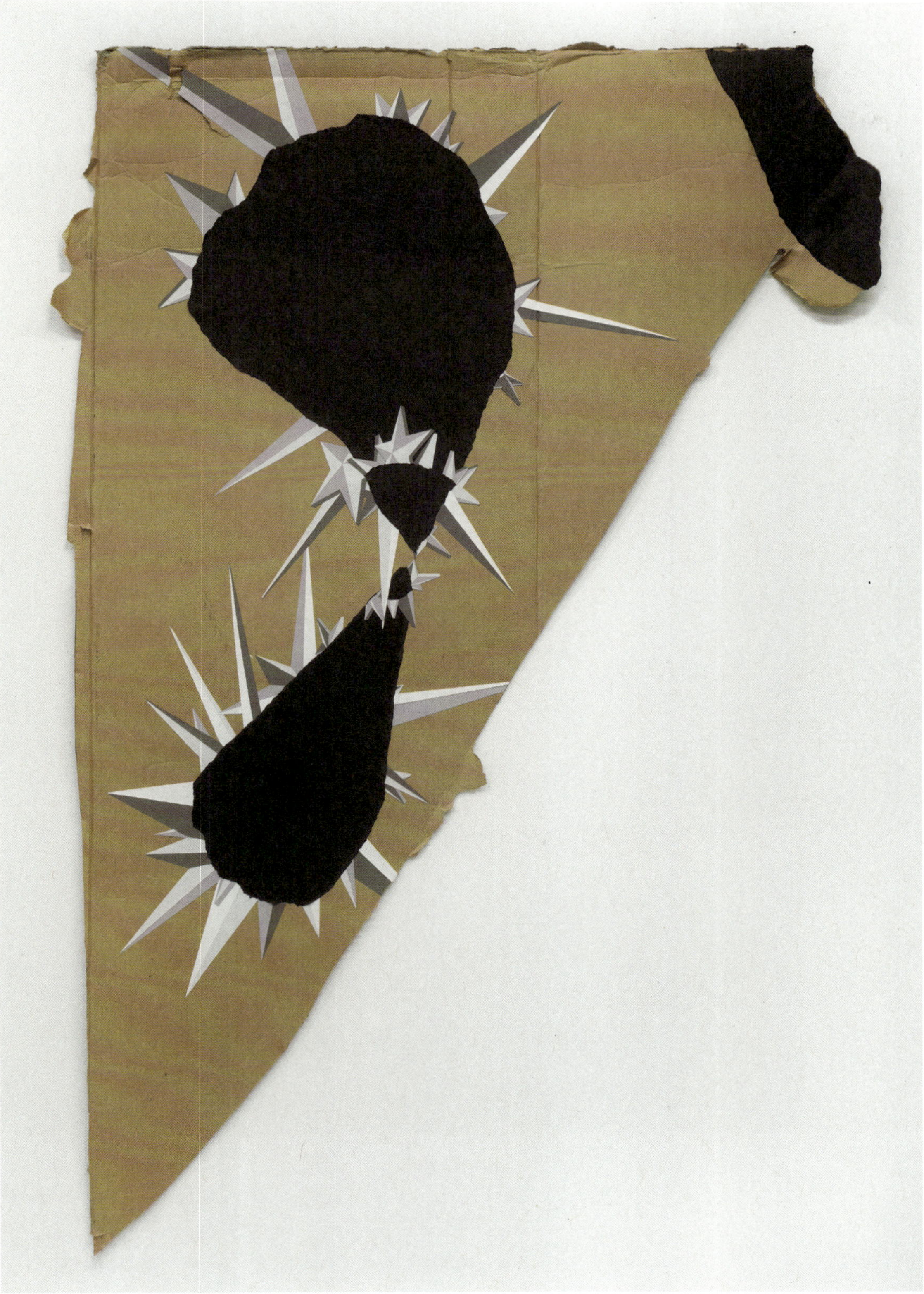

Plate 87
Pablo Vargas Lugo, Mexican, born 1968
Algunos Eclipses [Some Eclipses], 2008
Paper on cardboard
83 x 60 x 4 1/8 in. (210.8 x 152.4 x 10.2 cm)
Collection of Jack and Anne Moriniere

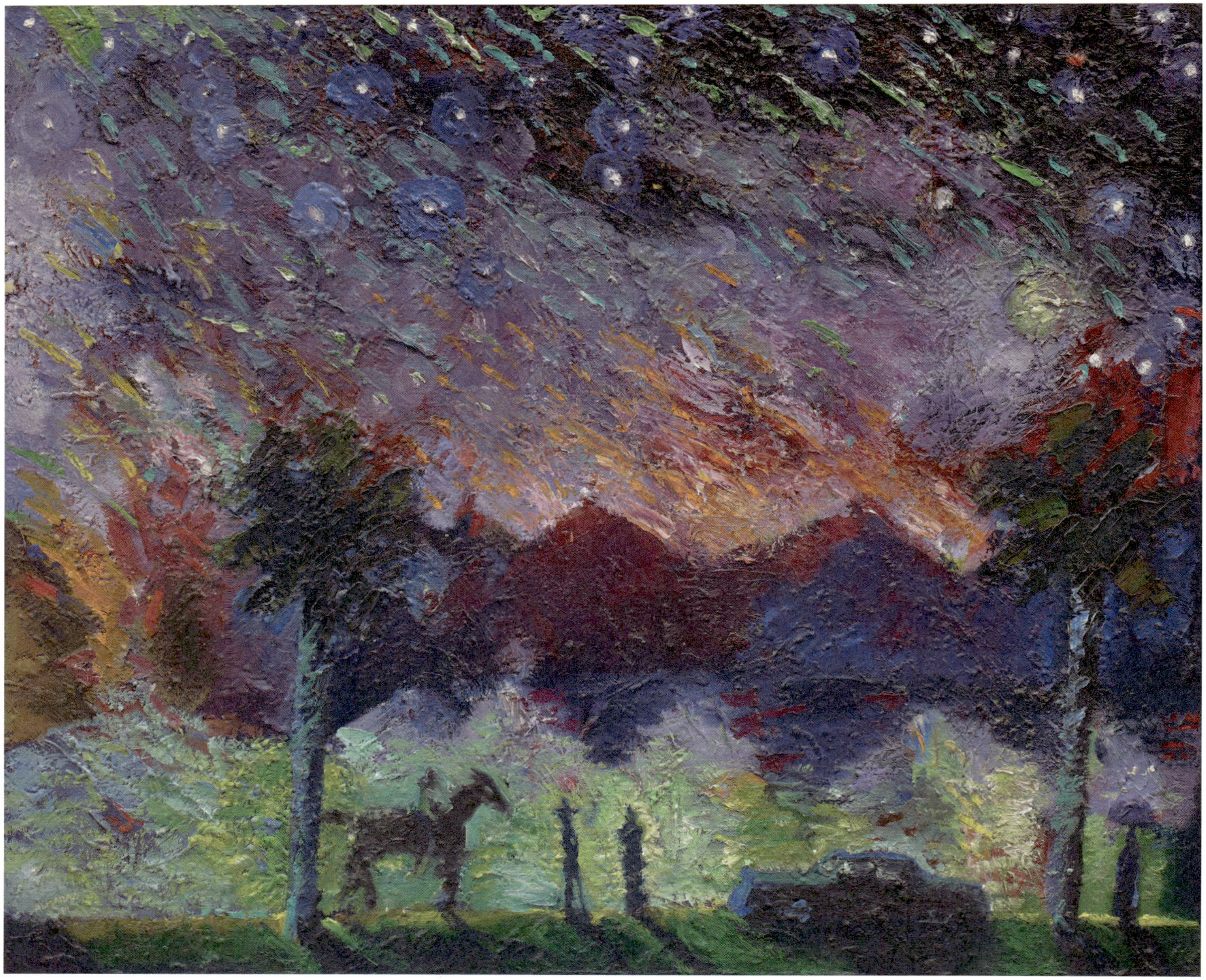

Plate 88
Carlos Almaraz, American, 1941–1989
Echo Park Series, c. 1980s
Oil on canvas
35 3/16 x 43 in. (88.9 x 109.2 cm)
Private collection

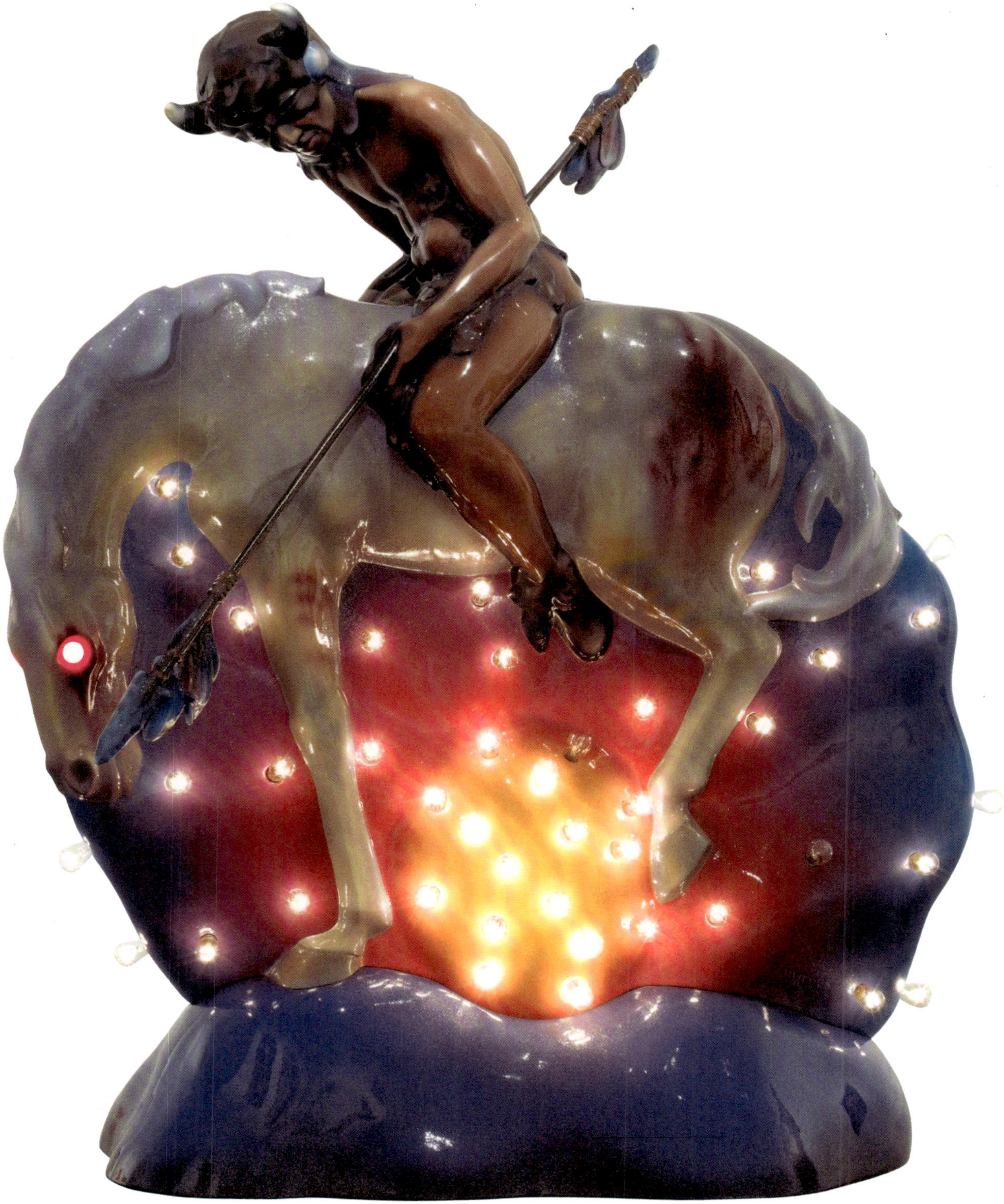

Plate 89
Luis Jiménez, American, 1940–2006
The End of the Trail (with Electric Sunset), 1971
Fiberglass, electric lighting
84 x 84 x 30 in. (213.4 x 213.4 x 76.2 cm)
The Museum of Fine Arts, Houston,
museum purchase with funds provided by the
Caroline Wiess Law Accessions Endowment Fund

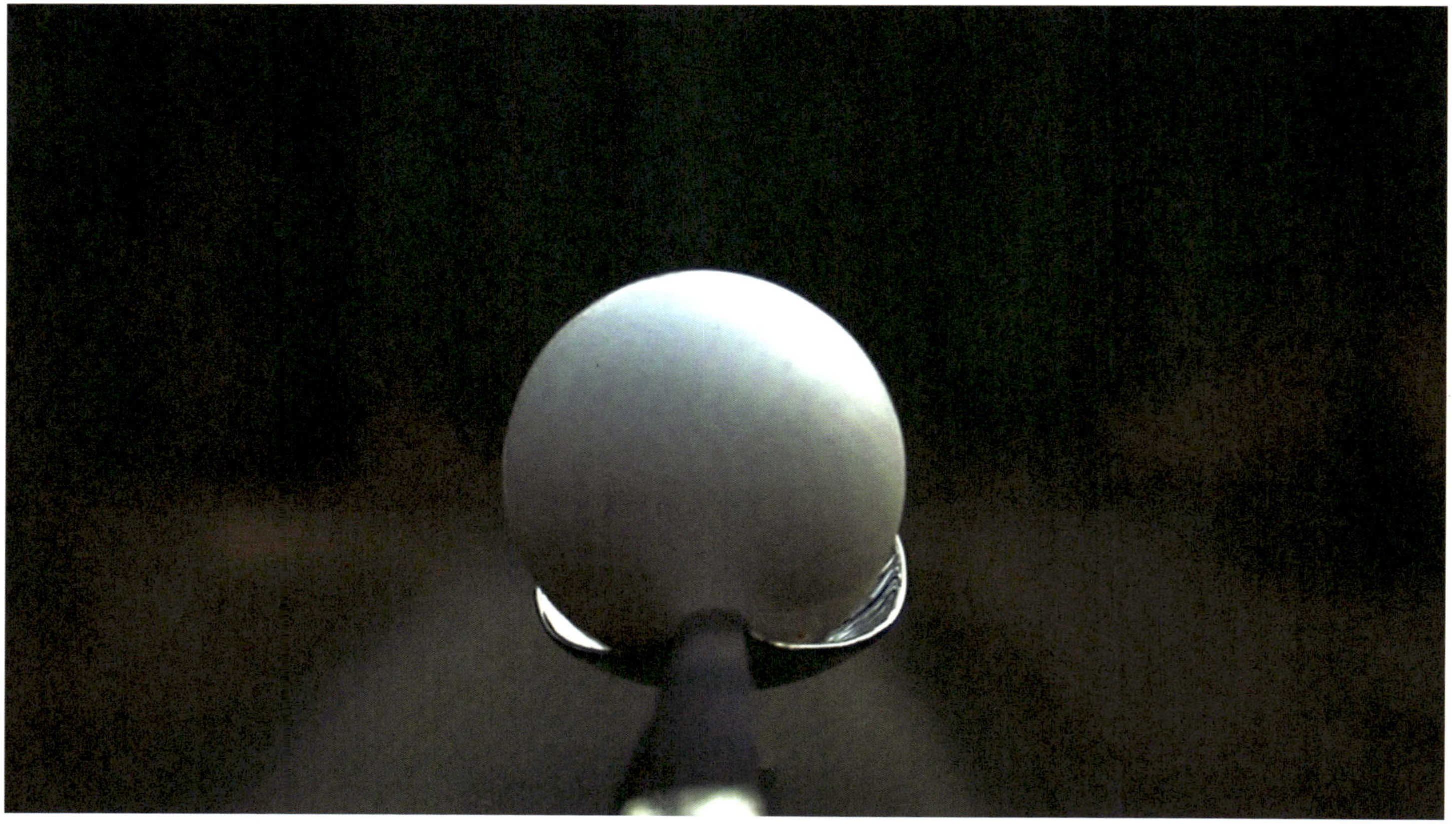

Plate 90
Rivane Neuenschwander, Brazilian, born 1967
The Fall, 2009
Digital video
14 minutes, 40 seconds
Collection of Diane and Bruce Halle

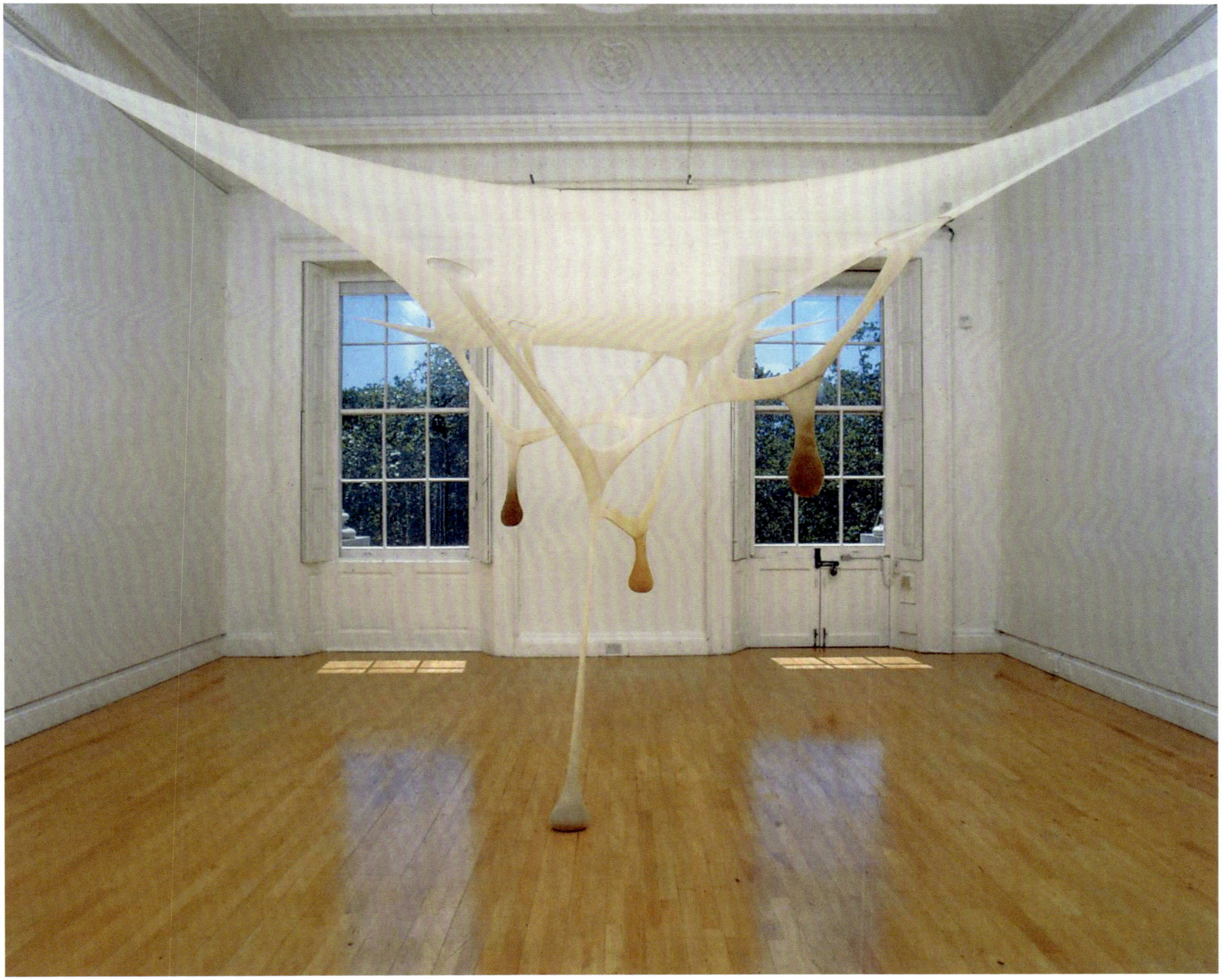

Plate 91
Ernesto Neto, Brazilian, born 1964
Pé de Três Sonhos [Tree of Three Dreams], 1999
Lycra tulle, stockings, saffron, urucum and sand
118 1/8 x 175 3/16 x 153 9/16 in. (300 x 445 x 390 cm)
Cecilia and Ernesto Poma Collection

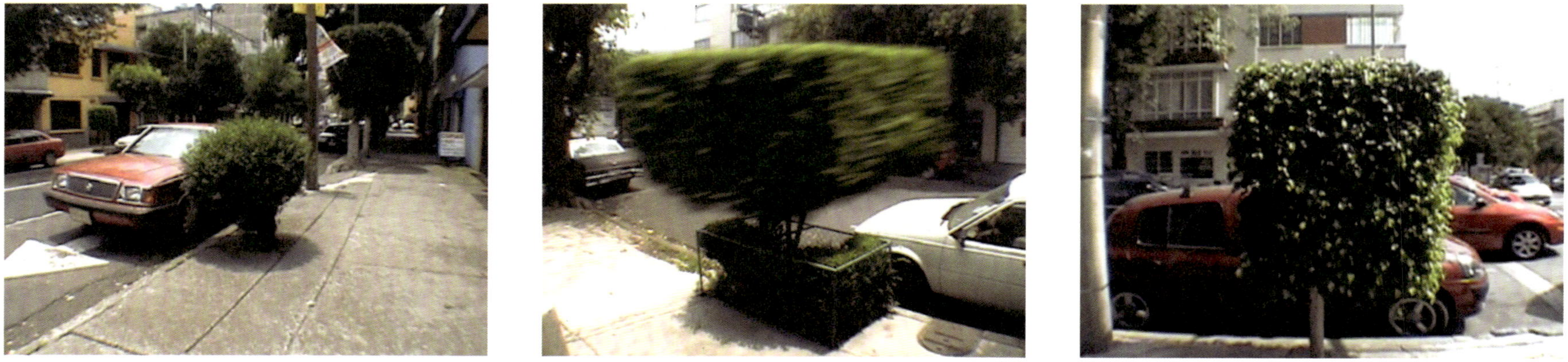

Plate 92
Gabriel Acevedo Velarde, Peruvian, born 1976
Parálisis [Paralysis], 2005
DVD
2 minutes, 30 seconds
Collection of Gail and Louis Adler

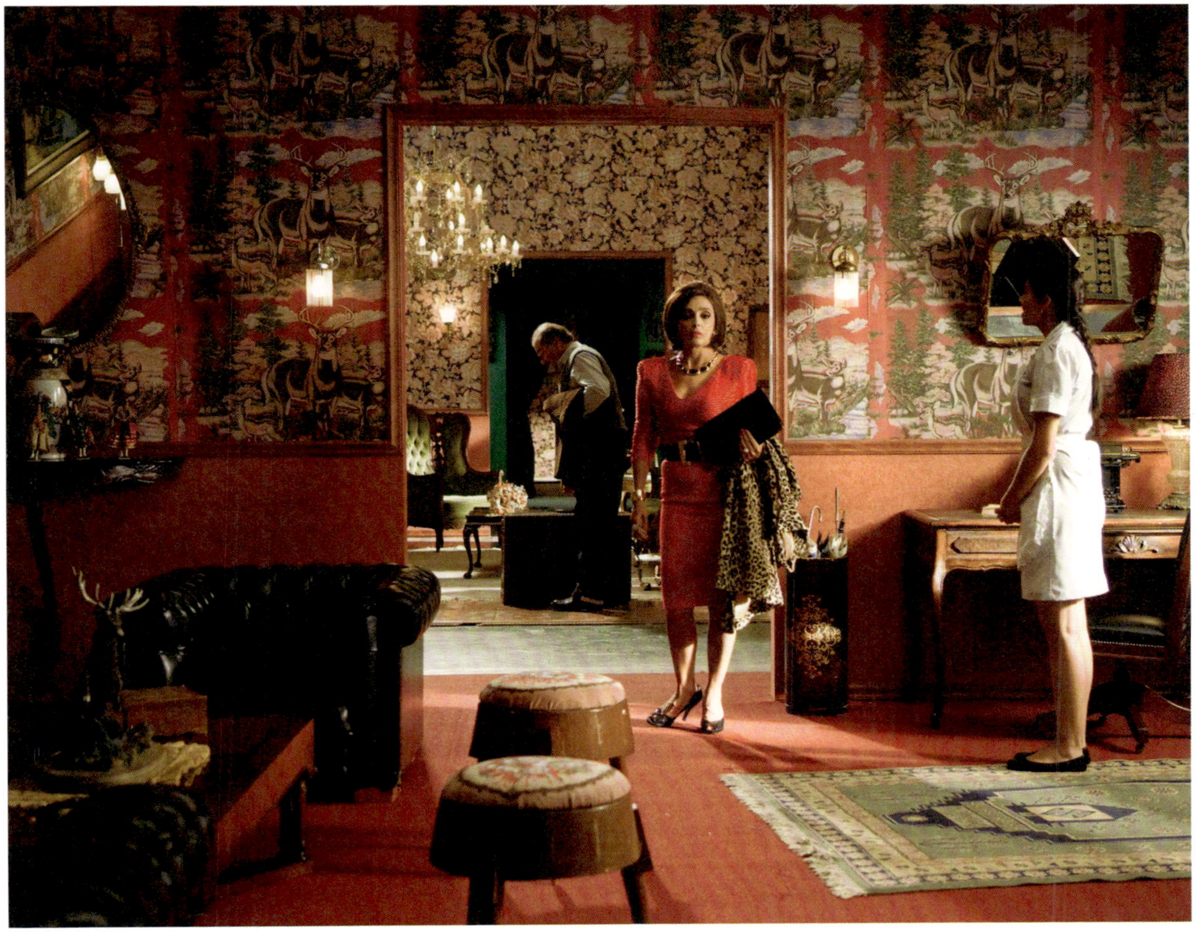

Plate 93
Phil Collins, British, born 1970
Soy mi madre (I Am My Mother), 2008
16 mm film transferred to digital video
28 minutes
Commissioned by the Aspen Art Museum
as part of the Jane and Marc Nathanson
Distinguished Artist in Residency
Collection of Dr. and Mrs. Bernard Arocha

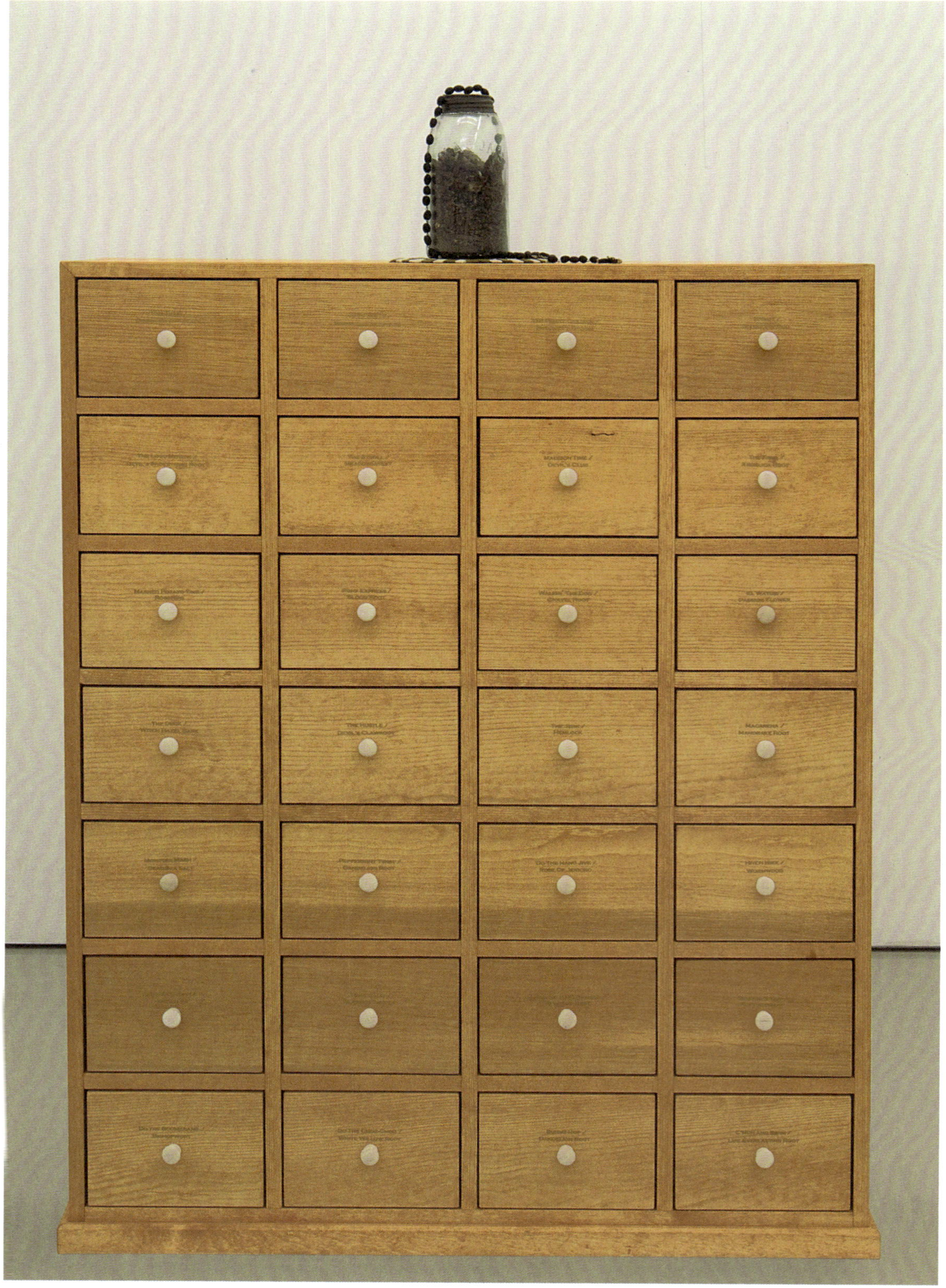

Plate 94
Dario Robleto, American, born 1972
Shaker Apothecary, 2007
Piner, hand-ground vinyl 45 rpm dance-craze records, various medicinal botanicals, carved bone calcium, typeset
40 x 60 x 15 in. (101.6 x 152.4 x 38.1 cm)

Salvation Cocktails, 2007
Veteran's old mason jar, soldiers' rosaries and crucifixes excavated from various battlefields, ground fulgurites (glass produced by lightning strikes when heat from blast melts surrounding sand), ground trinitite (glass produced during the first atomic test explosion when heat from blast melted surrounding sand), military buttons and medals, excavated fired bullets, spent shell casings and shrapnel from various wars, and military blanket wool from various wars
Overall: 9 x 4 1/2 x 4 1/2 in. (22.9 x 11.4 x 11.4 cm)

A Rosary for Rhythm, 2007
Melted and carved vinyl records of Jerry Lee Lewis's and Little Richard's "Whole Lotta Shakin' Goin' On," ground hip bone dust, cast pewter, and metal chain
Overall (Length): 26 in. (66 cm)
All Collection of Leslie and Brad Bucher

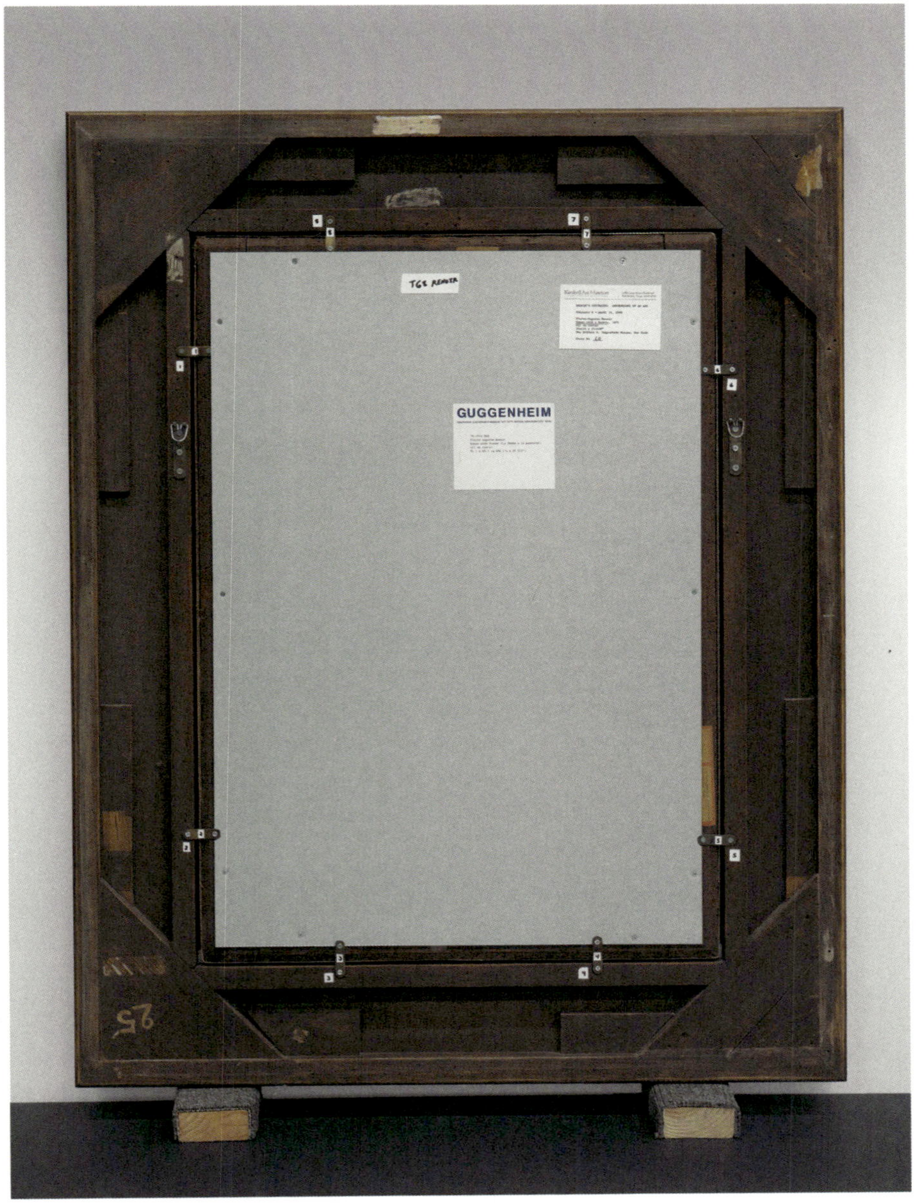

Plate 95
Vik Muniz, Brazilian, born 1961
Verso (Woman with Parrot), 2008
Mixed-media object
46 x 38 x 10 in. (116.8 x 96.5 x 25.4 cm)
Collection of Barbara and Michael Gamson

It can be argued that art collections tell stories, both at an institutional level and in the private domain of collectors' homes. The process of collecting – the methodology employed, the resources invested, and the single-minded focus directed toward specific objects and time periods – reveals a particular "collecting mindset or attitude." Furthermore, the actual accumulation of objects over time chronicles a practice analogous to the act of constructing a narrative.[1] My focus is not so much on what that narrative describes, though it certainly merits attention, but rather on how that narrative *functions*.

The Latin Maecenas have a unique relationship with the Museum of Fine Arts, Houston – both the institution that they support and the curatorial department that they have helped to build. Their relationship contributes to a larger story of narrative-making and community-building. One reading of that narrative follows a group of passionate individuals, who under the leadership of Mari Carmen Ramírez were inspired by the important vision of creating a definitive Latin American art collection and research center

CONSTRUCTING A NARRATIVE BUILDING A COMMUNITY ELIZABETH CEREJIDO

in the United States. The Maecenas then committed to embarking on a long-term journey to activate the objectives set forth by the department and to systematically implement them, which include the thorough study, exhibition, and collecting of Latin American and Latino art. Ultimately, they understood that this vision fundamentally included both steering away from and challenging the hegemony of previous North American models, which until recently were the primary sources of scholarly and curatorial material on the subject. Fueled by this ambitious mission, the Maecenas signed up for workshops and attended symposia that educated them on the subject. By participating in these activities, they laid the foundation for a new narrative that aims to reposition Latin American art in dialogue with mainstream modern and contemporary paradigms and to identify its own contribution and place in the Western canon.

Purposely resisting stereotypical depictions of Latin American art as solely figurative, exuberant, and colorful; and dispelling preconceptions of an art imbued with myth-making and "the fantastic," this new narrative recounts the history of Latin American art through key moments in early Modernism and twentieth-century avant-garde movements, up to current contemporary examples. The research and collecting strengths, thus far, have centered on abstraction and its many variants of nonrepresentational movements

Magdalena Fernández, Venezuelan, born 1964
2pmH0008N (Homenaje a Hélio Oiticica)
[2pmH0008N (Homage to Hélio Oiticica)], 2008
DVD
5 minutes
Collection of María Cristina and Pablo Henning

that includeJoaquín Torres-García and members of the School of the South; the Constructivist work of the Concrete and Neo-Concrete movements, principally represented in the acquisition of the Adolpho Leirner Collection from Brazil; and the kinetic explorations of Venezuelan Jesús Rafael Soto. The innovative exhibition curatorship of the work of previously under-recognized artists, such as the Venezuelan Gego (Gertrud Goldschmidt) and the Argentine Gyula Kosice, as well as the landmark exhibition *Inverted Utopias: Avant-Garde Art in Latin America* (2004), have positioned the department at the forefront of the production of new knowledge on art from this region. Additionally, the museum's active partnerships with the Cruz-Diez Foundation and the Gego Foundation not only have strengthened the permanent collection's focus in these areas, but they also have created a site for the methodical care of works by these two artists, the production of new scholarly materials about them, and the opportunity to produce exhibition projects that contextualize the artists' oeuvre within the larger arc of modern and contemporary practices in the Americas. Reinforced by the International Center for the Arts of the Americas (ICAA) at the MFAH, the research and publication arm of the department, this initiative provides a much broader context for and in-depth approach to the study and exhibition of Latin American art. As such, the initiative is distinct from Latin American art departments at other museums in the United States. Finally, the Maecenas' role in supporting this vision, coupled with their unwavering commitment, underscores not only the solid donor base of the department but also the grounded, long-term nature of this endeavor.

BUILDING COMMUNITY THROUGH COLLECTING

The act of collecting is inherently selfish and largely exclusive, and it is practiced by a select group of individuals with the resources to support an obsessive need to own objects for personal pleasure. Collecting with a philanthropic objective, or for another altruistic purpose, points toward alternate possibilities with regard to the collectors' accessibility to the public and to their potential function in the cultural fabric of a community. The scope of this essay, however, is not to delve into the history of art collecting nor to provide an exhaustive comparative study of collecting models. Instead, my objective is to provide contrasting models of philanthropy and collecting philosophies and their respective functions in community-building, in order to emphasize the singular character of the Latin Maecenas and their support of the Latin American Art Department at the MFAH.

In Latin America, specifically, philanthropy has been historically scant and virtually nonexistent. The culture of collecting has been traditionally defined by the notion of cultural patrimony being linked to a family's name, stemming from the continent's colonial heritage. In today's collecting climate, collections remain in the private domain of individuals who often wish to remain anonymous. This is attributed in large measure to a series of factors that combines reasons of personal safety with the manner in which cultural institutions are structured within governmental and civic entities. Because museums most often fall under the auspices of government agencies, directors' and curators' positions may shift and change, depending on the political agenda of an incoming government. This unstable climate often limits the kinds of opportunities available for cultivating donor relations and for articulating an institutional mission that might attract potential donors. Coupled with a lack of resources from government funding sources, museums tend to be at a constant disadvantage and, as such, collectors seldom think of gifting their collections to public institutions. Conversely, the philanthropic culture in the United States is vastly multifaceted and informed by the perception that collecting art is a sound investment practice. However, in addition to the fiscal benefits that donors derive from their collecting activities, there are several models that indicate the various strategies that act as the driving impetus in collection-building and their respective roles in furthering institutional mission, patron relationships, and community-building. Additionally, while the debate over the role and function of public institutions and their strategies for representing and attracting diverse communities is a contentious and complex issue, it is not the focus of this essay. What I want to emphasize is how the development of a new narrative, prompted by the visionary objectives of the Latin American Art Department and the renewed models of philanthropy and collection initiatives nurtured by the Latin Maecenas, has the potential to function as a catalytic force. This force will help the building of community that can both respond to local needs as well as establish an active network with a global reach.

In 2001, El Museo del Barrio in New York celebrated ten years of collection-building by organizing a group exhibition titled *Voices from Our Communities: Perspectives on a Decade of Collecting at El Museo del Barrio*. The introductory text in the accompanying catalogue explained that the driving force behind the museum's collecting philosophy was to demonstrate that "our public's voices provide an essential side of the equation that links persons and objects in that inexplicable transaction of beauty, interest and knowledge that museums mediate."[2] Furthermore, the role of community representation as one of the main objectives in its collecting strategy is underscored by this statement by the director: "to [acknowledge] important voices within our diverse constituency who inspire and support us in our work."[3] This type of community-building through collecting reinforces one identifiable strategy in which museums ". . . claim the right to assert their communities' point of view in the essential activities of the museums" or build their collections to "accommodate communities" that in turn reflect the specific needs of a particular group or various demographic groups.[4] Thus, in essence the communities exist and have become vocal agents prior to an institutional initiative such as that of building a collection is conceived and implemented.

Another vastly different model worth mentioning is that of the city of Miami, Florida. There, major collections exist primarily in the private domain of a handful of collectors who, during the last decade, have opened their own individual spaces that function as private museums. This evidences a troubling disconnect between institution and patron and the potentiality for community-building that stems from a joint effort between the two. It also produces the contradictory scenario that positions the collector, not the institution, as a leading protagonist, and casts the collector and the institution often in competing roles. As a result, few, if any, major public institutions in Miami have articulated a compelling long-term vision that acts as the unifying nexus from which patron, institution, and community work together to advance shared goals and to make a lasting impact.

The Latin Maecenas' support of the Latin American Art Department at the MFAH and its collecting efforts illustrates a contrasting model. Here, unlike El Museo del Barrio, the institution is articulating a vision with a broader role and function, without a specific target community in mind. Instead of upholding the model of representing or speaking on behalf of a particular group or an underserved audience, the MFAH's Latin American art initiative is building a program *first* that will in turn *create* community. Community (in this sense of collectors) follows vision.

The Latin Maecenas have expanded on a model of philanthropy that privileges a symmetrical relationship between supporter and institution. This more organic model places emphasis on the live, active *process* that comes with *building* a collection over time, instead of traditional paradigms of member/donor relations that tend to be hierarchical or donor-centric, and more passive. Although the majority of the Maecenas are based in Houston, numerous active members are also based in various cities in the United States, Latin America, and Europe, creating the kind of transnational dialogue and circuitous networking that propel a local effort into a global initiative. To this end, it may be argued that *Houston* beyond the physical site in which the institutional base lives and operates and the city in which many of these collectors reside, is in fact a microcosm that represents how an institution and its art patrons have a long-lasting impact and far-reaching effect on both local and international communities. On the institutional side, this model also reflects the social function of a contemporary collecting culture in an age of globalization and its capacity to "create spaces for intercultural encounters" that are both inclusive and groundbreaking.[5]

OPENING THE NARRATIVE AND EXPANDING THE COMMUNITY

Although the word "community" is invested with a social, political, and economic charge, community in its broadest definition can be described as "any group of individuals who build identity [. . .] around all manner of religious persuasions, political causes, lifestyle choices, and personal hobbies" or "within a common frame of reference."[6] The collecting community that the Latin Maecenas and the museum's Latin American Art Department have created lives in the realm of ideas and vision, outside of territorial demarcations and nationalistic impulses. In line with the aforementioned definition, the collecting community can be arguably described as one in which alliances are built around "lifestyle choices and personal hobbies" (the Maecenas' passion for collecting) and a shared "frame of reference" (the vision and singular point of view of Latin American art set forth by the institution). However, the operative phrase *frame of reference*, and the complex factors that it constitutes, is one of the core future challenges worth tackling at this particular juncture.

The celebration of this milestone and the occasion for this exhibition project – the ten-year anniversary of the Latin American Art Department at the MFAH and its tribute to the Latin Maecenas – represent a propitious opportunity to identify new directions and to embrace future challenges. In keeping with the department's mission, museum staff will continue to follow the trajectory of researching and exhibiting the work of under-recognized artists from important movements of the twentieth century. The MFAH will simultaneously move into the sphere of contemporary art and into geographic areas that are still untapped in scholarship and exposure. These include countries that encompass the Pacific coast of the region, as well as Central America, Colombia, Venezuela, and the

Caribbean (in its broadest definition). Focusing on the heterogeneous cultural production of these distinct sites should also present compelling challenges that circumscribe areas of scholarship and curatorship to the social, political, and economic forces that drive the aesthetic work of these various regions. Advancing into these areas will stimulate the exploration and continuation of new narratives that fall well outside established discursive notions of center and periphery. Additional challenges to (re)consider should include the term *Latino* and questioning its role and function within a discourse on Latin American art that increasingly positions itself within a global context.

If we return to the premise of the narrative (read "implementation of a vision") and its functional potentiality for creating community, it behooves us to ask not so much *what* the story narrates as "what a story *does*: what relations it creates, how it morphs its environment, what it negates, and what intensities it creates. . . ." And, perhaps most important, the story should be about *its possibility* and the options and practices it *authorizes and enables*."[7] As storytellers armed with the resources to *enable, empower, and authorize*, the Latin Maecenas and the staff of the Latin American Art Department are continuing to construct a new narrative. In doing so, they must ask themselves these important questions: Whose voices will be empowered as participating actors in an institutionally-driven art market? Which social areas will become sites for possibility? How can the community of shared ideas and vision created by both the collectors and the department expand into the province of engagement – producing the kinds of concrete results that are generated by citizens involved in the sectors that the institution purportedly serves? These questions point toward the need to expand that "shared frame of reference" inherent in the building of a community into unchallenged and contested geographic, conceptual, scholarly, social, and political arenas, thus creating the conditions for a plurality of points of references to emerge. These are challenges worth taking on, and both the Latin Maecenas and the Latin American Art Department at the Museum of Fine Arts, Houston, are uniquely poised to undertake them.

NOTES

1 Mieke Bal, "Telling Objects: A Narrative Perspective on Collecting," in *The Cultures of Collecting*, eds. John Elsner and Roger Cardinal (London: Reaktion Books, 1994), 97.

2 Susana Torruella Leval, "Our Collection, Its Voices: Introduction from the Director," in *Voices from Our Communities: Perspectives on a Decade of Collecting at El Museo del Barrio*, ed. Susana Torruella Leval (El Museo del Barrio, 2001), ii.

3 Ibid.

4 Ivan Karp, "Introduction: Museums and Communities: The Politics of Public Culture," in *Museums and Communities*, eds. Karp, Ivan, Christien Mullen Kreamer, and Steven D. Lavine (Washington, D.C.: Smithsonian Institution, 1992), 12.

5 Tomás Ybarra-Frausto, "Latin American Culture and the United States in the New Millennium," in *Collecting Latin American Art for the 21st Century*, ed. Mari Carmen Ramírez with Theresa Papanikolas (Houston: International Center for the Arts of the Americas, The Museum of Fine Arts, Houston, 2002), 55.

6 James Bau Graves, *Cultural Democracy: The Arts, Community, and the Public Purpose* (Urbana and Chicago: University of Illinois Press, 2005), 155.

7 Roger M. Buergel, Anselm Franke, Maria Lind, and Nina Möntmann, "Curating with Institutional Visions: A Roundtable talk with: Roger M. Buergel, Anselm Franke, Maria Lind, and Nina Möntmann," in *Art and Its Institutions: Current Conflicts, Critique and Collaborations*, ed. Nina Möntmann (London: Black Dog Publishing, 2006), 40.

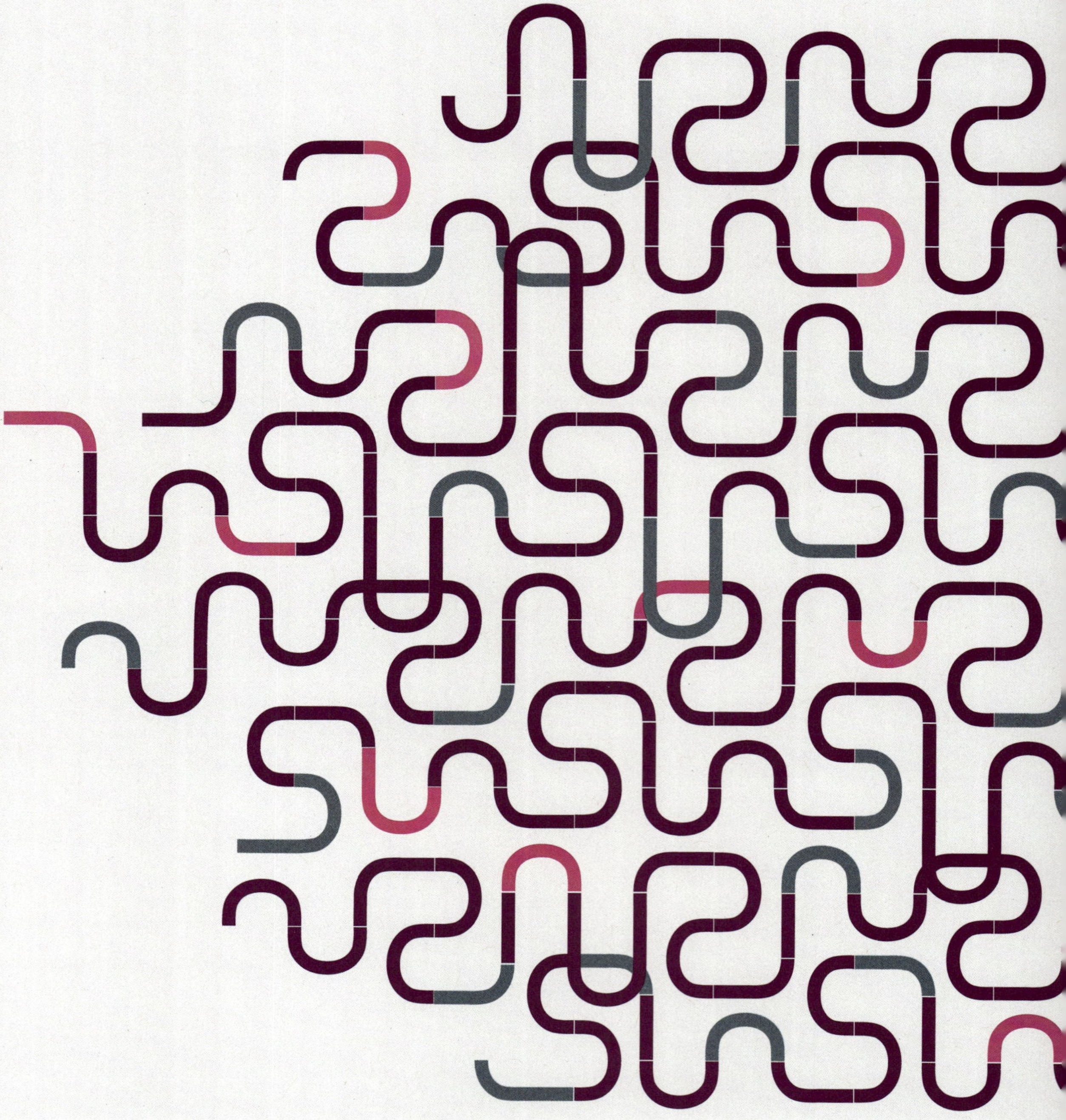

THE LATIN MAECENAS IN PICTURES
2002-2009

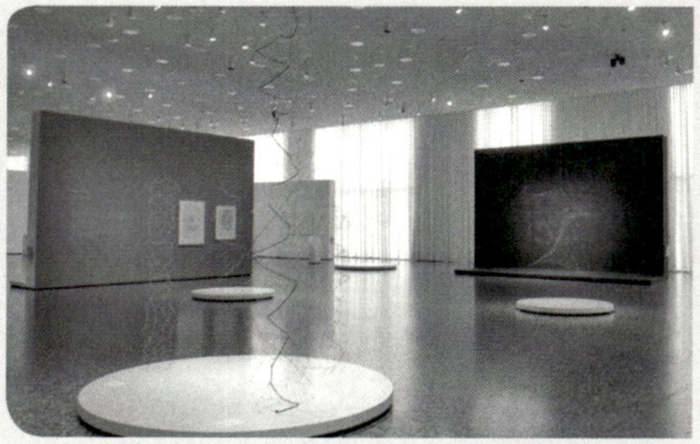

Questioning the Line: Gego, A Selection, 1955–1990, installation view

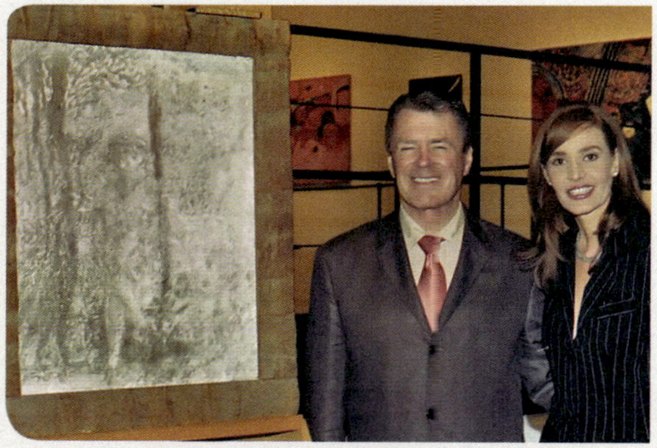

Peter Marzio and Carmen María Lechin

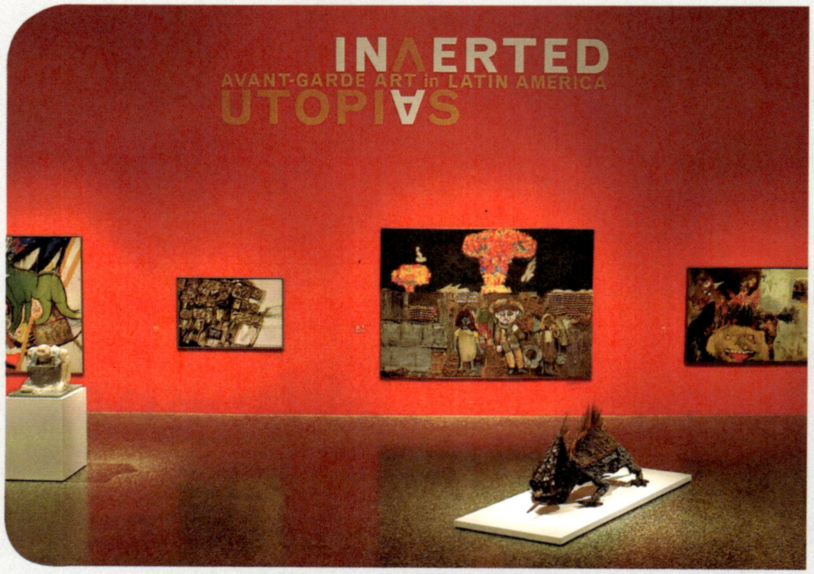

Inverted Utopias: Avant-Garde Art in Latin America, installation view

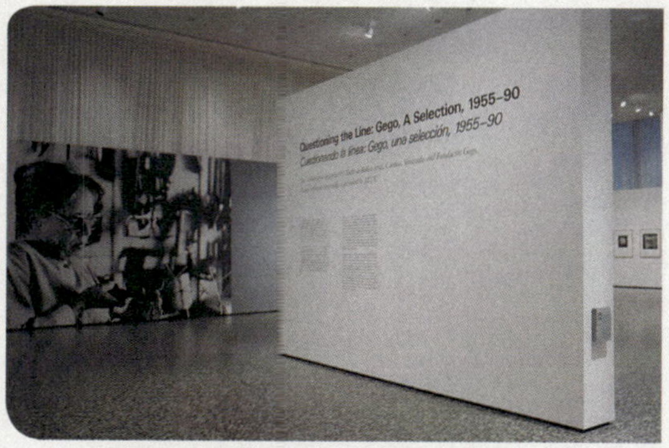

Questioning the Line: Gego, A Selection, 1955–1990, installation view

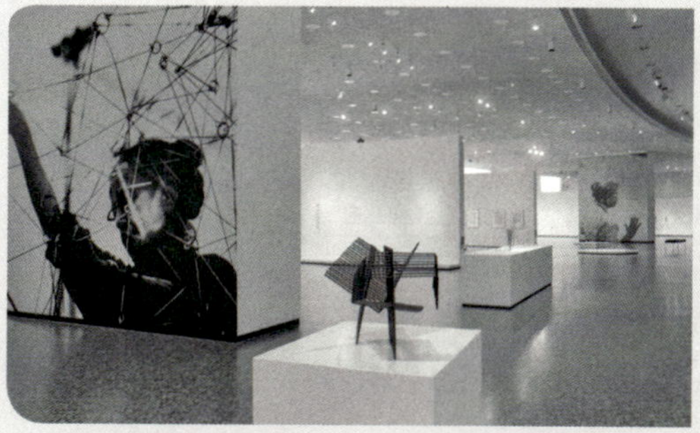

Questioning the Line: Gego, A Selection, 1955–1990, installation view

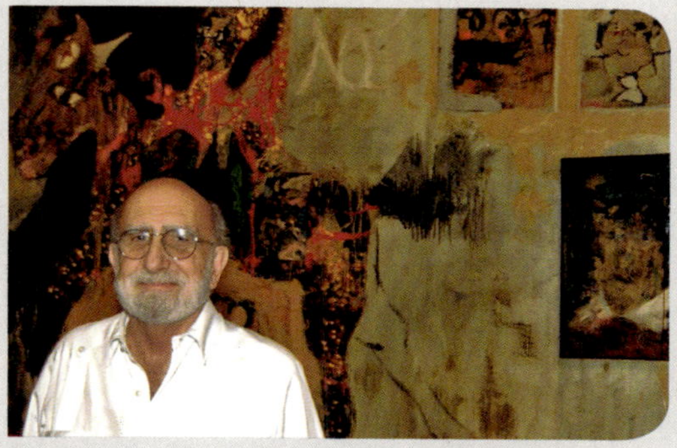

Inverted Utopias artist Luis Felipe Noé

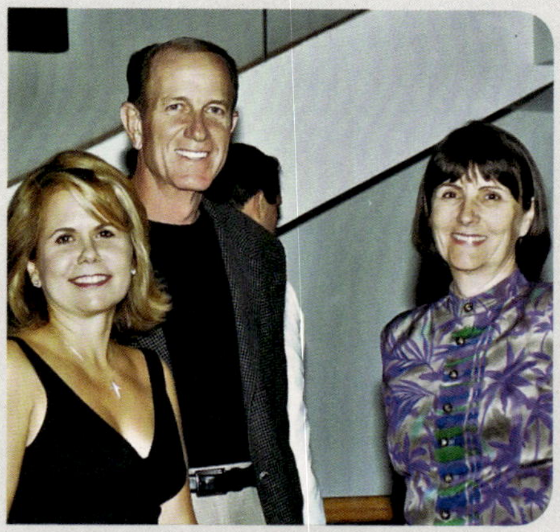

Leslie and Brad Bucher, Mary Arocha

THE LATIN MAECENAS 2002-2004

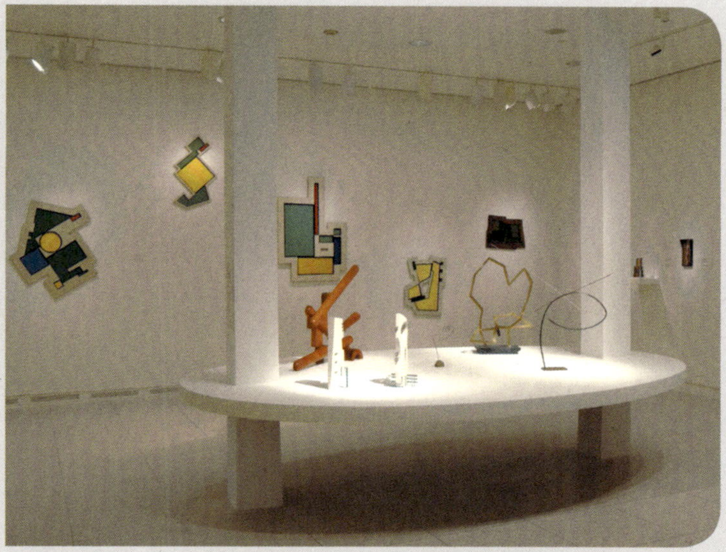

Inverted Utopias: Avant-Garde Art in Latin America, installation view

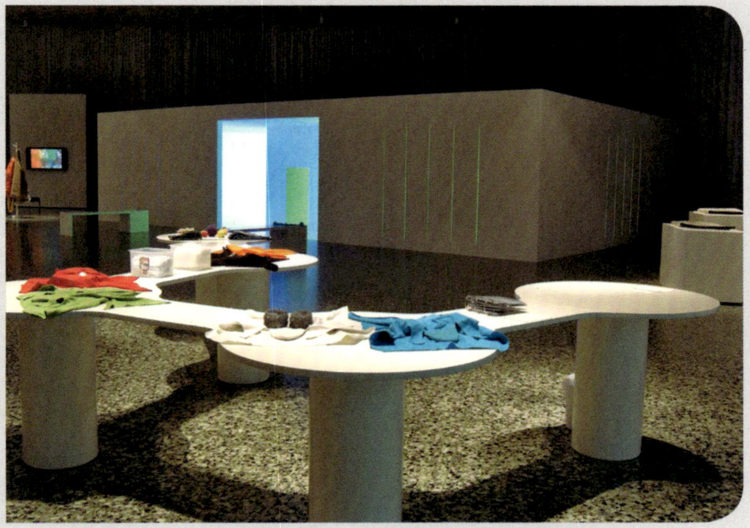

Inverted Utopias: Avant-Garde Art in Latin America, installation view

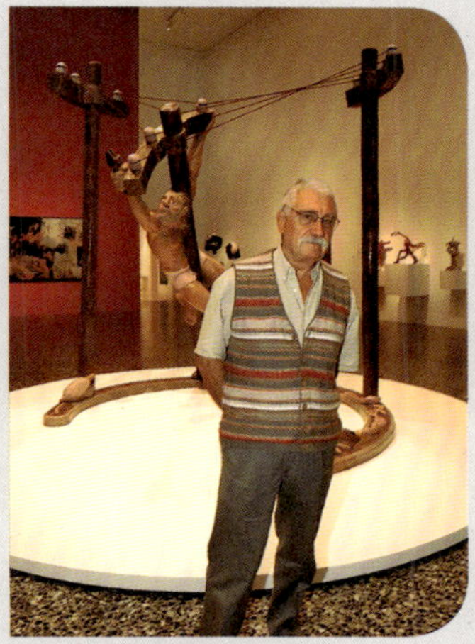

Inverted Utopias artist
Juan Carlos Distéfano

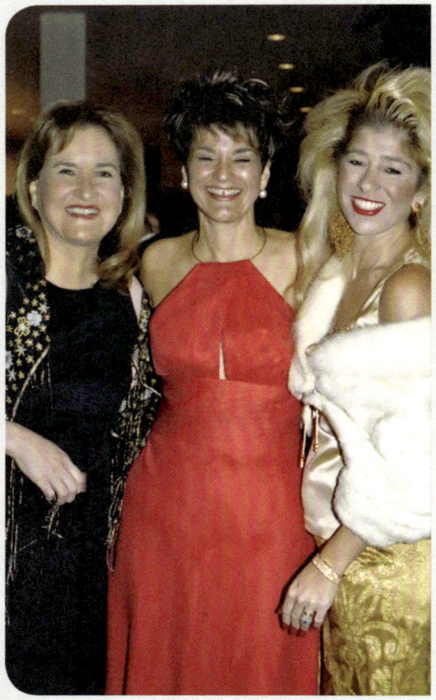

Latin American Experience Gala and Auction, Harris County Commissioner Sylvia García, Mari Carmen Ramírez, and Sofia Adrogué

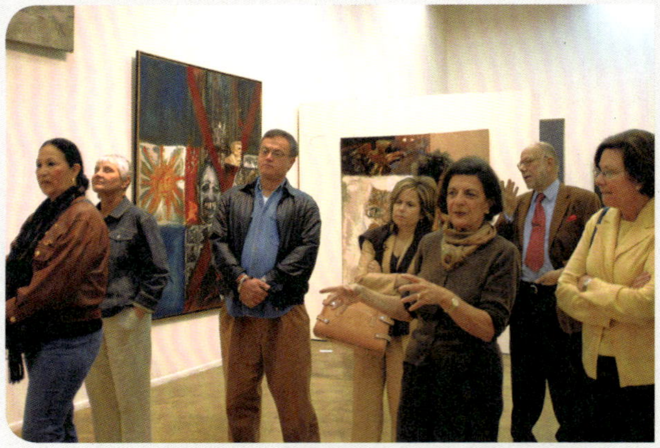

Latin Maecenas visiting the Jorge and Marion Helft Collection, Buenos Aires, Argentina

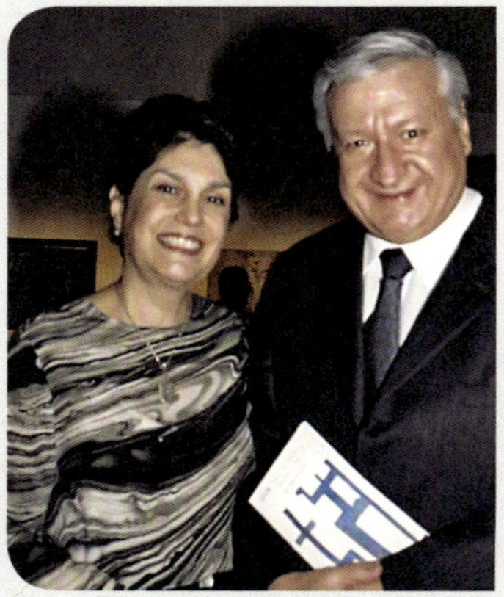

Latin American Experience Gala and Auction, Cecilia and Dr. Luis Campos

THE LATIN MAECENAS
2005

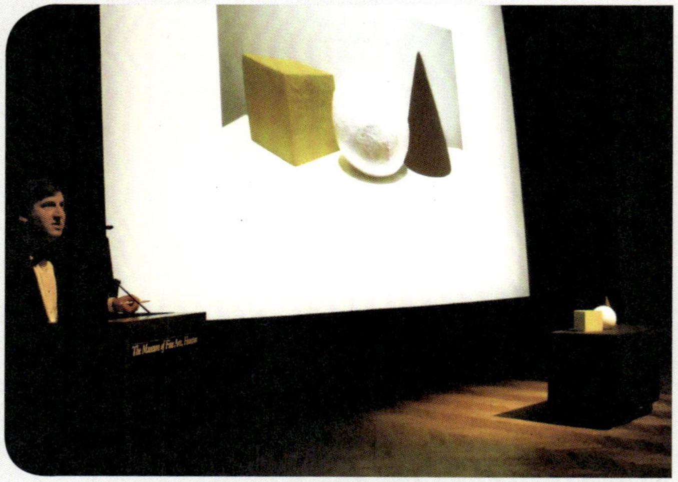

Latin American Experience Gala and Auction with auctioneer Augie Uribe of Sotheby's

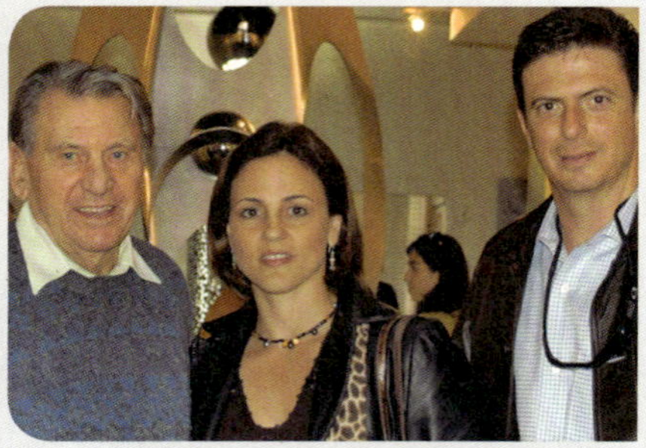

Artist Gyula Kosice with Carolina and Sergio Weitzman, Buenos Aires, Argentina

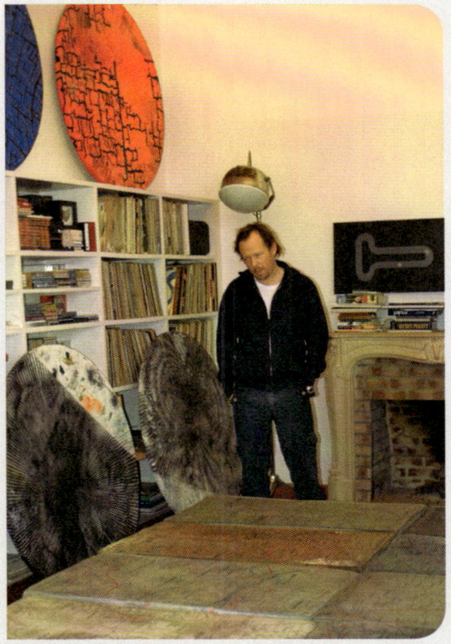

Guillermo Kuitca studio visit,
Buenos Aires, Argentina

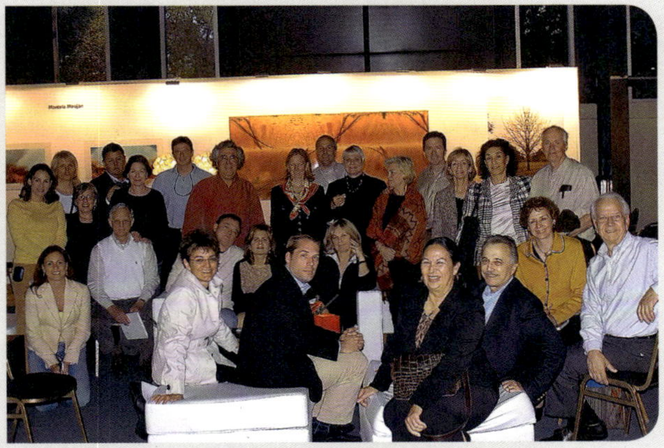

Latin Maecenas group photo at Arte BA, Buenos Aires, Argentina

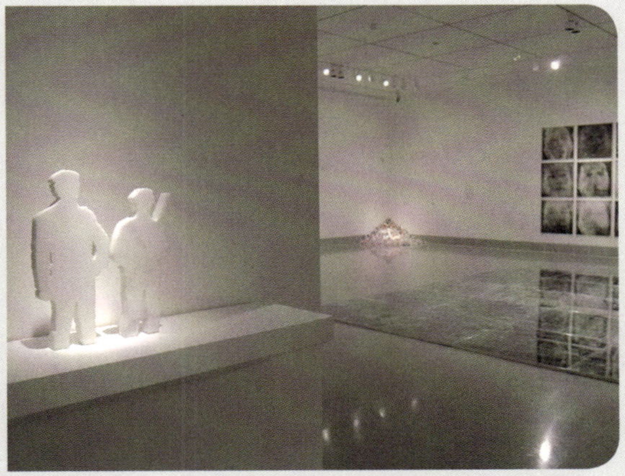

Indelible Images installation view, Daniel Joseph Martinez

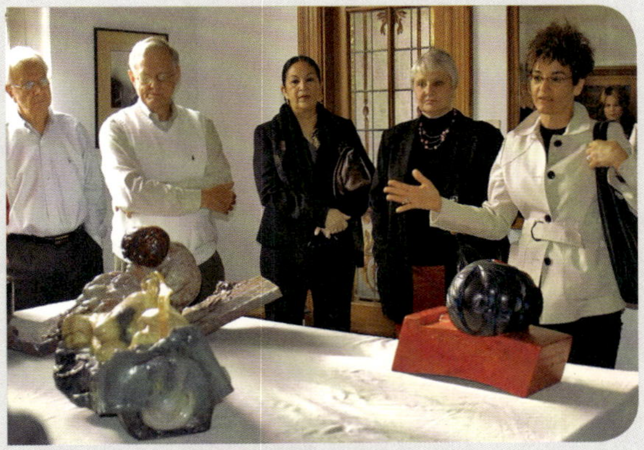

Studio visit with Juan Carlos Distéfano,
Buenos Aires, Argentina

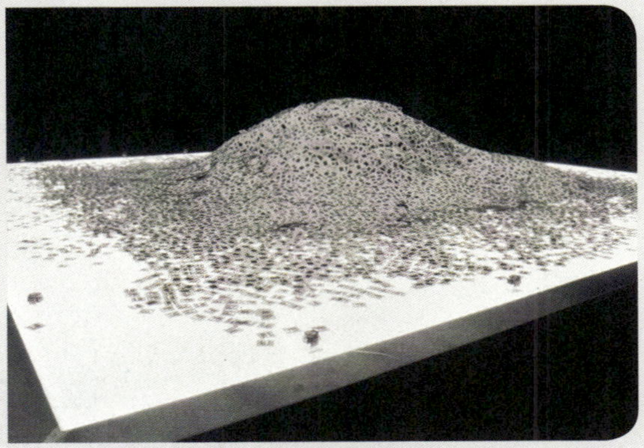

Alfredo Jaar: The Eyes of Gutete Emerita, installation view

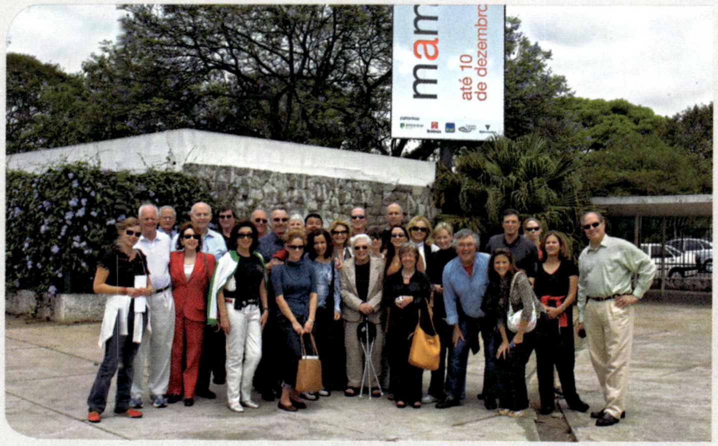

Latin Maecenas group photo at São Paulo Biennale, Brazil

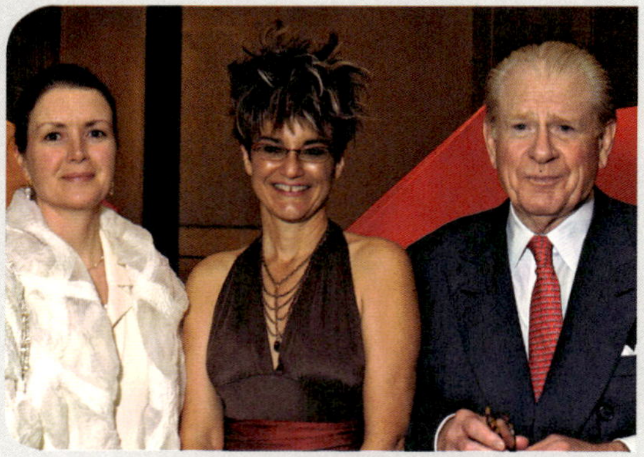

Johanna Wortham, Mari Carmen Ramírez, and
Rusty Wortham, opening of *Hélio Oiticica: The Body of Color*

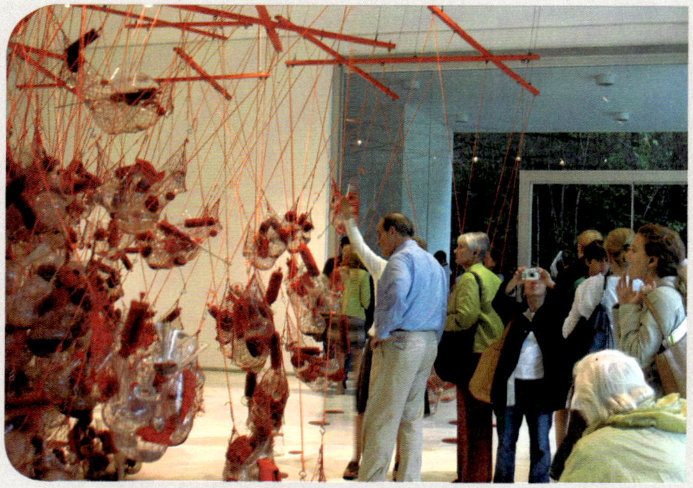

Visit to Instituto Cultural Inhotim, Belo Horizonte, Brazil,
installation view of work by Tunga

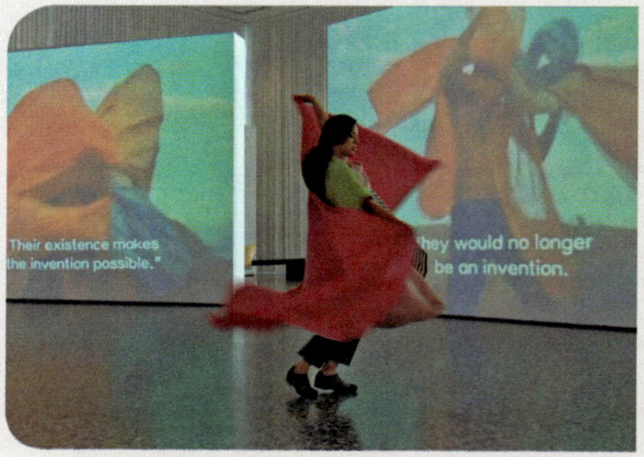

Hélio Oiticica: The Body of Color, installation view
with *Parangolé* performance

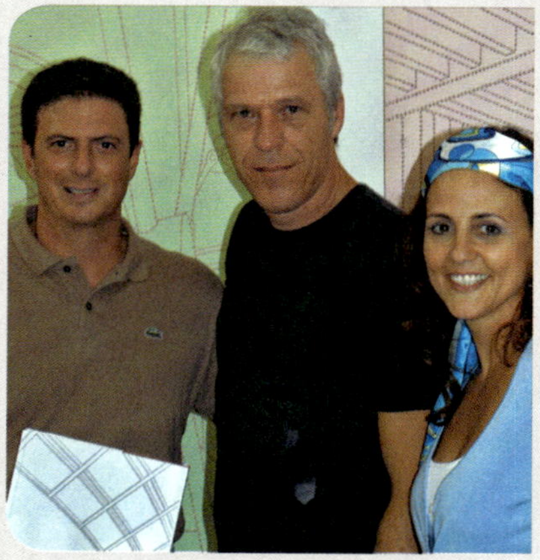

Artist Paulo Climachauska with Sergio and
Carolina Weitzman, São Paulo, Brazil

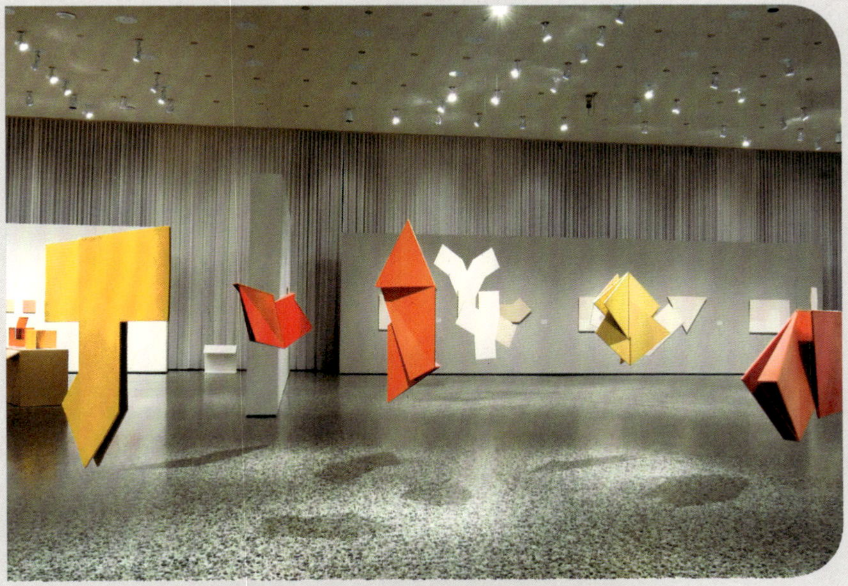

Hélio Oiticica: The Body of Color, installation view with *Relevos espaçiais*

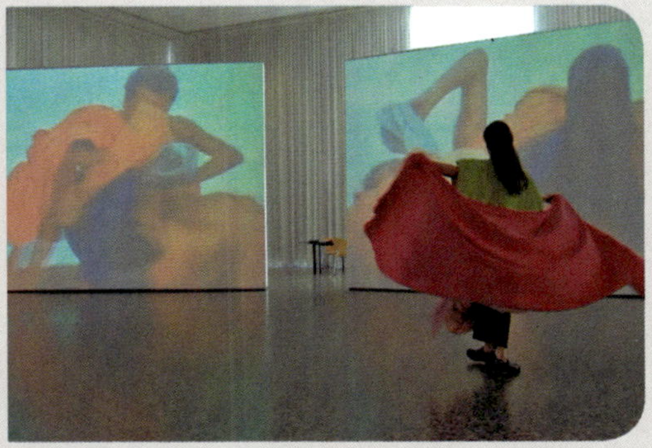

Hélio Oiticica: The Body of Color, installation view with *Parangolé* performance

THE LATIN MAECENAS 2006

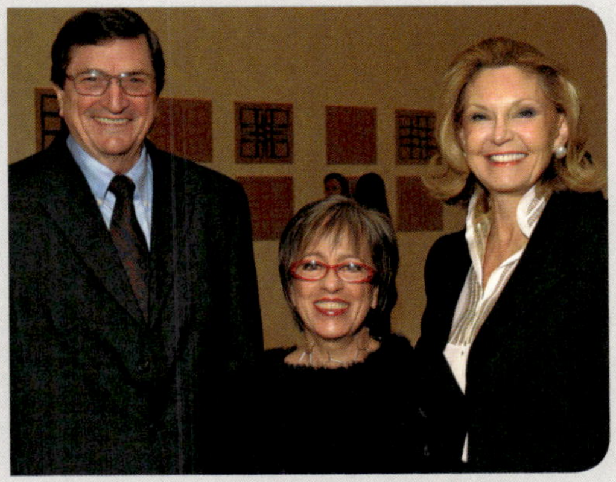

Frank Ribelin, María Inés Sicardi, Karen McRae

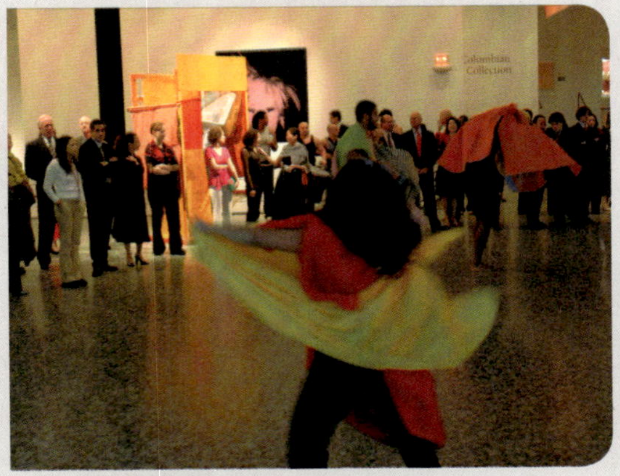

Hélio Oiticica: The Body of Color, opening

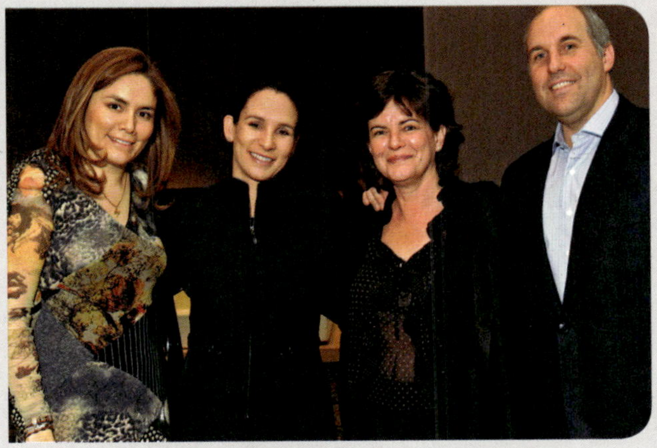

Marigel Rodríguez, Maria Christina Henning, Carmen Mélian, and Pablo Henning

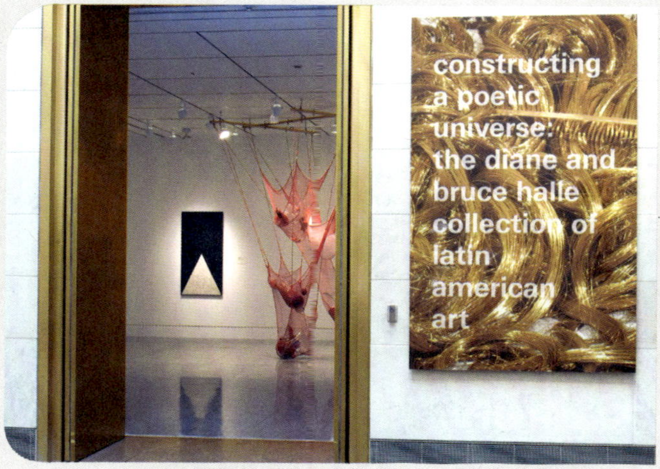

Constructing a Poetic Universe: The Diane and Bruce Halle Collection of Latin American Art, installation view

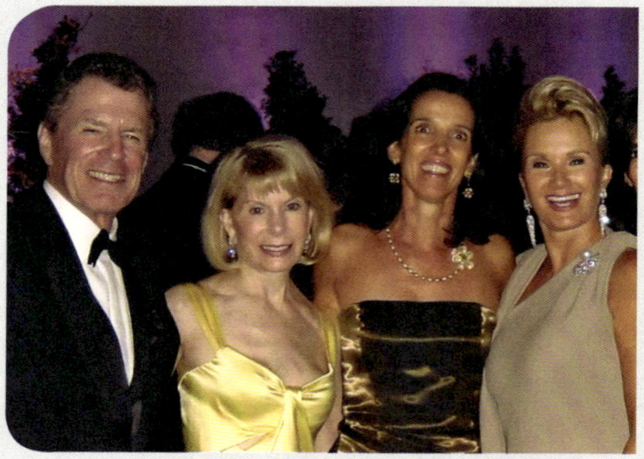

Peter and Frances Marzio, Eugenia Grüneisen, Diane Halle

THE LATIN MAECENAS 2007

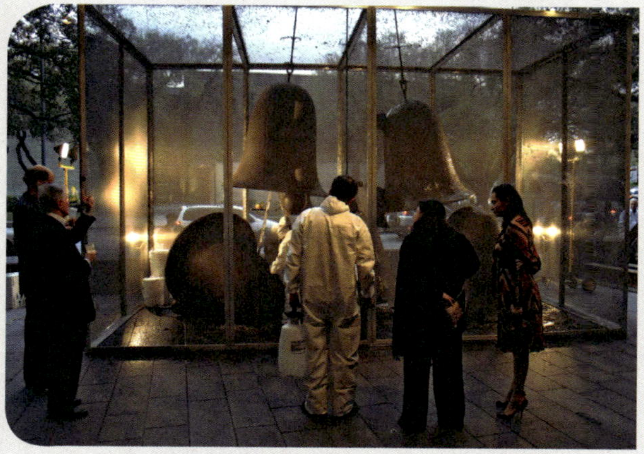

Constructing a Poetic Universe: The Diane and Bruce Halle Collection of Latin American Art, performance by Tunga

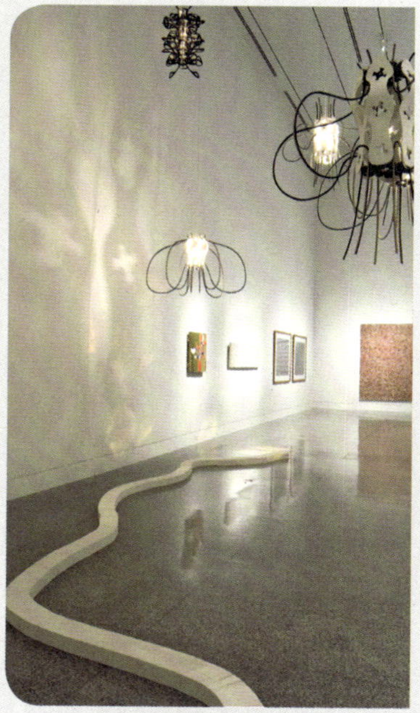

Constructing a Poetic Universe: The Diane and Bruce Halle Collection of Latin American Art, installation view

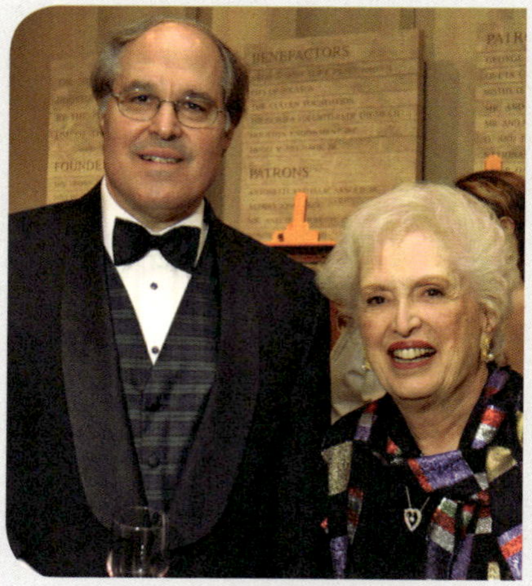

Dr. Robert Card, Renée Wallace

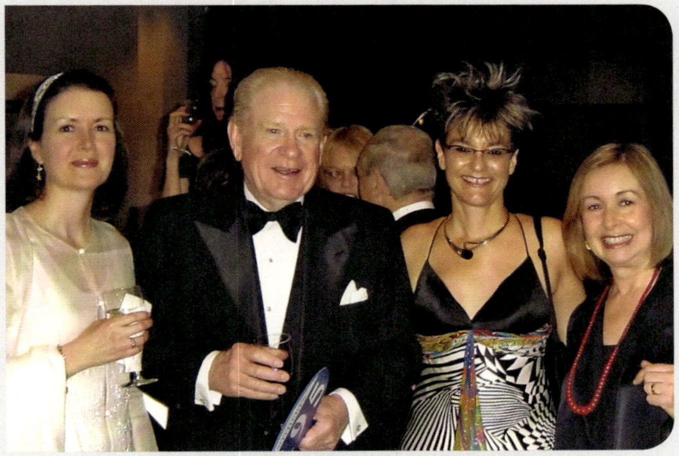

Johanna and Rusty Wortham, Mari Carmen Ramírez, and Cecilia de Torres

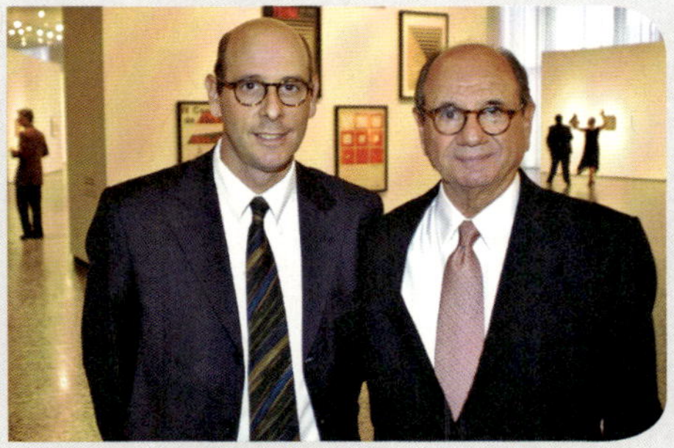

Adolpho and Ricardo Leirner

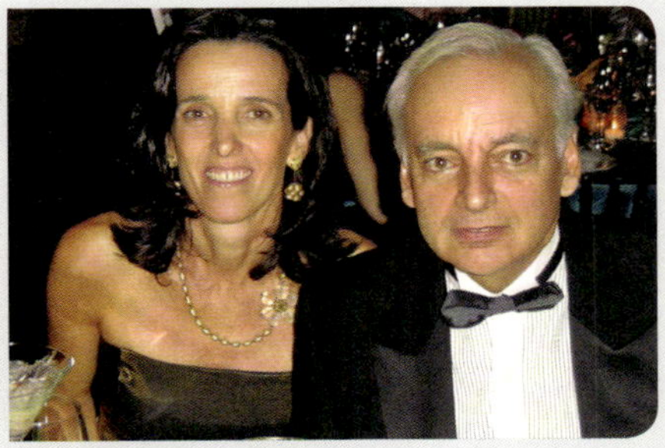

Eugenia and Eduardo Grüneisen

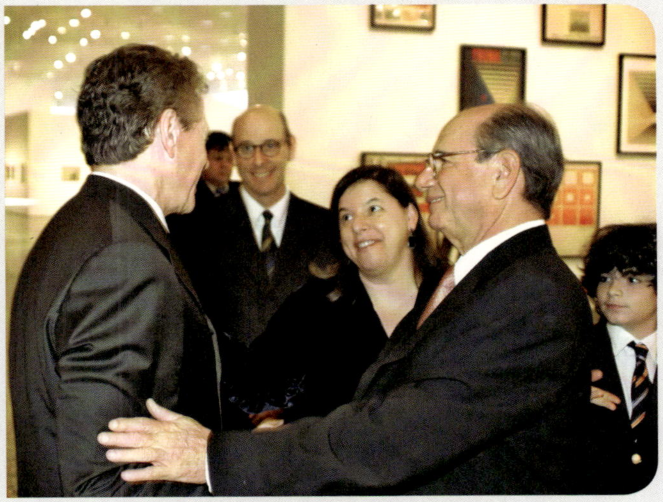

Peter Marzio with Adolpho Leirner and family

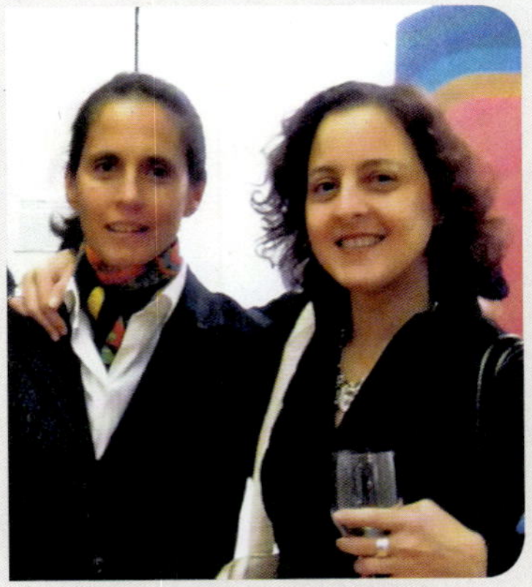

Pinta Art Fair, Natalia Majluf and her sister

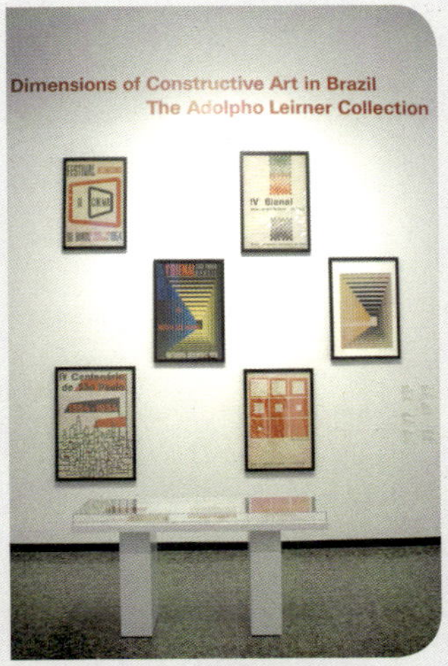

Dimensions of Constructive Art in Brazil: The Adolpho Leirner Collection

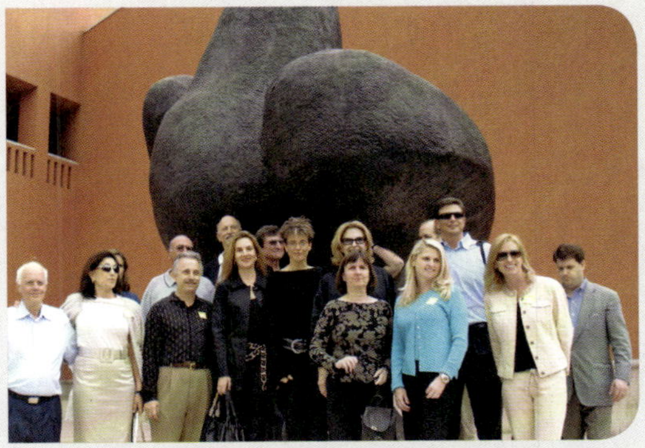

Latin Maecenas group photo, MARCO, Monterrey, Mexico

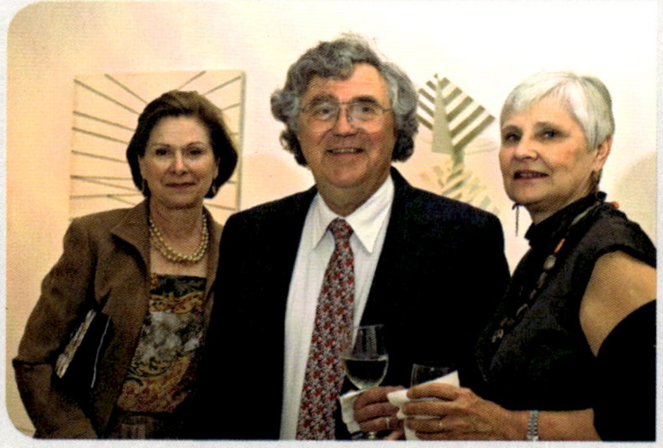
Latin Maecenas Annual Dinner, Anne Moriniere, Tom and Barbara Solis

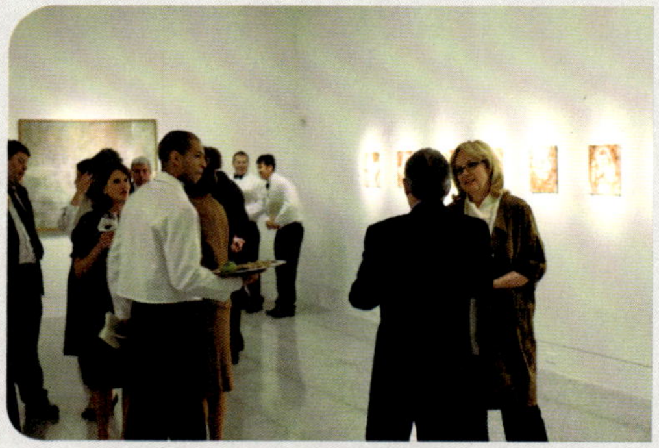
Latin Maecenas Annual Dinner, installation of recent acquisitions

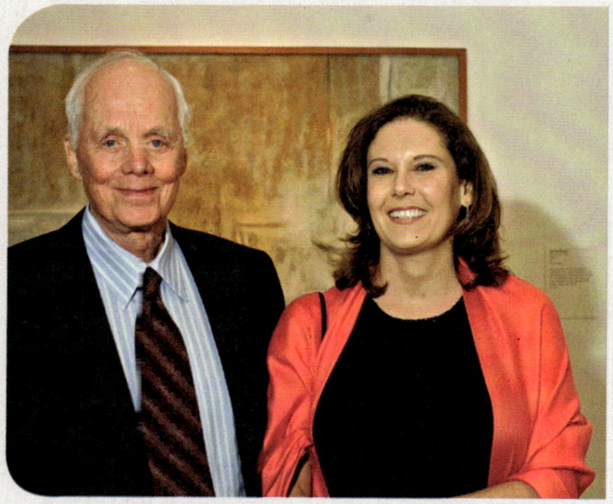
Latin Maecenas Annual Dinner, Roy Cullen, Rebecca Leach

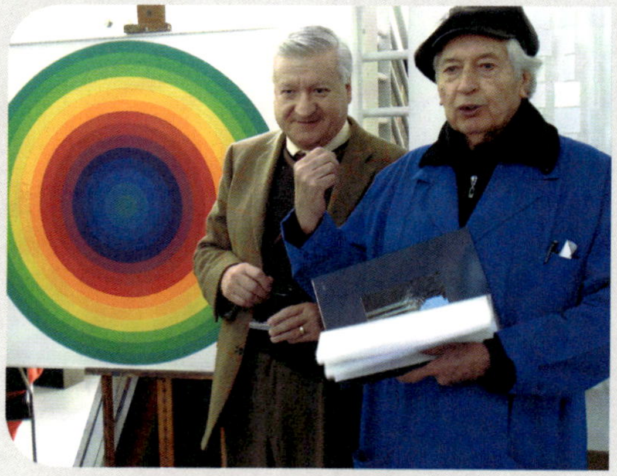
Dr. Luis Campos with Julio Le Parc at the artist's studio in Paris

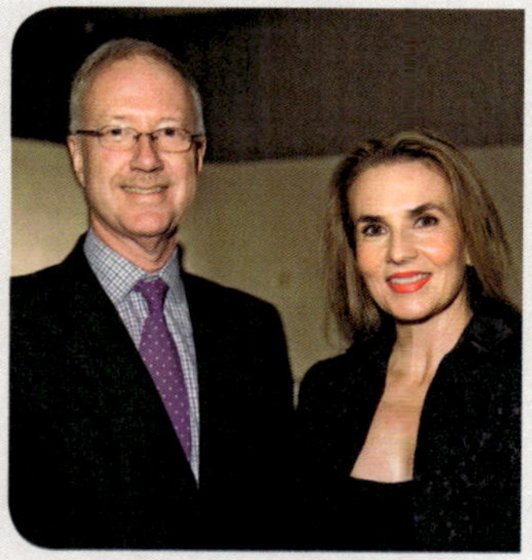
Latin Maecenas Annual Dinner, Mauro Herlitzka, Celina Hellmund

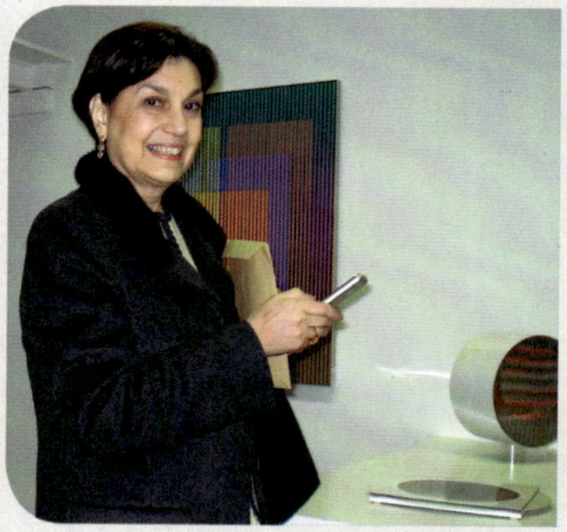
Cecilia Campos at Carlos Cruz-Diez studio in Paris

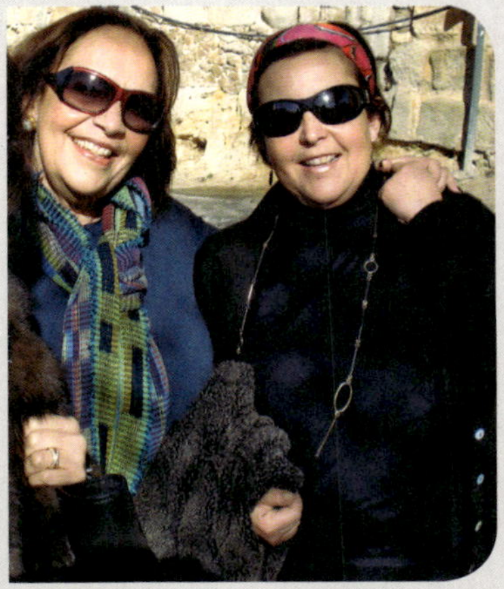

Latin Maecenas trip to ARCO Madrid, Marilyn Oshman, Karen Diesenberg

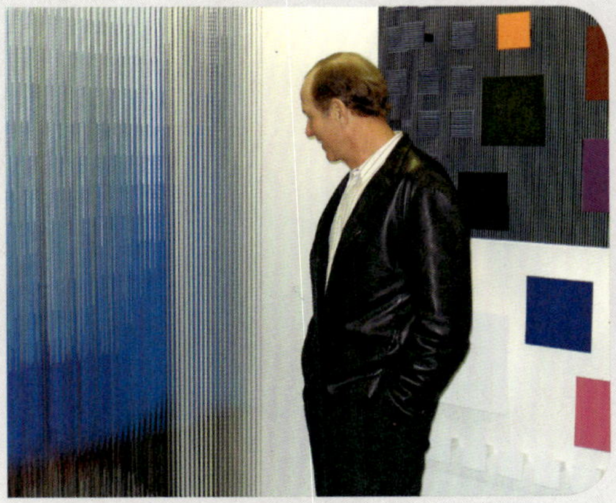

Brad Bucher at Atelier Soto in Paris

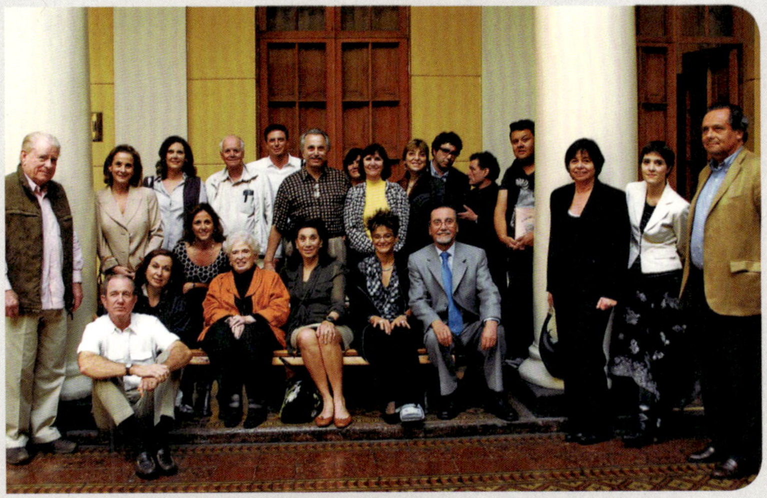

Latin Maecenas group photo, Santiago, Chile

THE LATIN MAECENAS 2008

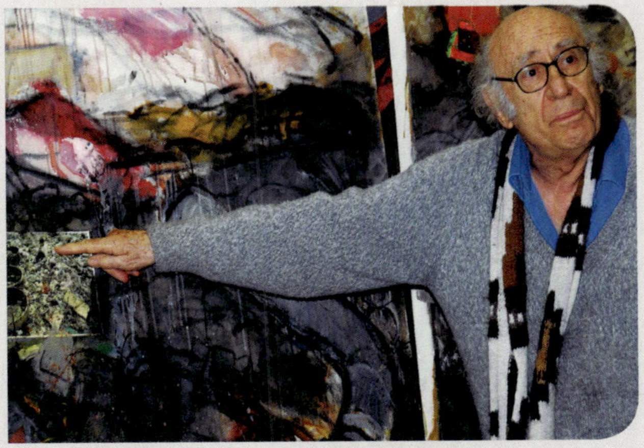

Artist José Balmes at his studio in Santiago, Chile

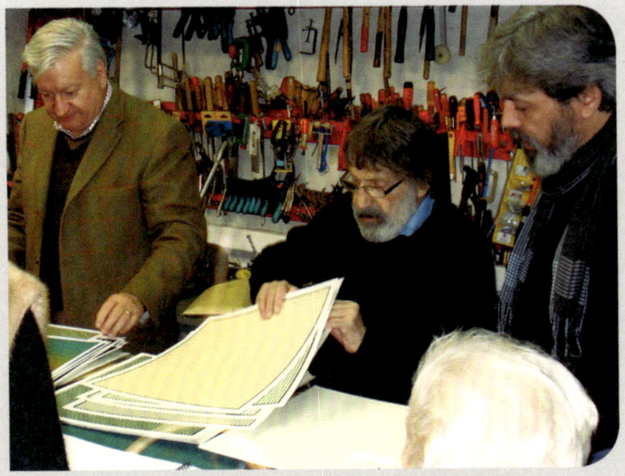

Dr. Luis Campos and Carlos Cruz-Diez at the artist's studio in Paris

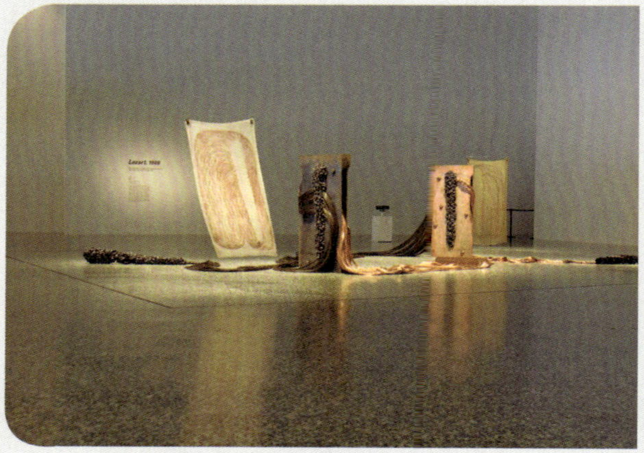

Tunga: Lezart, 1989, installation view

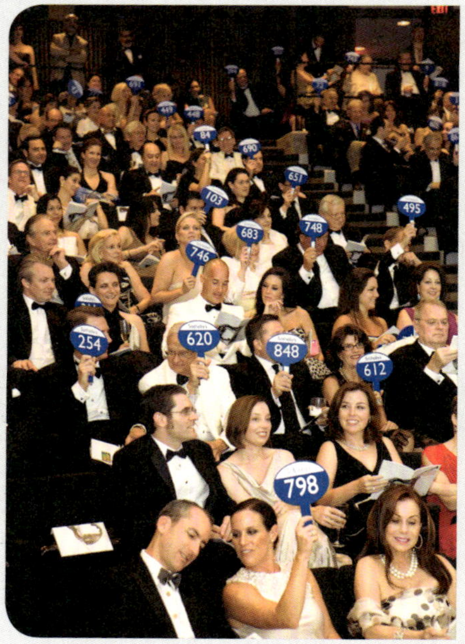

Latin American Gala and Auction, audience view

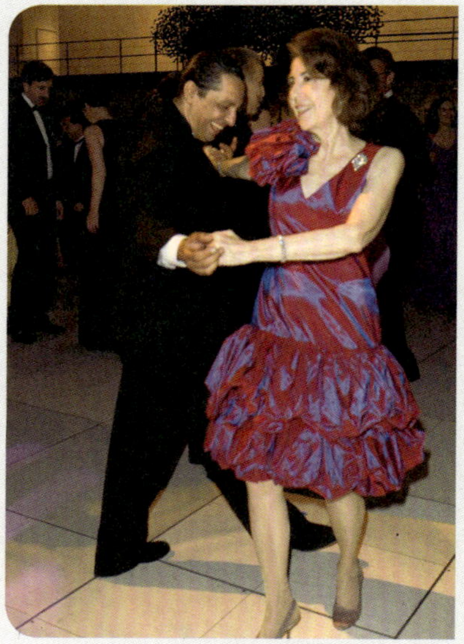

Latin American Gala and Auction,
Gail Adler with Norberto "El Pulpo" Esbrés

THE LATIN MAECENAS
2009

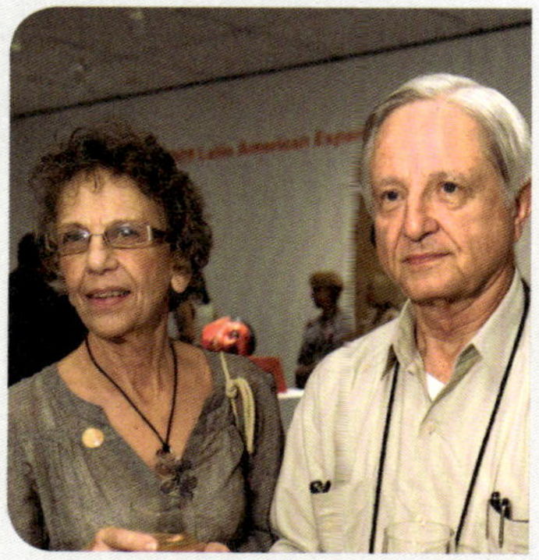

Barbara Gunz, Tomás Gunz

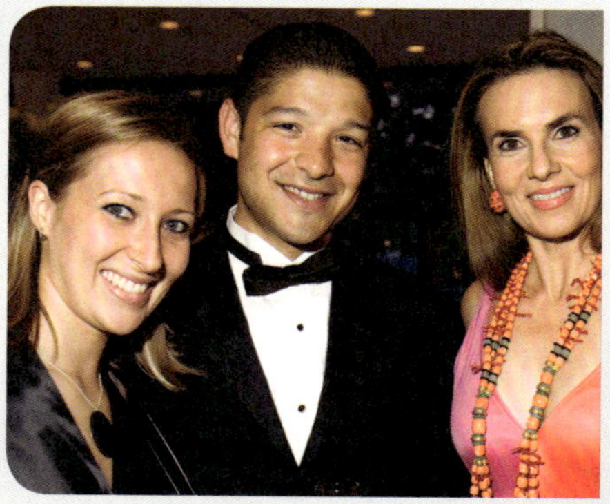

Latin American Gala and Auction,
Sophie Imbert, Gabriel Cruz, and
Celina Hellmund

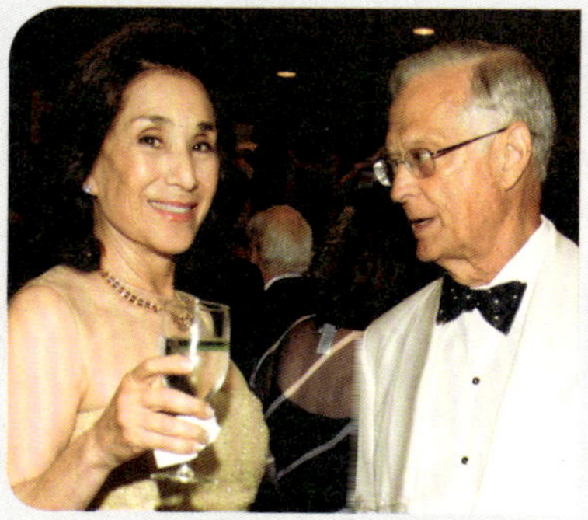

Latin American Gala and Auction,
Mary Cullen and Jack Moriniere

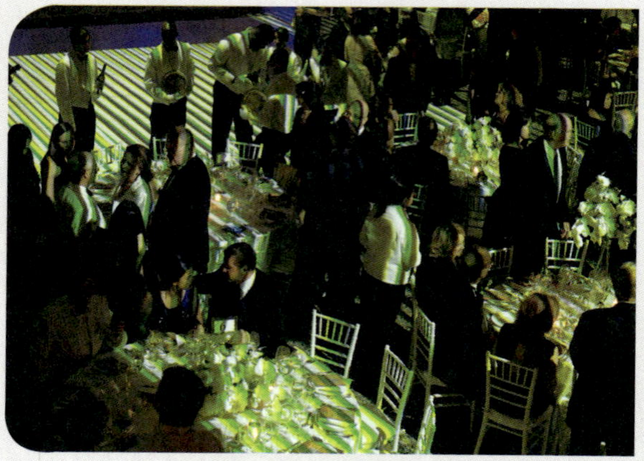

Latin American Gala and Auction,
Carlos Cruz-Diez *Chromo-interference*, 2009

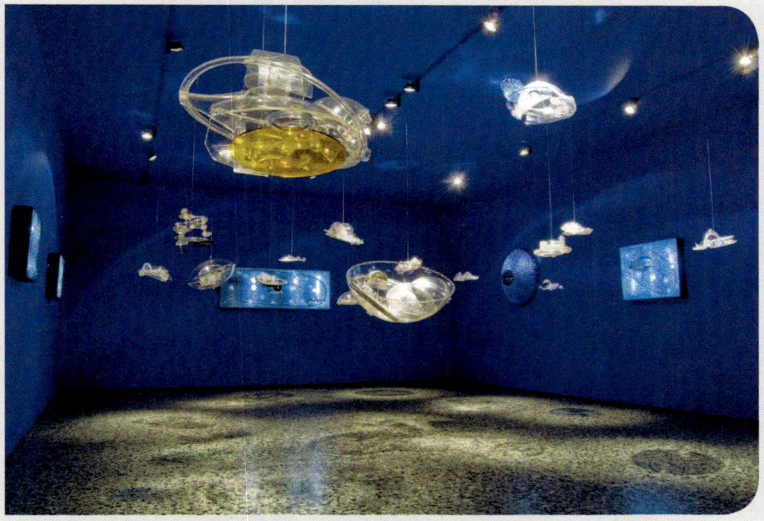

North Looks South: Building the Latin American Art Collection, installation view, Gyula Kosice's *La Ciudad Hidroespacial* [The Hydrospatial City]

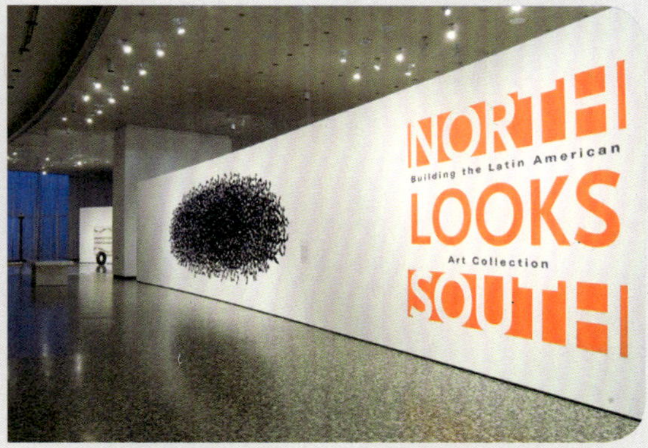

North Looks South: Building the Latin American Art Collection

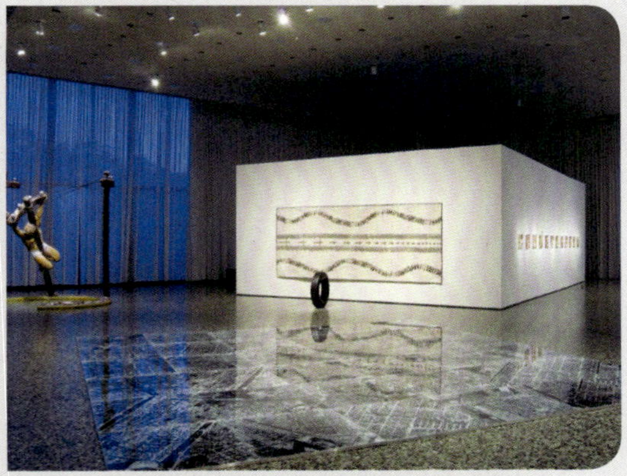

North Looks South: Building the Latin American Art Collection, installation view

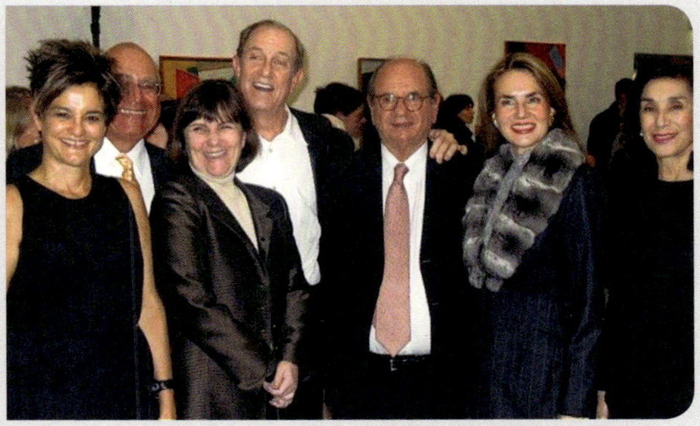

Opening of *Dimensions of Constructive Art: The Adolpho Leirner Collection* at Haus Konstruktiv, Zürich, Switzerland: Mari Carmen Ramírez, Sam Gorman, Leslie and Brad Bucher, Adolpho Leirner, Celina Hellmund, and Mary Cullen

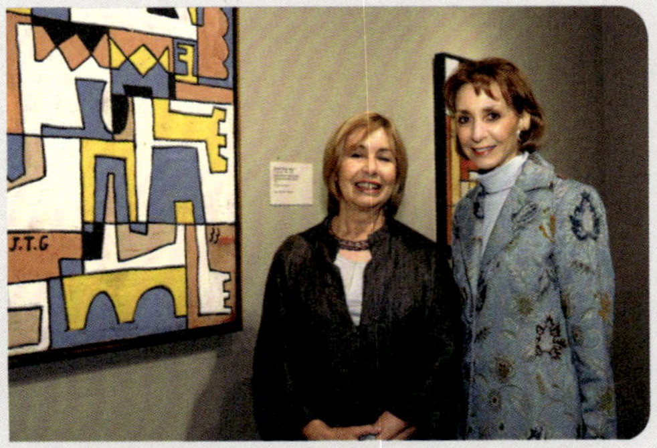

Opening of *Joaquín Torres-García: Paintings in Houston Collections*, Cecilia de Torres, Mimi Kilgore

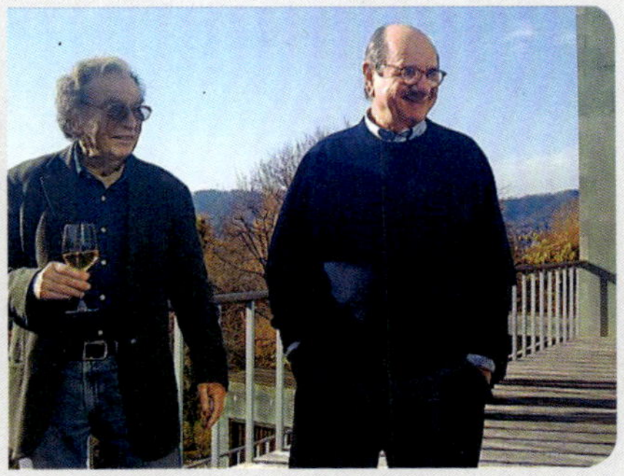

Alexander Wollner, pioneering graphic designer and artist, and Adolpho Leirner, Zürich, Switzerland

COLOPHON

Book design by Studio Blue

Typeset in Van Condensed

Color separations and printing by Capital Offset Company, Concord, New Hampshire

REPRODUCTION CREDITS

PHOTOGRAPHY

Photographs by Thomas R. DuBrock: pp. 13, 26, 28, 30 (left), 34, 37, 50–56, 61–63, 65 (right), 68–69, 72–73, 75–80, 86–89 (top), 90–91, 98–105, 107, 111, 119; Paul Hester, Hester + Hardaway Photography, Houston, TX, p. 33; Will Michels: pp. 21, 30 (right), 38, 40–41, 43 (top), 47–49, 57–60, 64, 65 (left), 66–67, 70–71, 81, 89 (bottom), 108–9, 110, 112–13; and Gustavo Sosa Pinilla, Buenos Aires: pp. 18, 22, 42, 43 (bottom), 44–46, 82–84, 92–94. Photographs courtesy of Magdalena Fernández: p. 120; Collection of Diane and Bruce Halle: pp. 75, 107; Meredith J. Long and Company, Houston: p. 25; Carlos Cruz Puga: p. 85; res: p. 95; Dario Robleto: p. 118; Sicardi Gallery, Houston: pp. 96–97. Video stills and photography courtesy of Tanya Bonakdar Gallery: pp. 114–15, 117; video stills courtesy of Galeria Leme, Sao Paulo, Maribel López Gallery, Berlin: p. 118.

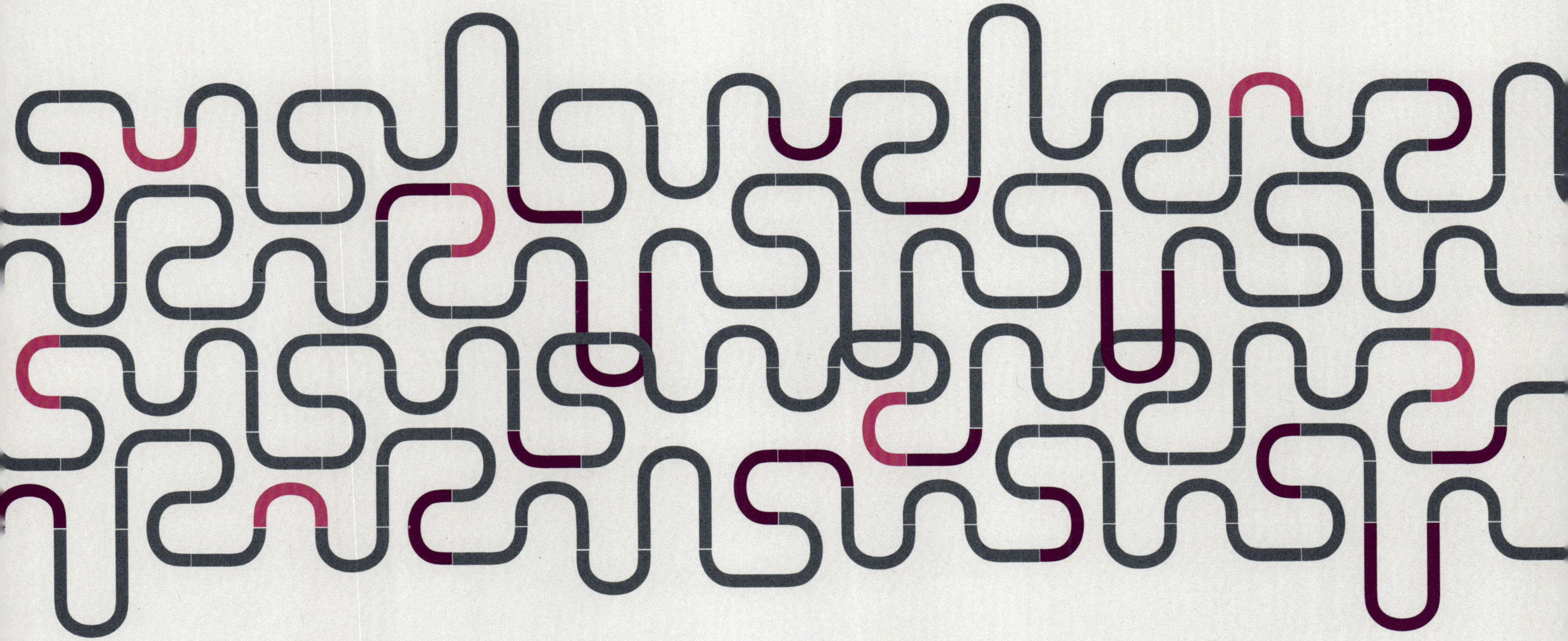

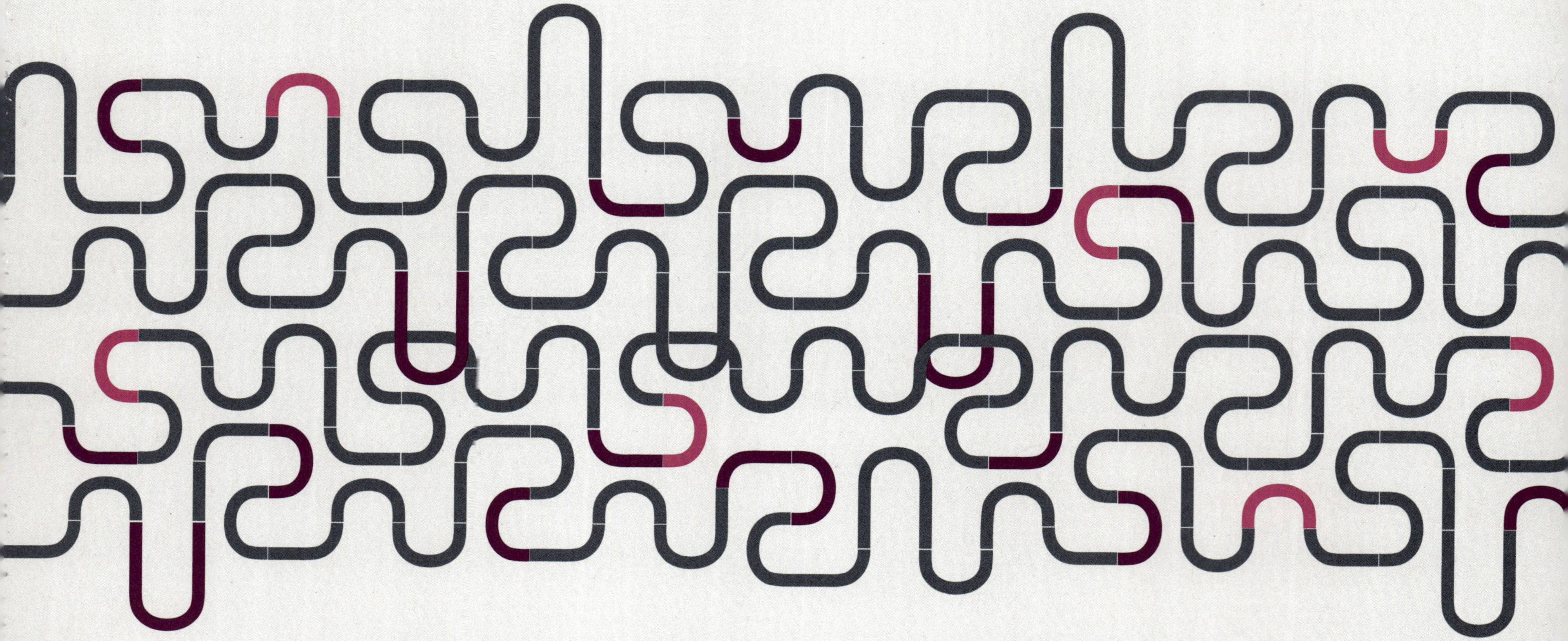